FINGER LAKES PANORAMAS

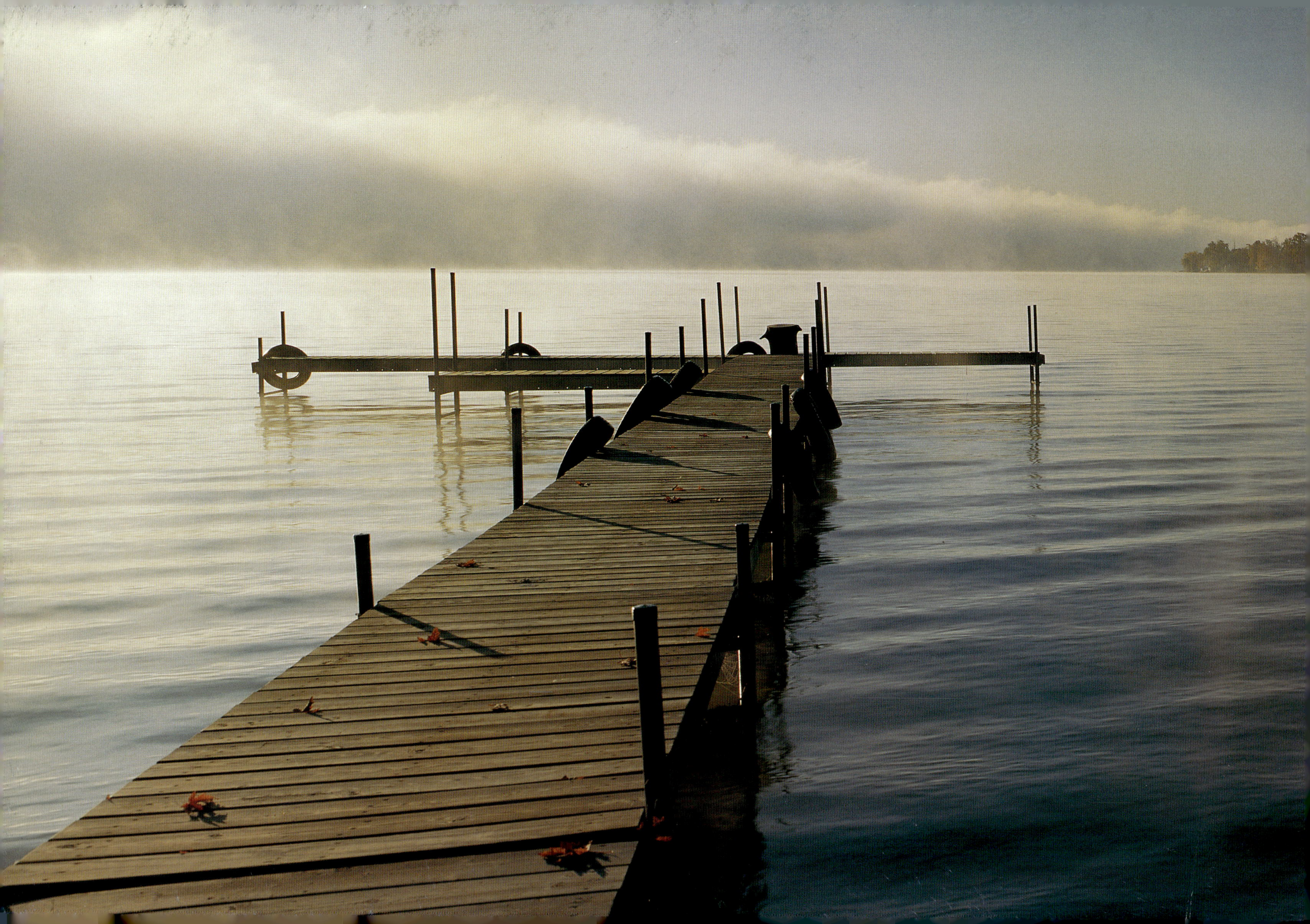

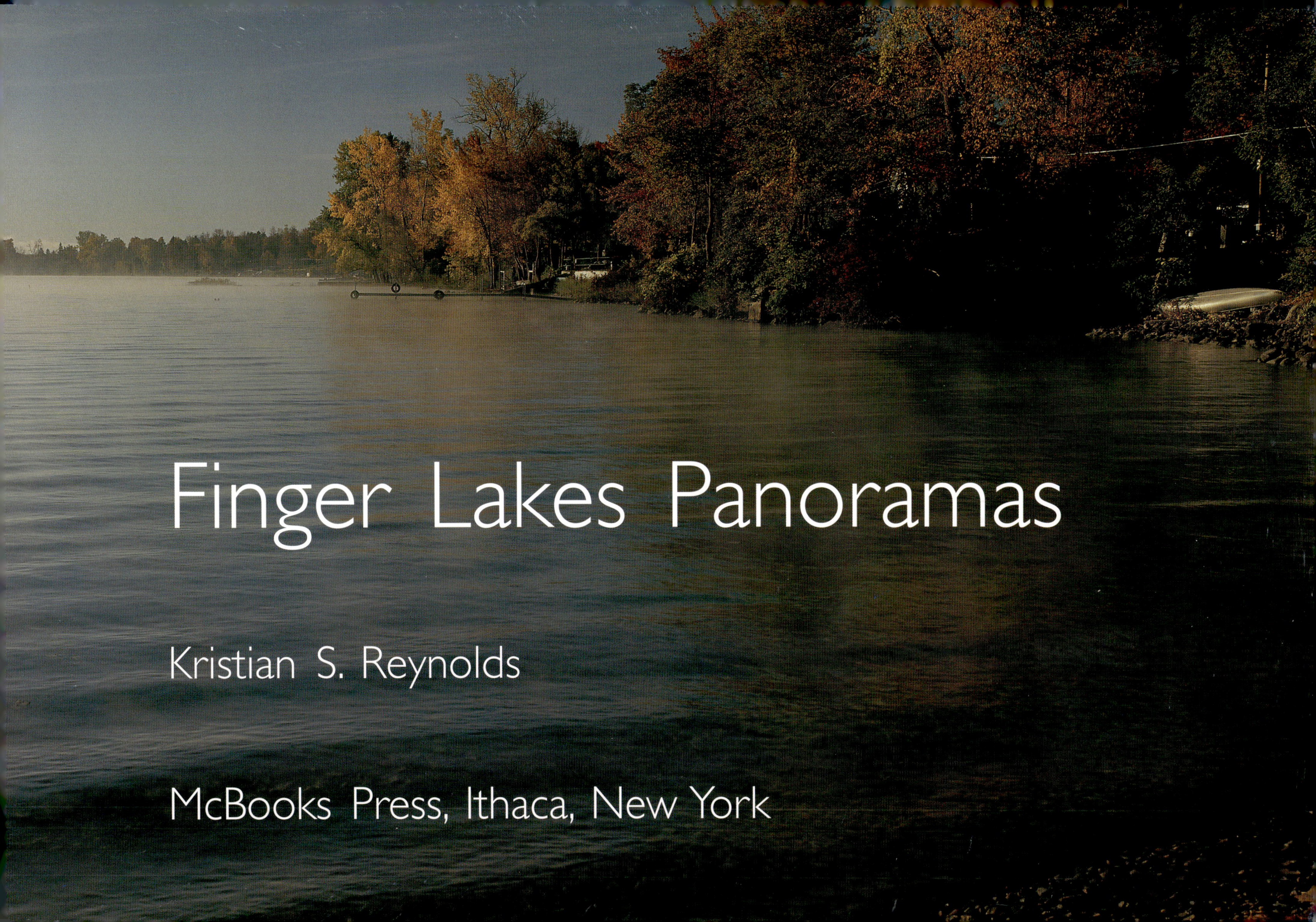

Finger Lakes Panoramas

Kristian S. Reynolds

McBooks Press, Ithaca, New York

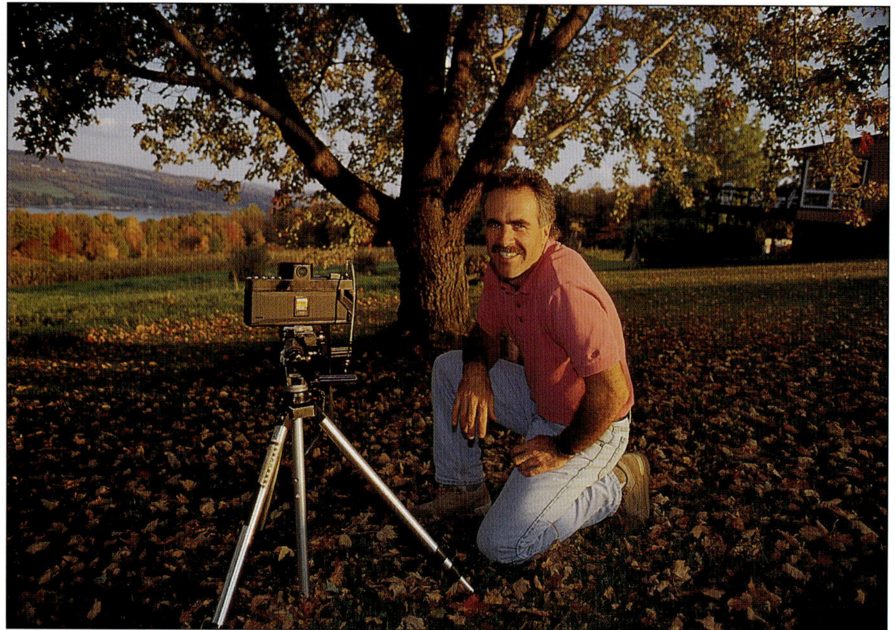

About the Photographer

Kristian S. Reynolds, photographer and videographer, specializes in landscapes, sports and recreation, and industrial imagery. After taking a bachelor's degree in professional photography from Rochester Institute of Technology in 1975, he set out to merge photography with his love of downhill skiing, which led to work for major ski resorts in the Rockies and New England. But the beauty of the Finger Lakes region eventually drew him back. His freelance work has served a variety of clients, including, in New York, Dunlop Tire (Buffalo), *SKI* Magazine (New York City), the New York State Department of Economic Development (Albany), Greek Peak Ski Resort, Suit-Kote Corporation, and Gutchess Lumber (all in Cortland), Glenora Wine Cellars (Dundee); in Vermont, Mt. Mansfield Resort (Stowe); in Florida, Divi Beach Resorts (Miami); and *Snow Country* Magazine (Connecticut).

Mr. Reynolds lives near Cortland with his wife Tricia, daughters Paige and Taylor, and son Kristian.

Photo by Paige Reynolds

Cover photo by Kristian S. Reynolds

Library of Congress Cataloging-in-Publication Data

Reynolds, Kristian S., 1953–
Finger Lakes panoramas / Kristian S. Reynolds.
p. cm.
ISBN 0-935526-55-2 (hc.)
1. Landscape photography—New York (State)—Finger Lakes Region.
2. Photography, Panoramic— New York (State)—Finger Lakes Region.
3. Finger Lakes Region (N.Y.)—Pictorial works. I. Title.
TR660.5.R49 1999
779'.36747'8—dc21 99-20187
CIP

Distributed to the trade by National Book Network, Inc.,
15200 NBN Way, Blue Ridge Summit, PA 17214
800-462-6420

Additional copies of this book may be ordered from any bookstore or directly from McBooks Press, Inc., ID Booth Building, 520 North Meadow St., Ithaca, NY 14850. Please include $4.00 postage and handling with mail orders. New York State residents must add sales tax All McBooks Press publications can also be ordered by calling toll-free 1-888-BOOKS11 (1-888-266-5711). Please call to request a free catalog.

Visit the McBooks Press website at www.mcbooks.com.

Printed in China

9 8 7 6 5 4 3

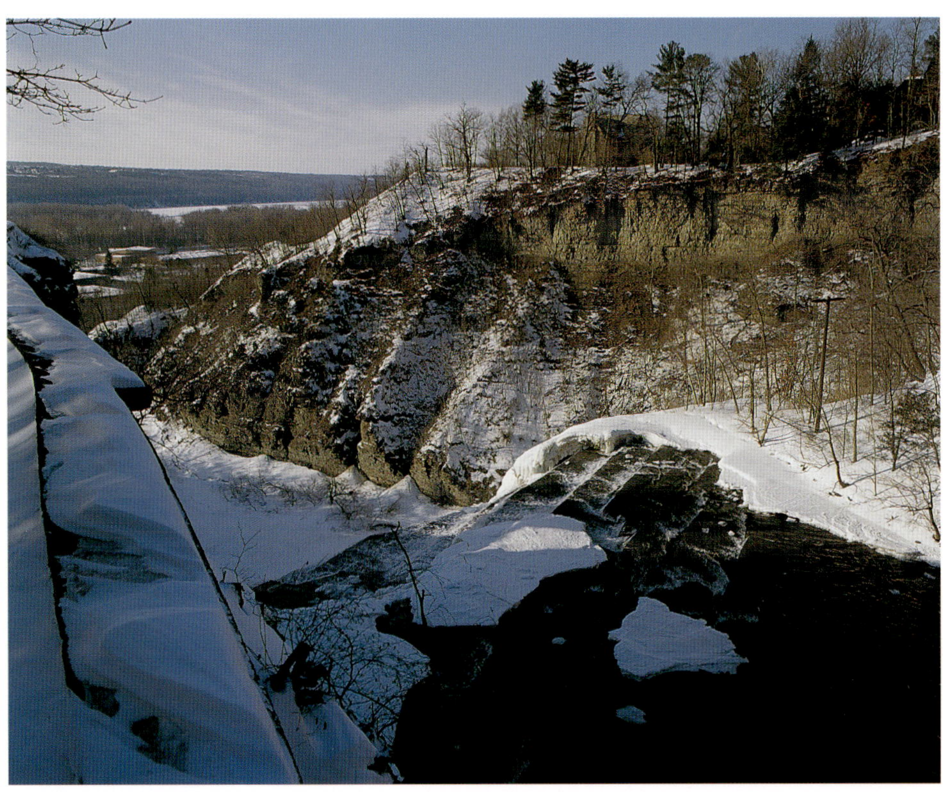

CAYUGA LAKE from Ithaca Falls, looking west.

Contents

This book is dedicated to my parents, who taught me that success is not a destination; it's a journey.

For Tricia, Paige, Taylor, and Kristian.

I would like to thank Bill and Mary and the countless individuals whose generosity and kindness made this project truly enjoyable.

Foreword

When people from other regions think about New York State, more often than not their vision is formed by images of the City of New York and its suburbs. There is little awareness of or appreciation for other areas of the state. This can be true even for New Yorkers who live downstate and spend most of their work and leisure time there.

My wife and I were once typical of this genre. We were raised in "the City," and, while we were quite familiar with Long Island, upstate communities were foreign to us. This all changed in 1965, when, after the birth of our first child, we decided to look for a more placid environment to raise our family. The City was still a special place, and, to this day, we enjoy its unique tempo and culture, but, as others had before us, we discovered in our search the extraordinary attractions of upstate New York.

And in particular, we discovered the Finger Lakes. As the photographs in this impressive book demonstrate, it is a region of unusual beauty. Kristian Reynolds, the author and photographer, has, by virtue of his talent and his love of the land, light, and water, captured this beauty for us. He has captured, as well, the region's diversity—its changing seasons, its agriculture and small towns, its flat lands and rolling hills.

He has done so by patiently traversing the territory, covering 28,000 miles over a four year period, and by bringing to his project an appreciation for the area that is manifest in virtually every photo.

If one has visited the Finger Lakes, or has lived here, there are scenes that will have particular resonance. For me, the view of Cayuga Lake from Ithaca College evokes special memories. In 1965, when our family visited the region for the first time, this was the scene that spread before us when we drove into Ithaca, and it helped inspire us to make this community our home.

However, one does not have to be a resident or a frequent visitor to enjoy the panoramas presented here. Indeed, for one who is totally unfamiliar with the region, this collection is a striking introduction to a lovely, peaceful part of our world, one which, as the author says, rivals in beauty any other in the country.

MATTHEW F. MCHUGH
Member of Congress (1975–1992)
Ithaca, New York

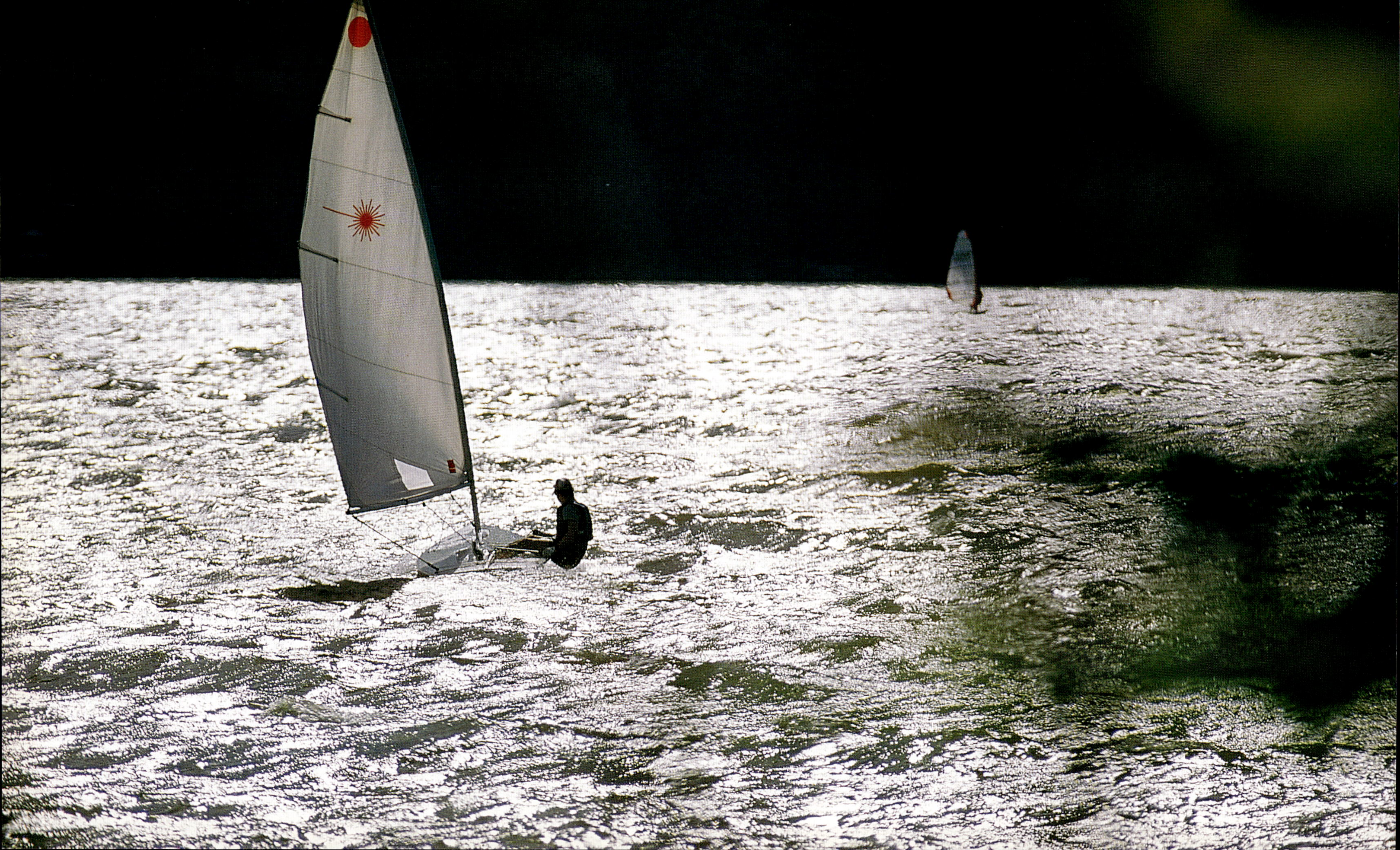

Introduction

My earliest memories are of sitting at the edge of a lake, playing with stones and watching sunlight sparkle and dance on the water. The lake was Keuka, one of the long, narrow bodies of water which are the Finger Lakes of central New York. My family lived on Keuka Lake year-round, so my days were filled with swimming and water skiing all summer, and ice skating and snow skiing all winter.

Over time, it became clear to me that I had developed an enduring fascination with light and water, and the way they interact. Perhaps, in part, that's because the Finger Lakes region is very much a place where light and water meet. They produce a distinctive character in the look of the land which residents love and which also captivates many visitors, drawing them back again and again. The stunning geography of the region may challenge our lives but it always comforts our souls.

In my work as a professional photographer, light and water are the very essence of what I do. In making a photograph, the effects of light are recorded on film—a liquid emulsion dried onto plastic. Liquid chemistry then draws the light-based image out of that emulsion. For me, photography has always offered a natural vehicle to combine my personal vision with glorious events in the natural world. My work has taken me all over the United States, but I still find that the beauty of the Finger Lakes territory rivals anything I've seen. That's why making this book was a dream come true for me, the chance to create images, with light, of the water I love.

Making these images, I worked in an area encompassed roughly by the relatively flat lands near the New York State Thruway (Route 90) in the north, to the steeper regions near Routes 13 and 17 in the south, from Route 390 in the west to Interstate 81 in the east. I have included images taken from locations around eleven lakes and have also mixed in a few favorite spots along the fringes of those boundaries. In some cases, to help orient a viewer, I have indicated in which compass direction the center of a given photo faces.

Overall, my goal has been to capture the beauty which is all around the Finger Lakes via emphasis on its waterways. I have tried not only to offer glimpses of little-known spots in this lovely region, but also to show very familiar locations in a new light.

The characteristic long, slender topography of the lakes defines their individuality but is also the source of special problems for the photographer. Since traditional cameras provide an aspect ratio of 1:1 or 1:1.5, they can't do justice to the broad landscapes of the region. That's why most of the subjects in this book were shot using a special panoramic format of 1:3. Simply put, a panoramic photo is equivalent to placing three regular photos side by side. This format creates a seamless visual sweep of the land, perfect for the broad, open landscapes so typical in the Finger Lakes.

To get technical, I shot for 190 days over four years and traveled over 28,000 miles. The majority of the photos in this book were shot with a Fuji 617 panoramic camera. I also used a Horizon 202 (35mm panoramic), Pentax 67, Nikon F4, Nikon N90S, and a Nikon 8008. For film, I used 300 rolls of Kodak Lumiere and Fuji Velvia. I kept filters to a minimum, usually using only UV, polarizing, or graduated neutral density.

In most cases, I took the picture I wanted by returning to the same location many times. Each time, because of the variable nature of light, the results were different. Most of my photos were taken in the minutes just before and after sunrise and sunset. To my eye, this light produces the most dynamic images.

I have another purpose in capturing the beauty of the Finger Lakes on film. Almost 250 years ago, Ben Franklin wrote, "When the well's dry, we know the worth of water." The centerpiece of the Finger Lakes region is its bright shining clean water. Those who live or visit here are blessed with an abundance of drinkable, swimmable fresh water. But that luxury is in danger. A glaring example of flagrant abuse of this precious, limited resource lies just to the northeast, near Syracuse, in the sorely polluted waters of Onondaga Lake, where swimming has been banned for almost half of this century.

People the world over are facing a critical shortage of clean, fresh water. According to a 1993 article in *National Geographic,* if we imagine all of the water in the world fitting into a one-gallon jar, the amount of drinkable water inside would measure just over one tablespoon. That amount is shrinking each day.

A human being can live for a month without food, but less than a week without fresh water. And yet we take water for granted. It comes from the tap on command and disappears down the drain to somewhere else. The Finger Lakes region may be water-rich but, like people everywhere else, its inhabitants must begin to show more care and concern for how that water is used. It's my hope that, in some way, this book will inspire all of us to more vigilance in protecting and preserving the purity of our waters. Our health and our future depend upon it.

1 *Finger Lakes country offers rich variety…*

KEUKA LAKE, near Red Jacket Park, Penn Yan, looking west

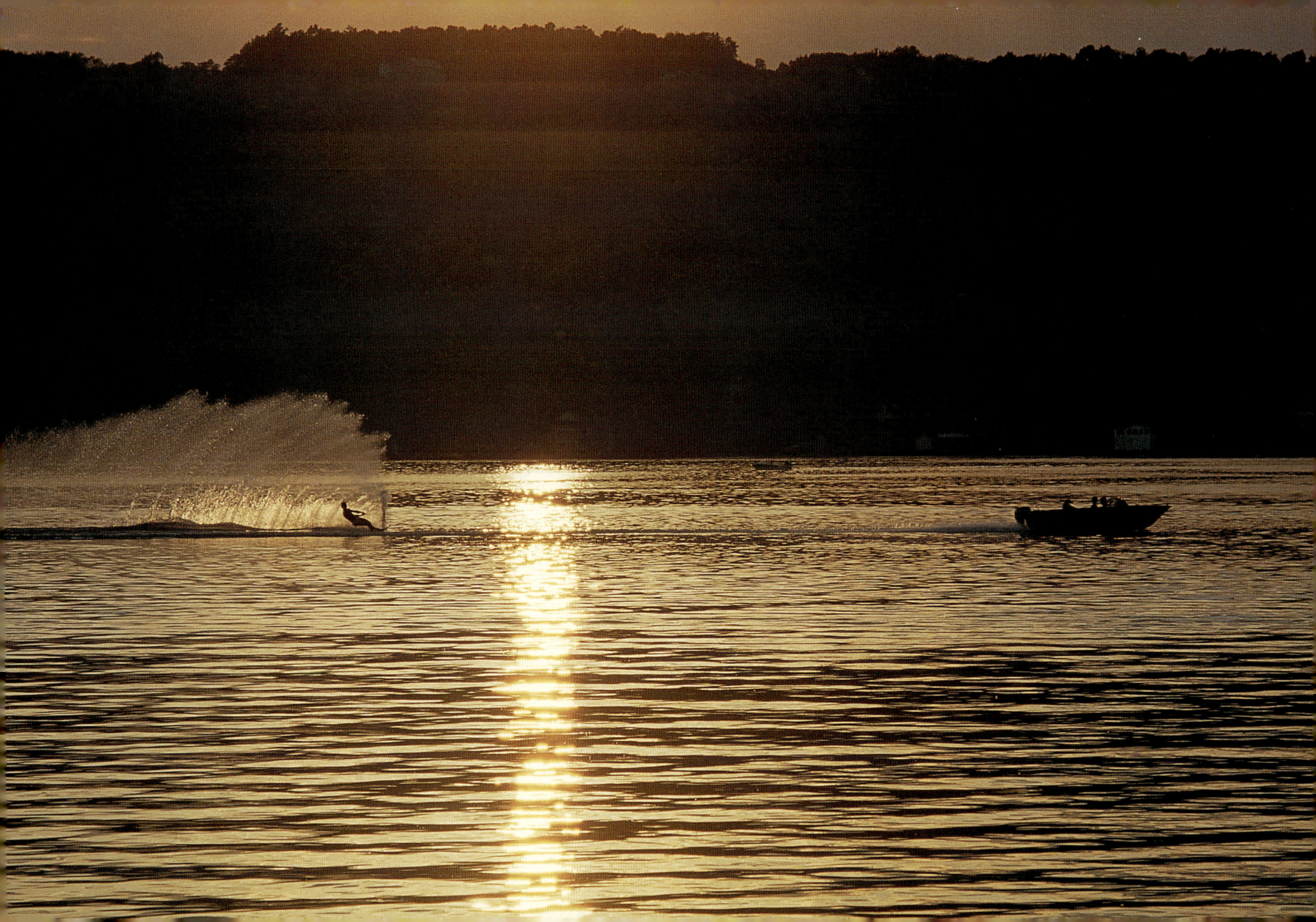

Lush vineyards . . .

KEUKA LAKE and Bluff Point, from Taylor Vineyards, looking northeast

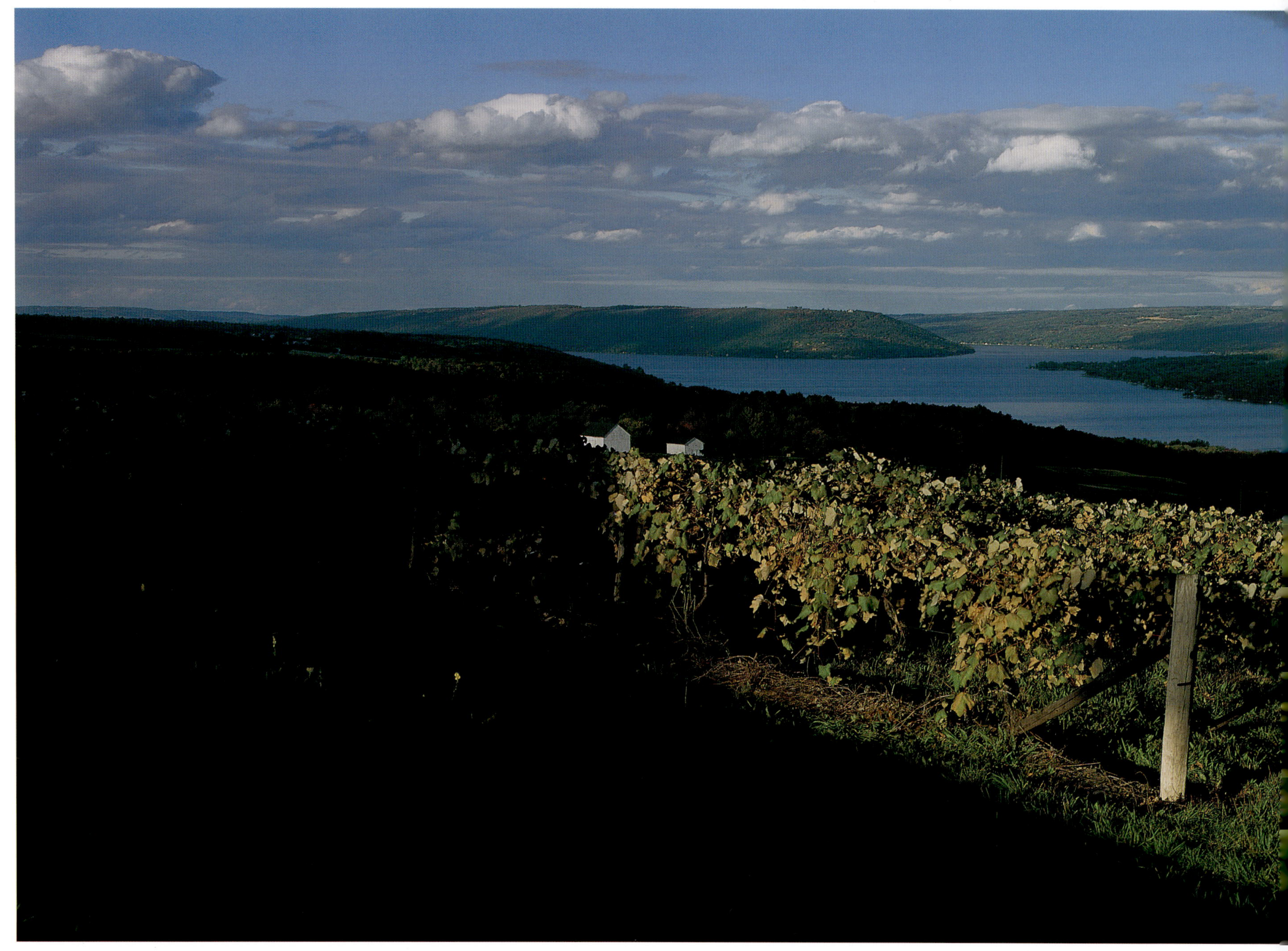

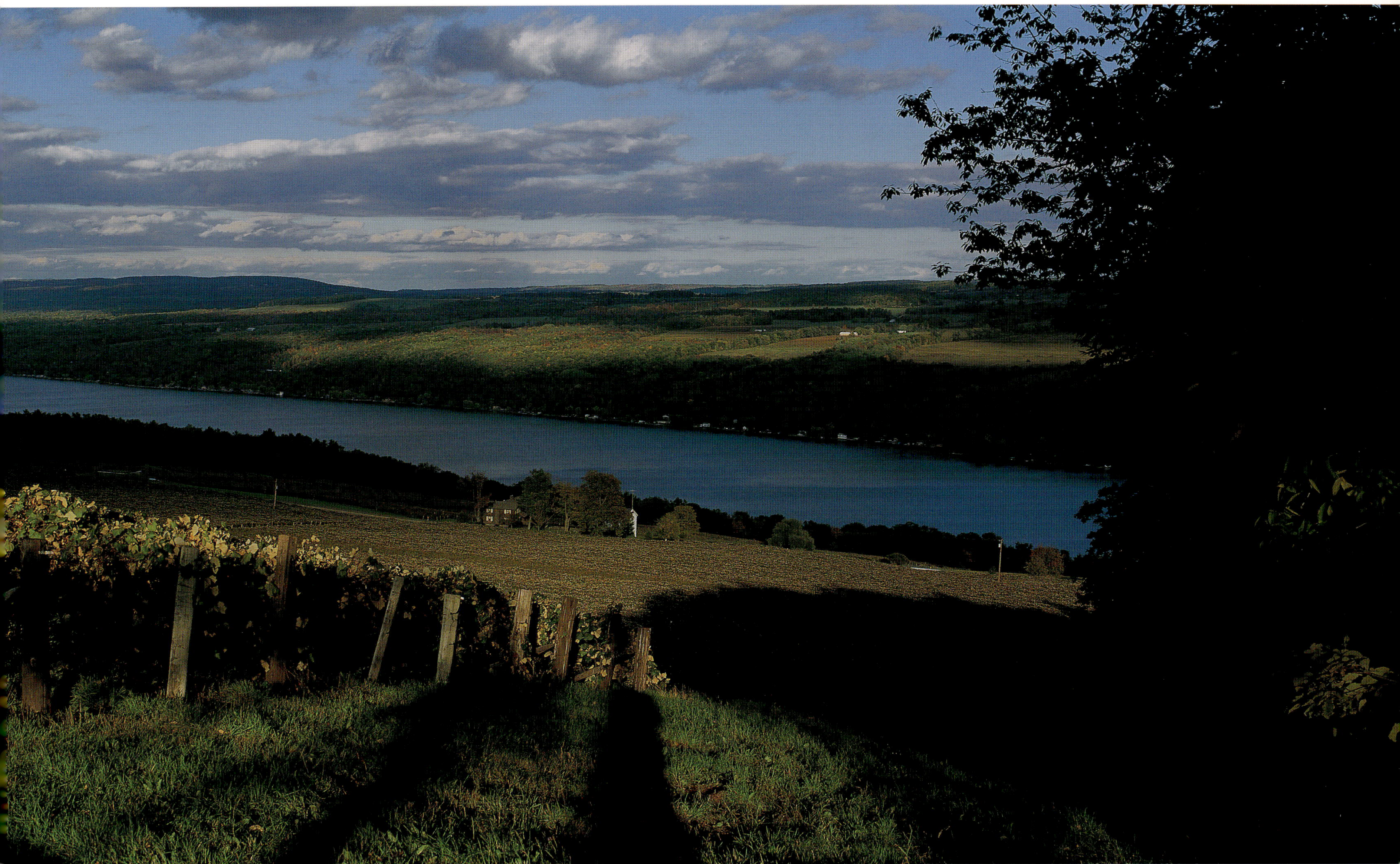

Geological wonders . . .

LETCHWORTH STATE PARK, Lower Falls.

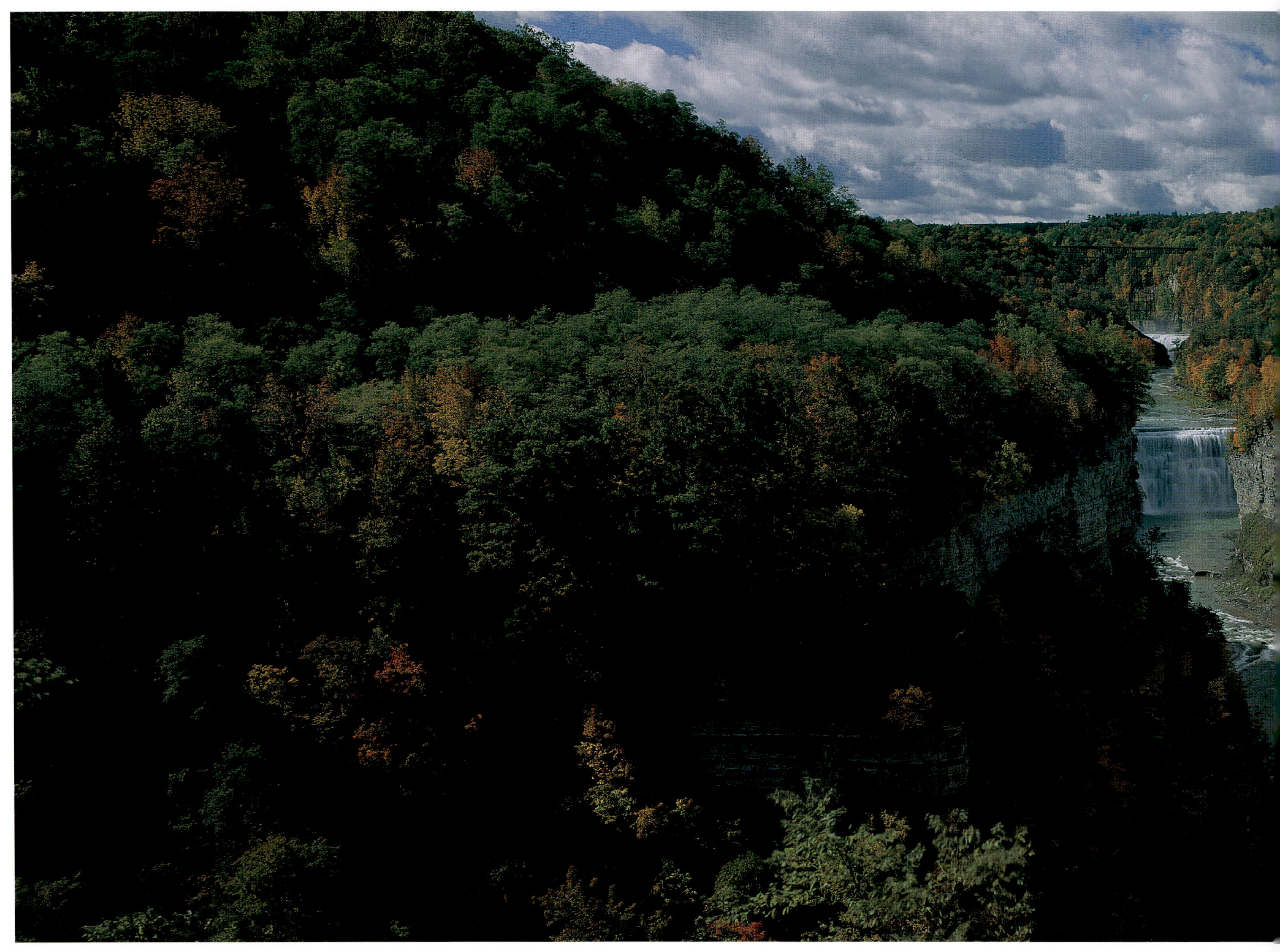

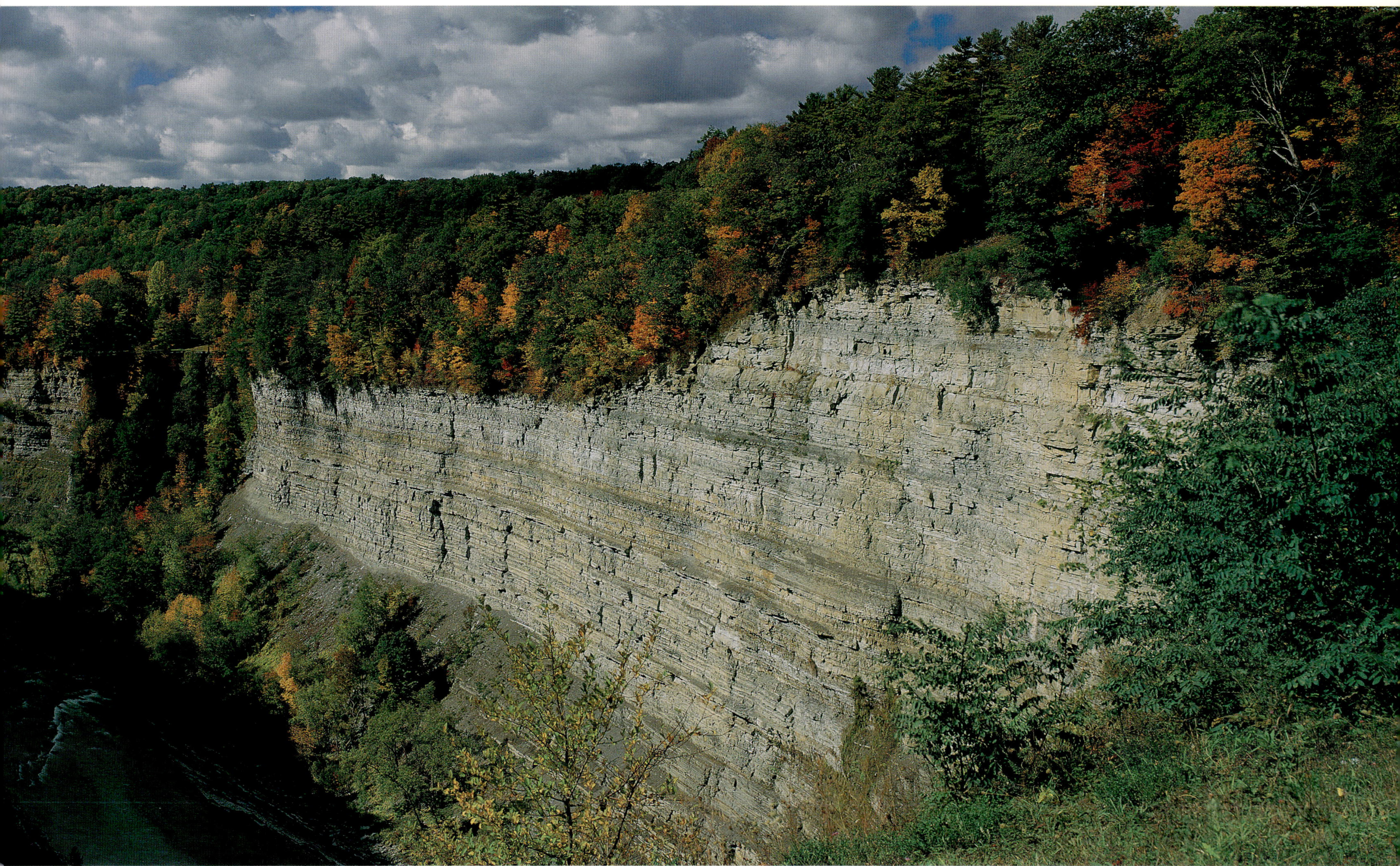

The hush of sunrise . . .

SENECA LAKE, from Geneva On The Lake, looking east.

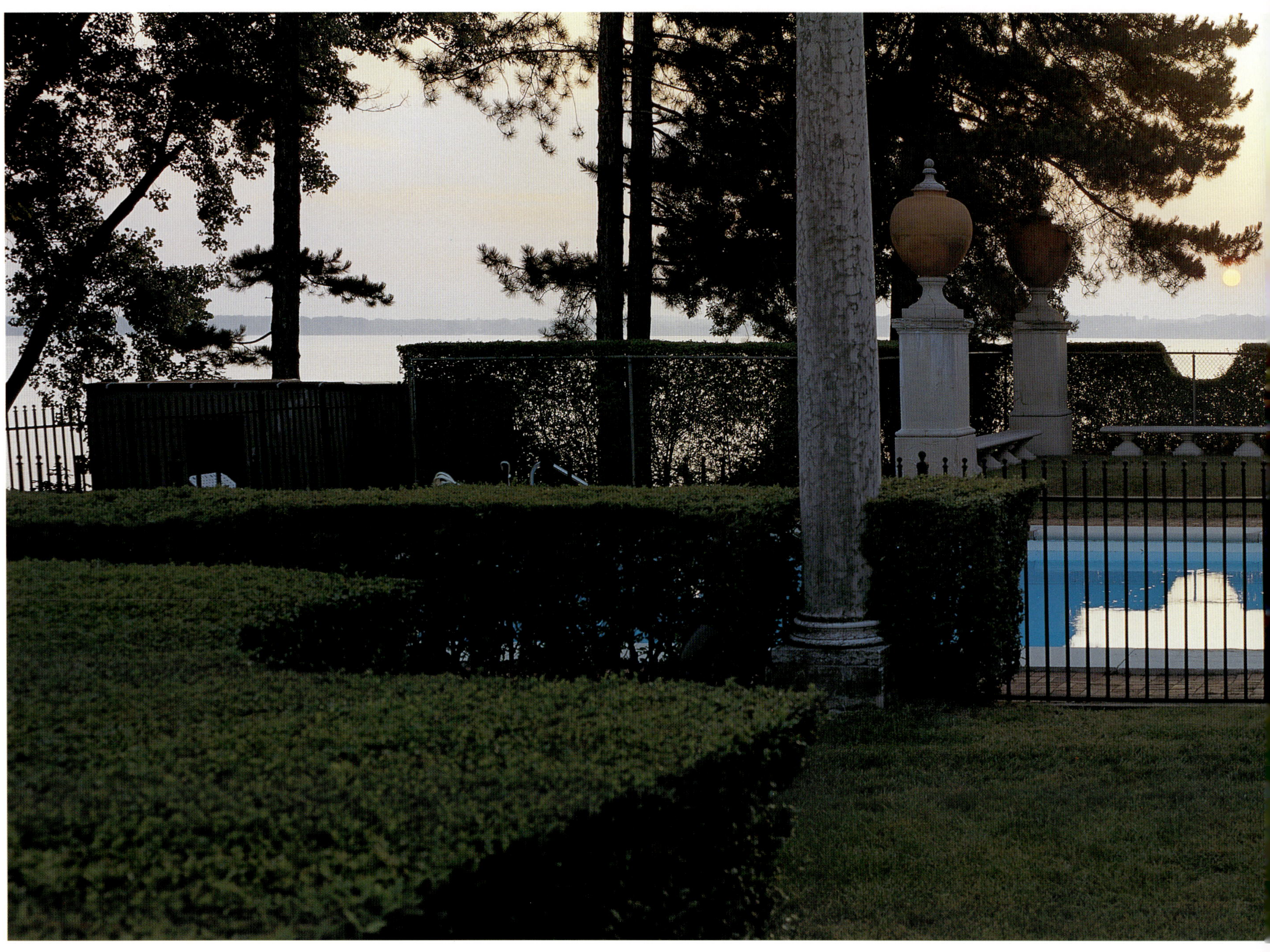

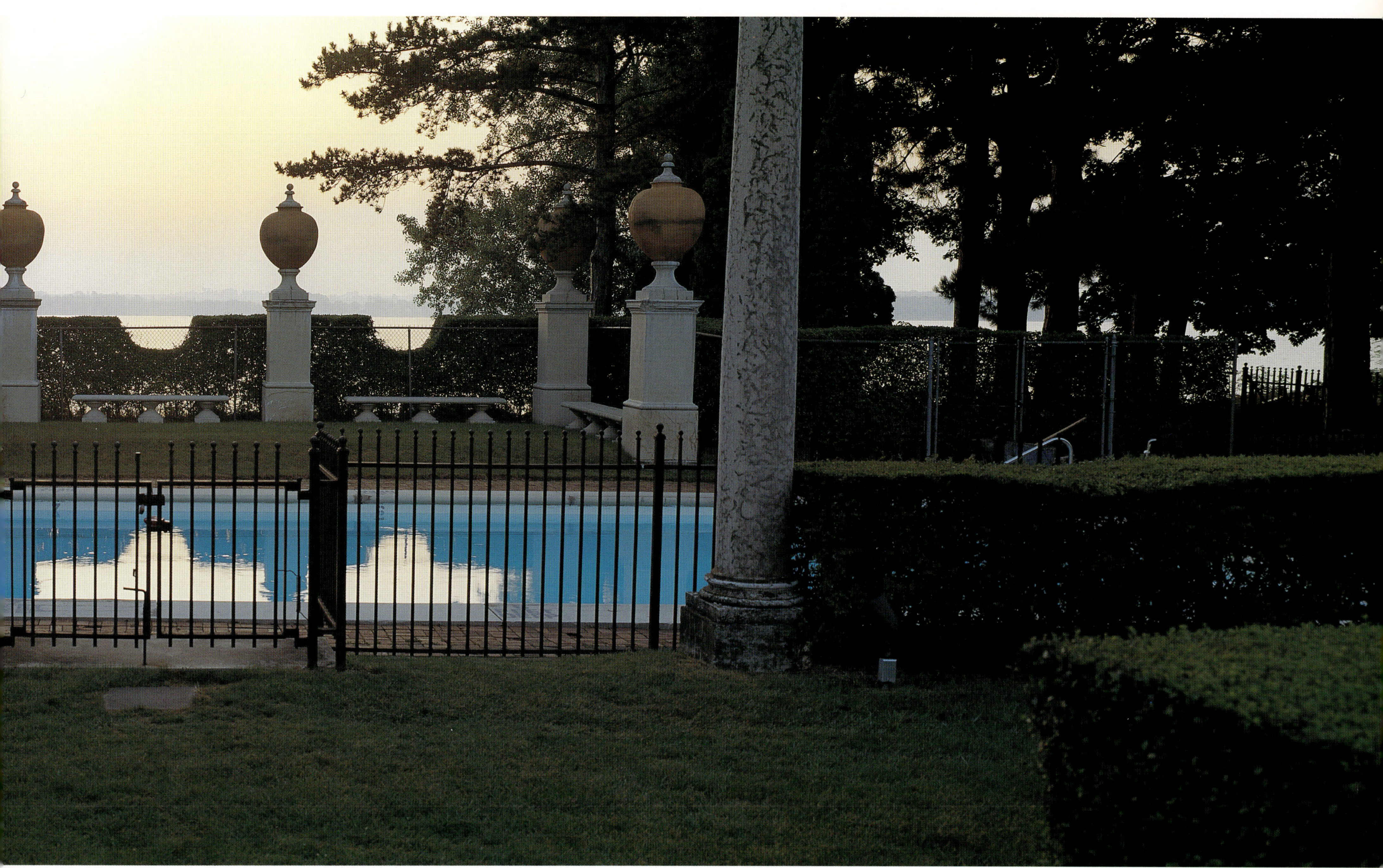

Charming villages . . .

SKANEATELES from the west shore of Skaneateles Lake, looking north.

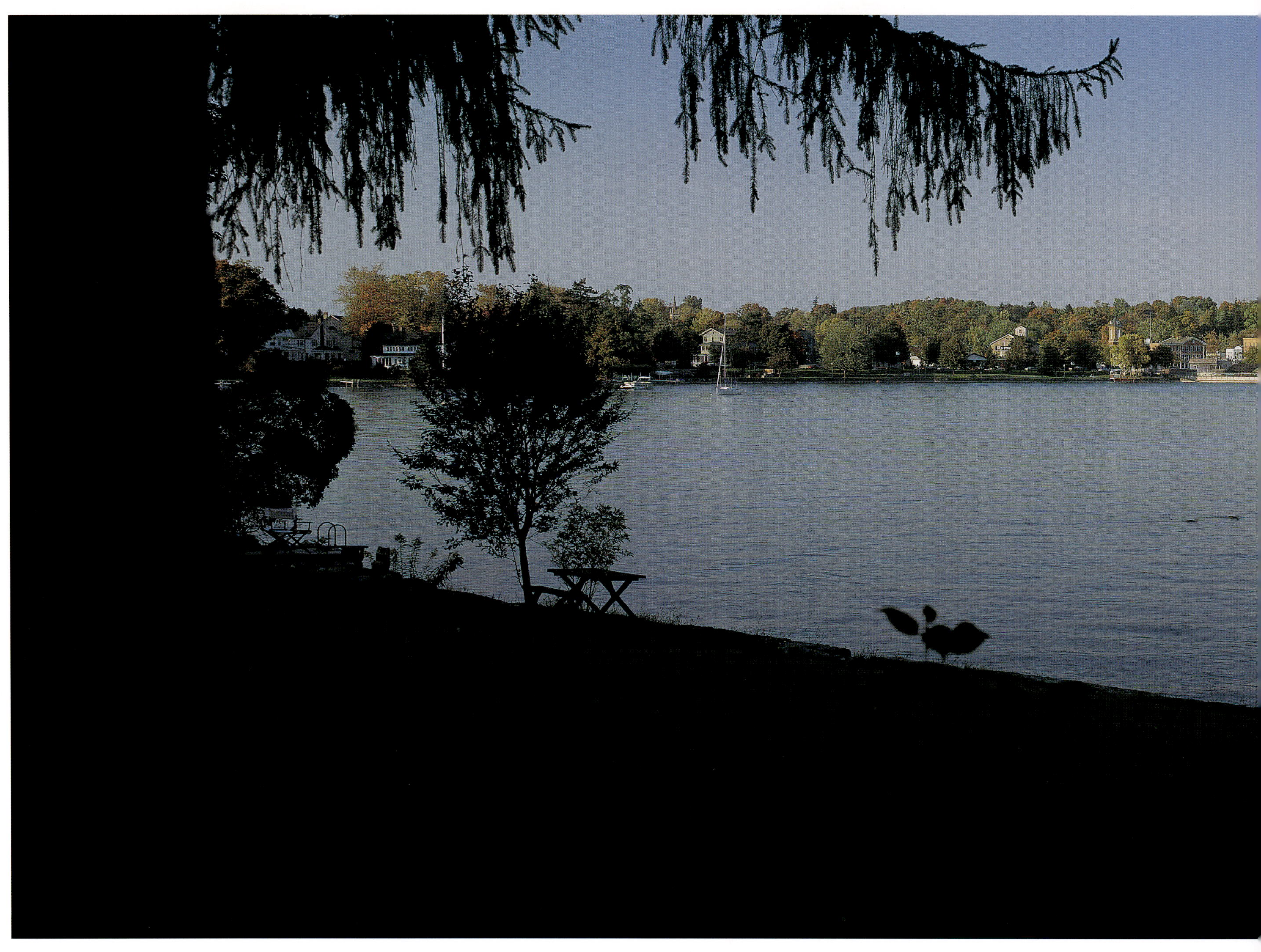

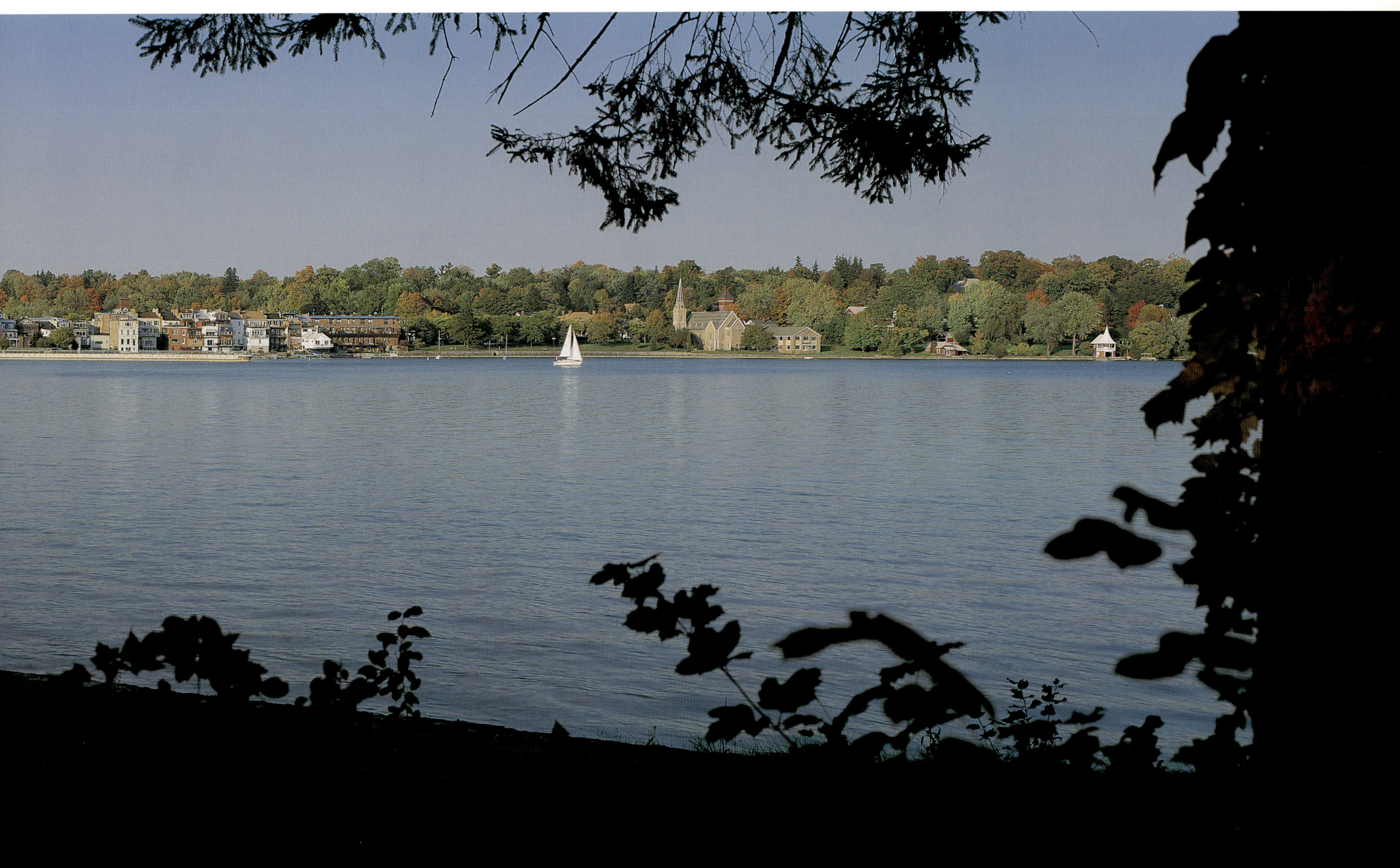

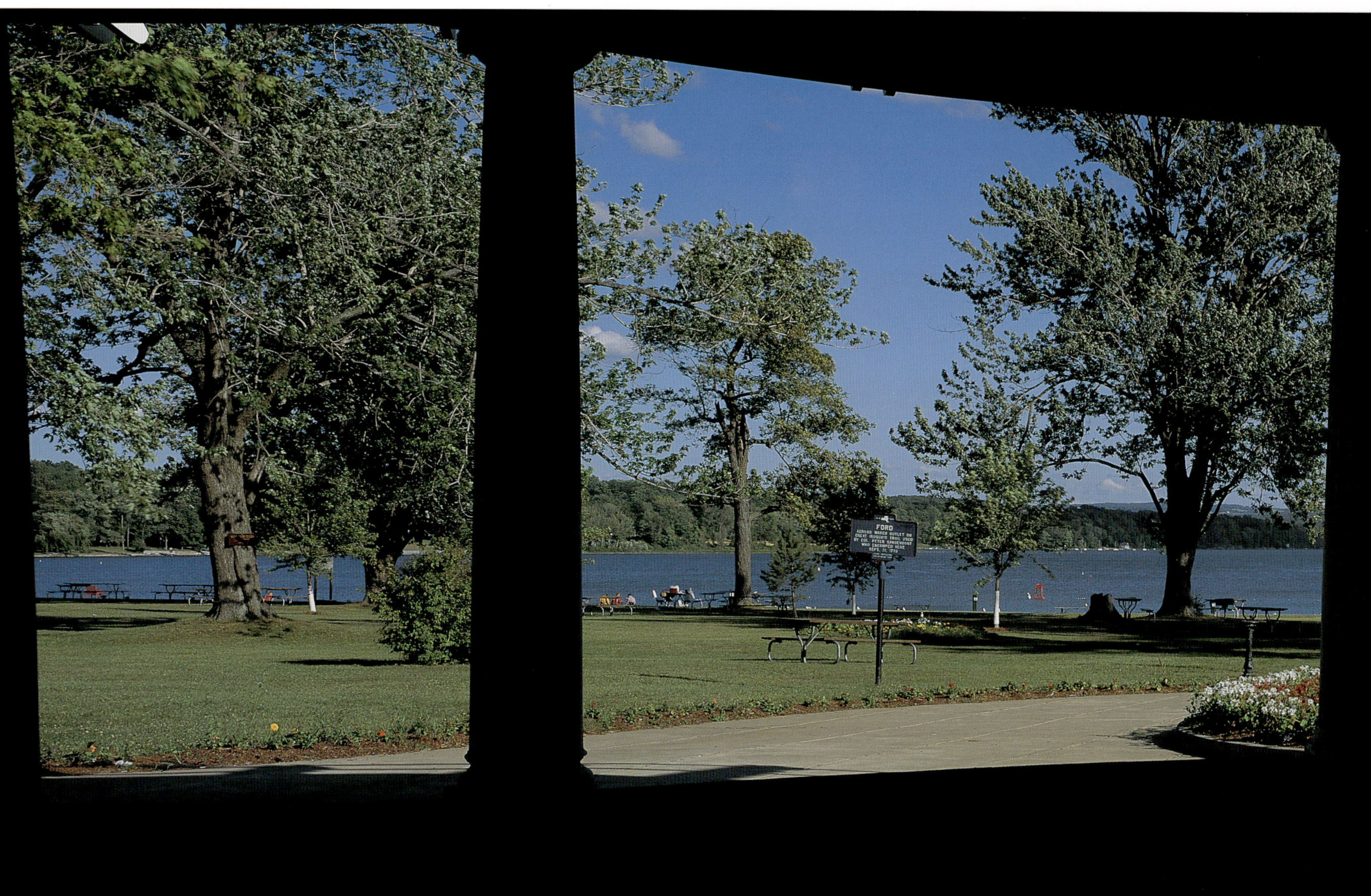

Hometown landmarks . . .

OWASCO LAKE from Emerson Park Pavilion, looking south.

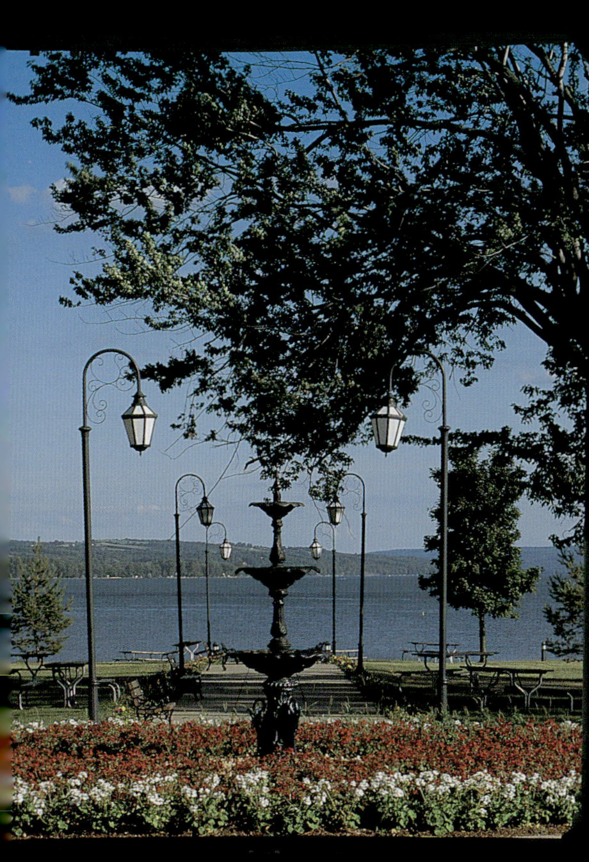
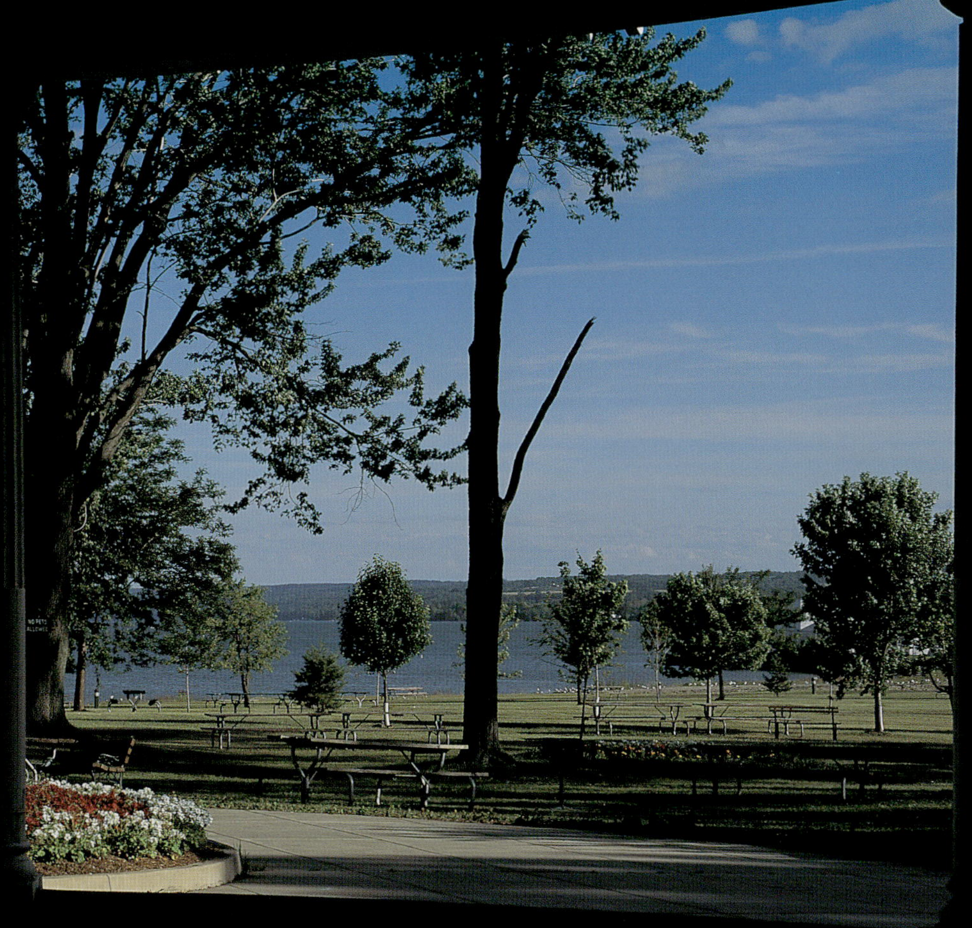
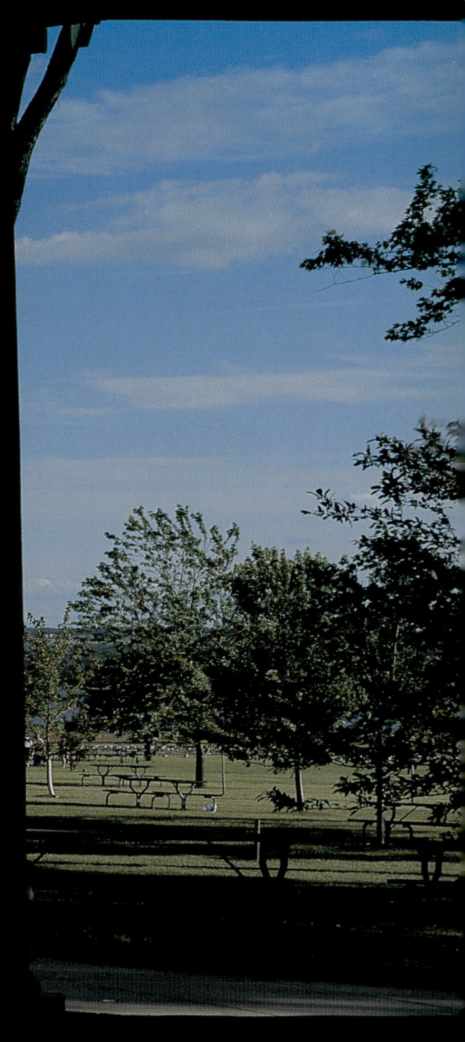

Prosperous cities . . .

CORNING and the Centerway Bridge

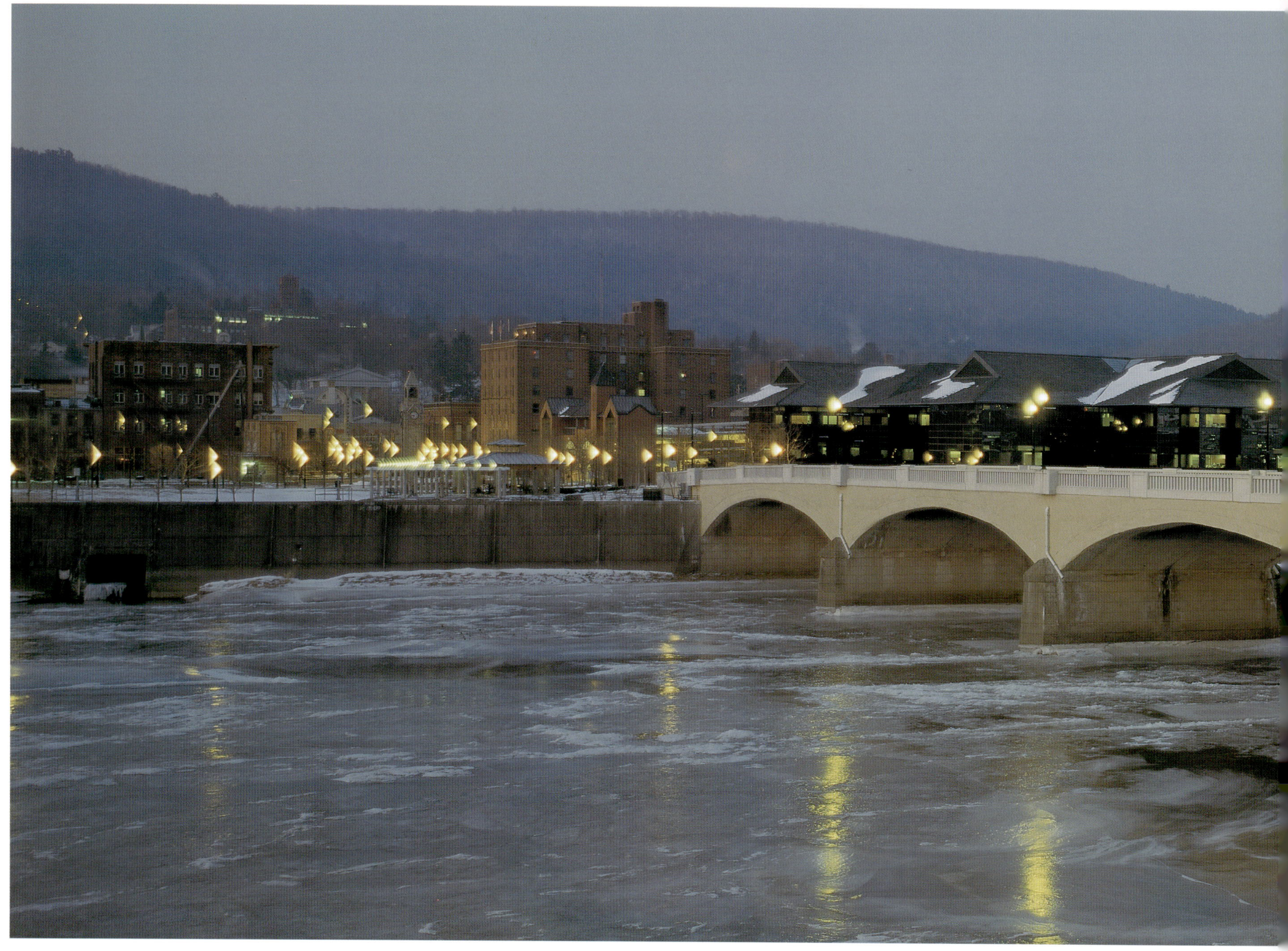

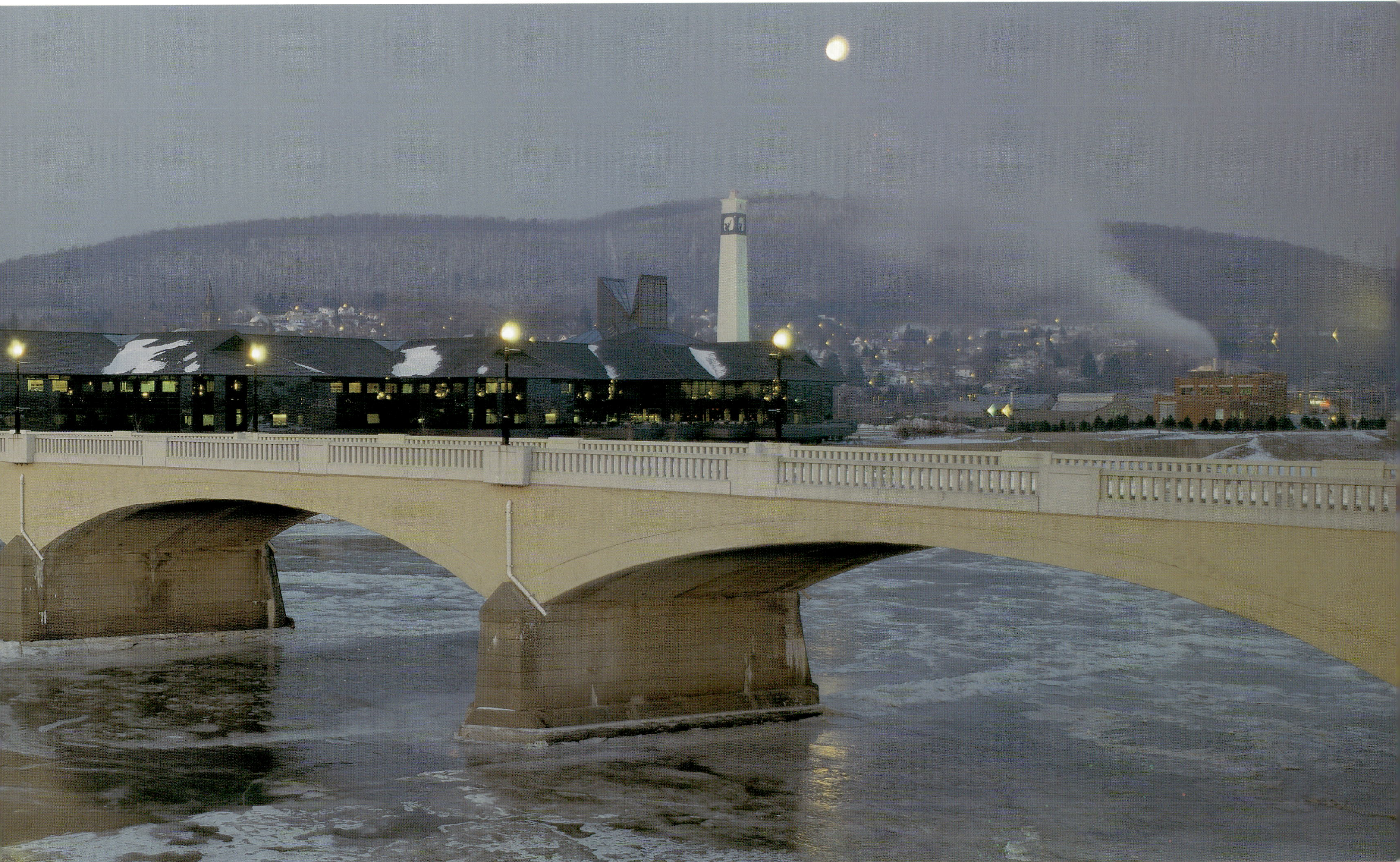

Boating paradise . . .

CAYUGA LAKE,
Treman State Marine Park, Ithaca

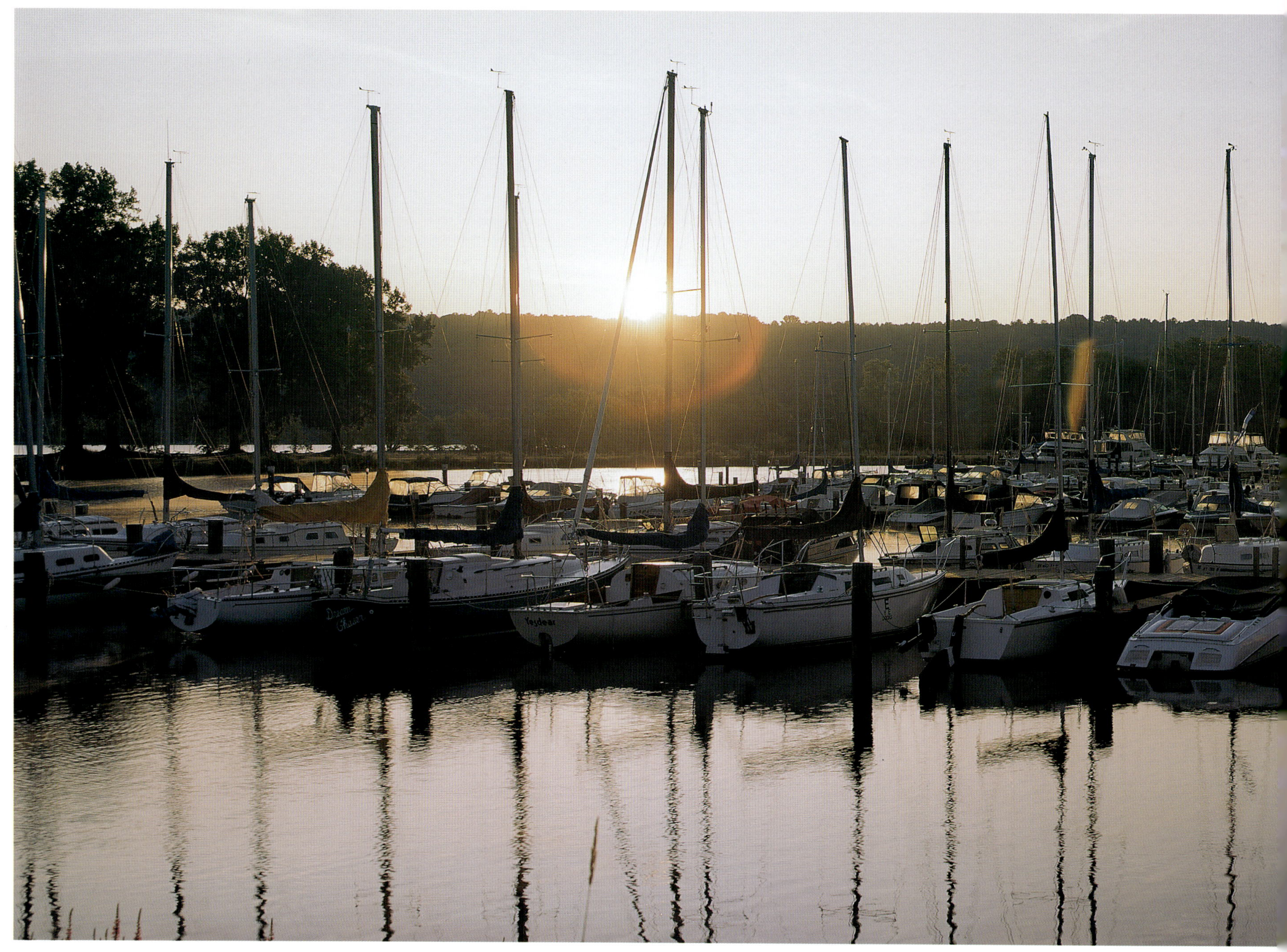

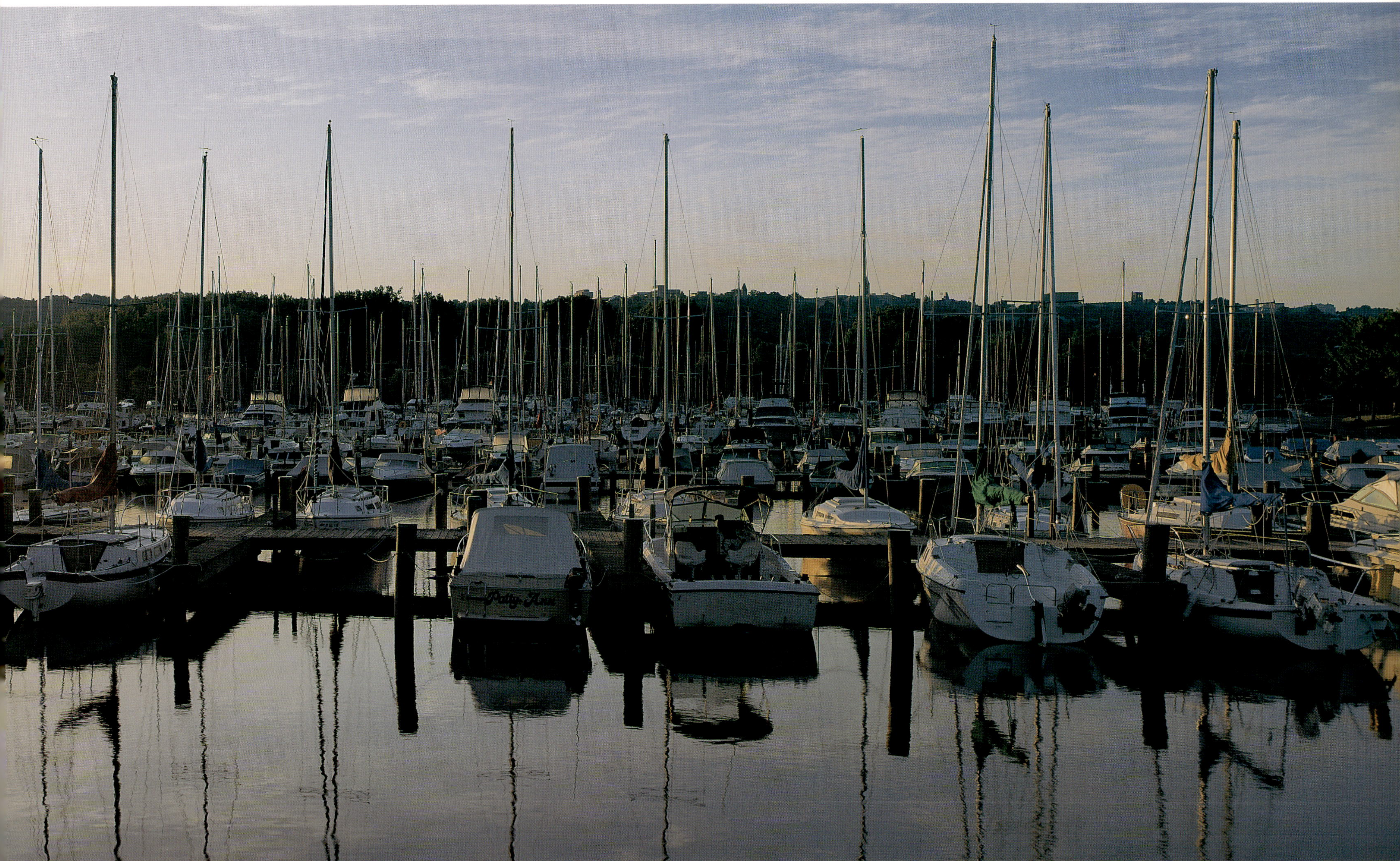

2 Letchworth State Park and Conesus Lake

CONESUS LAKE from McPherson Point, looking south.

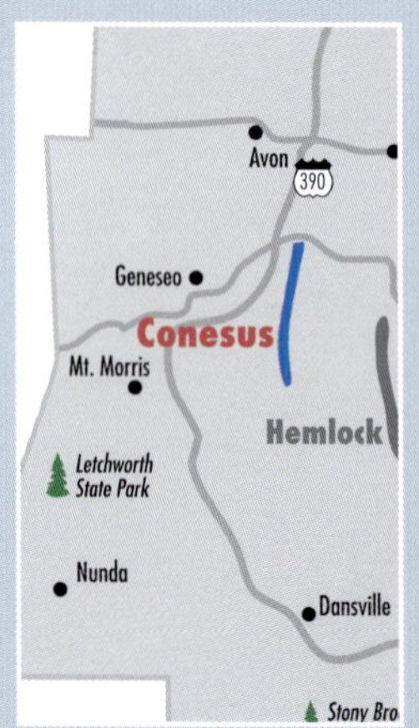

Letchworth State Park and Conesus Lake form the western gateway to the Finger Lakes region. Because of its thrilling depth, breadth, and beautiful waterfall scenery, the gorge in Letchworth has been called the "Grand Canyon of the East." Six-hundred-foot shale and sandstone walls channel the Genesee River through a course which roars over three major waterfalls, including one 107 feet high.

Heading east from Letchworth, you'll cross Canaseraga Creek and begin a gentle climb to a gorgeous view of nine-mile-long Conesus Lake, located due south of Rochester. Lakeville marks the north (outlet) end of the lake, site of an ancient Indian village. Near the south end lies the town of Conesus.

The lake is relatively shallow at 59 feet, perfect for hooking walleyes, pike, perch, and bass. McPherson Point, perhaps the most distinctive landmark along the shore, practically pinches the lake in half near its midsection.

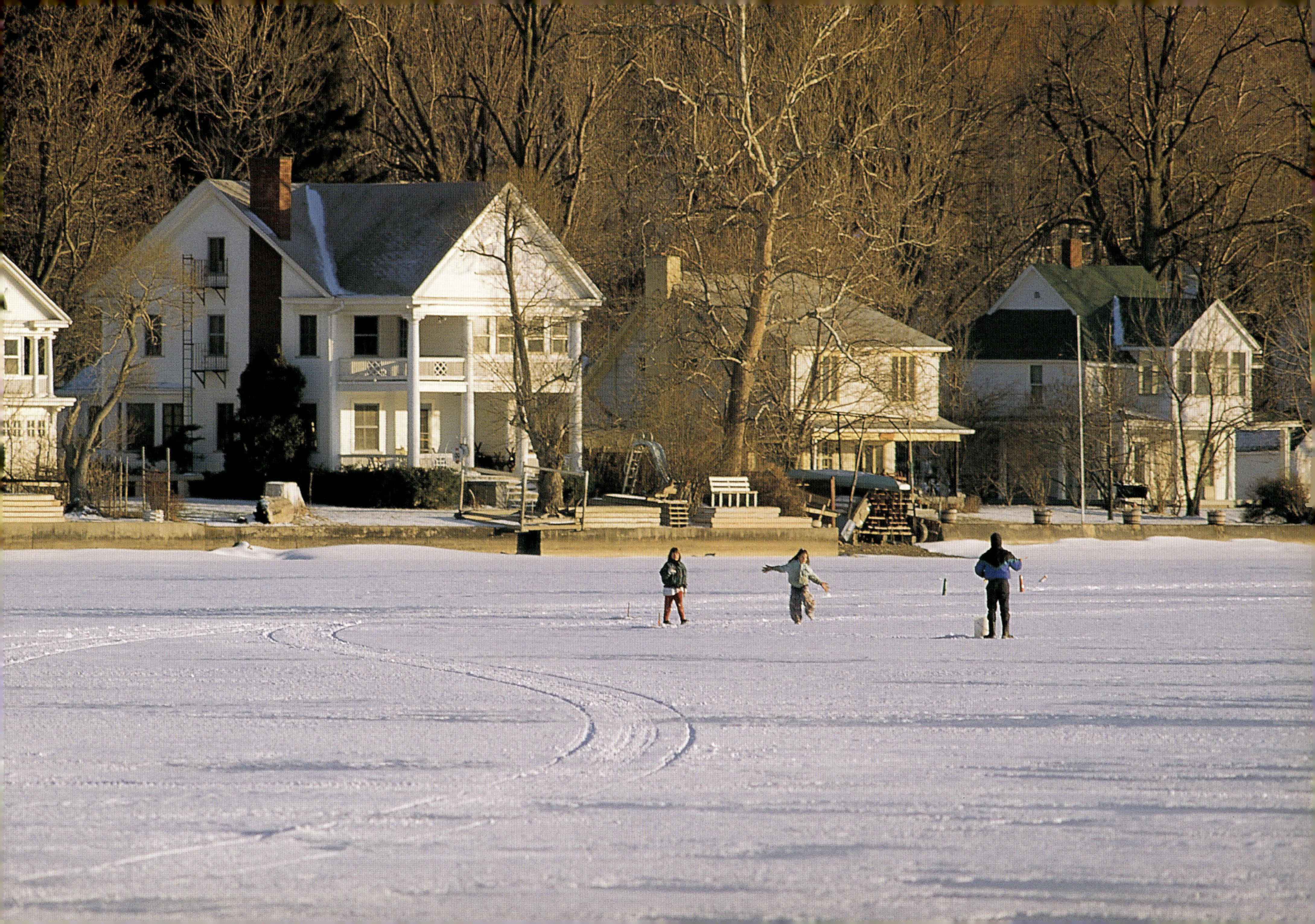

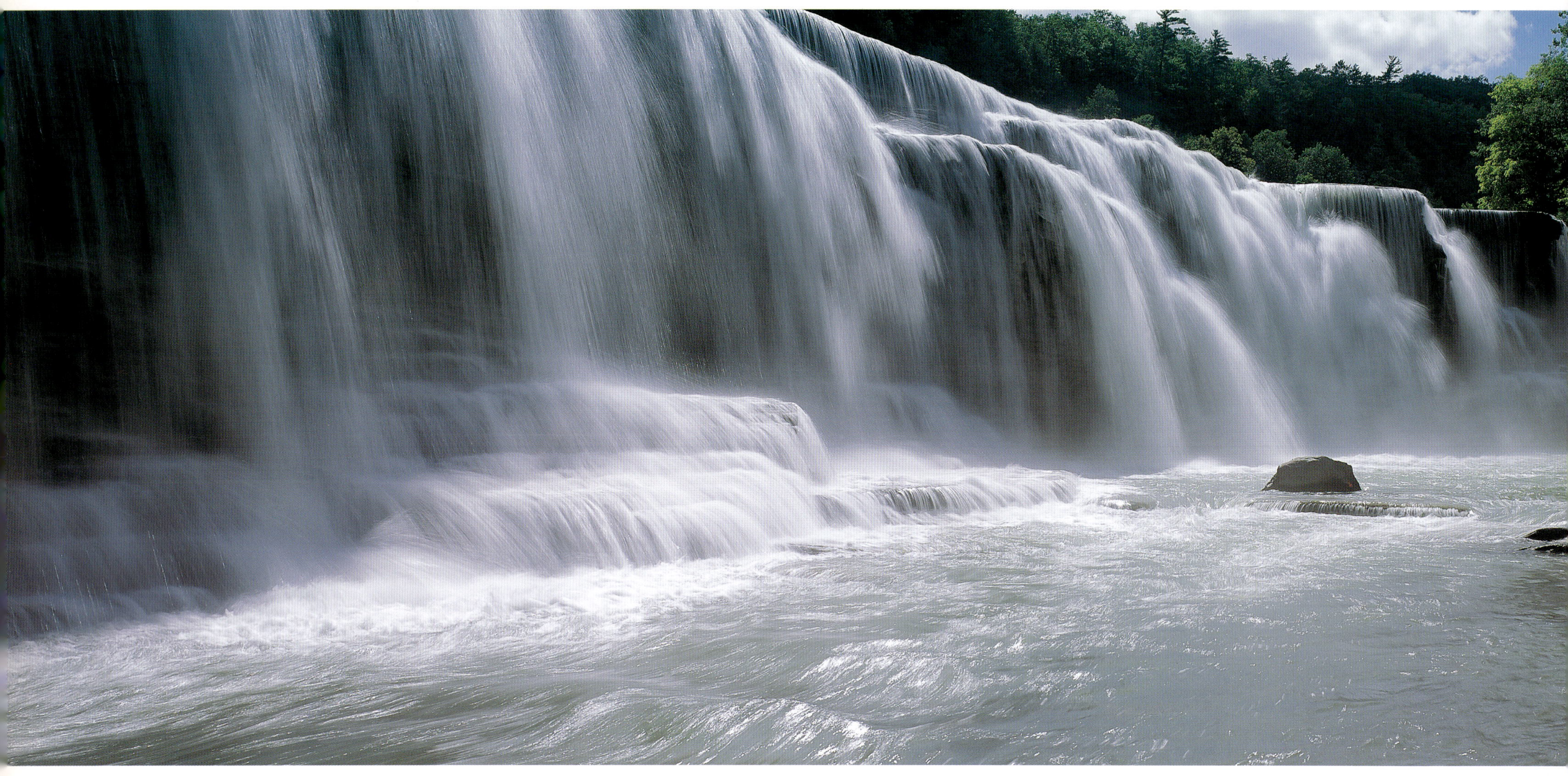

Above: LETCHWORTH STATE PARK, Lower Falls.

Right: LETCHWORTH STATE PARK, Middle and Upper Falls, from the Finger Lakes Trail.

GLACIERS deposited large masses of soil and rock which once blocked an ancient river bed, creating the gorge and its spectacular waterfalls.

The most popular scenery in the park, Middle Falls is seen at right from atop an enormous cliff on a branch of the Finger Lakes Trail. (The famous Glen Iris Inn is just out of the photo, to the right of the falls.) The Finger Lakes Trail, a hiking path system of some 785 miles, stretches from the Pennsylvania border in Allegheny State Park, across the southern ends of the Finger Lakes, to connect with the Long Path in Catskill Park. It's a favorite for hikers, backpackers, cross-country skiers, nature lovers, bird-watchers, and photographers.

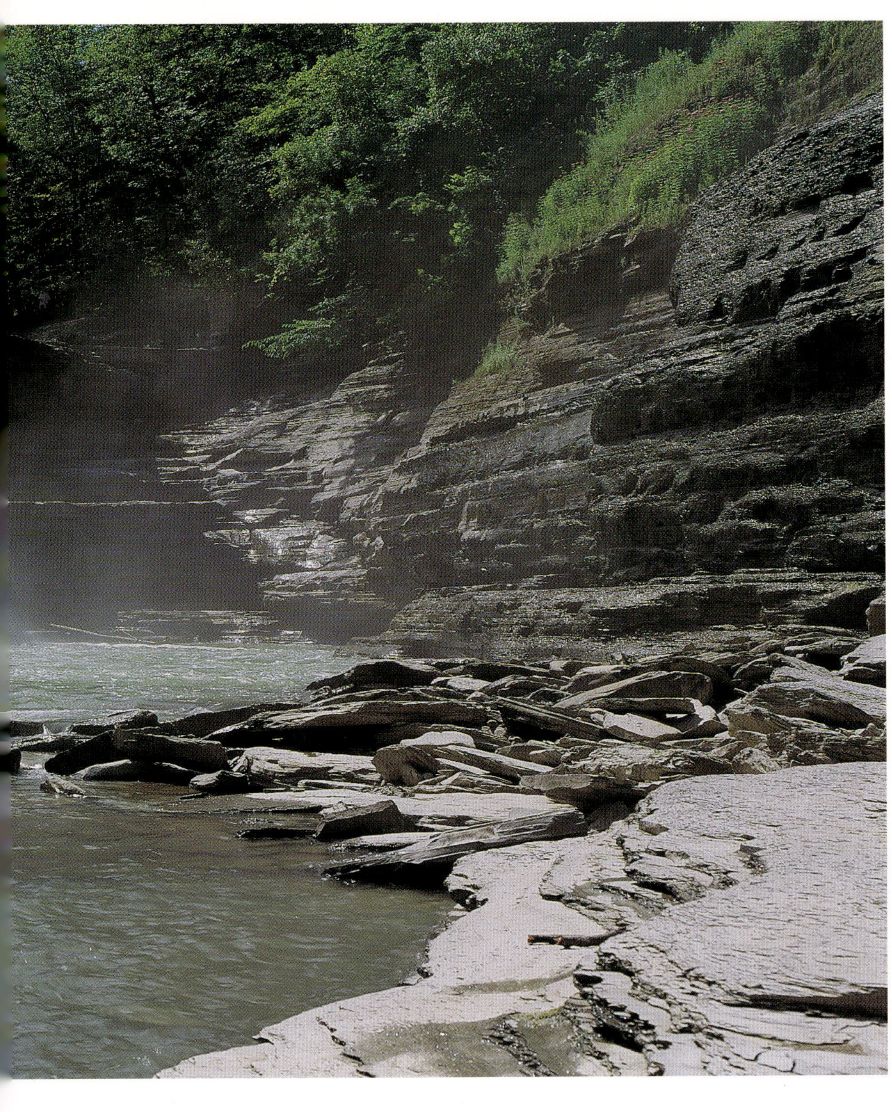

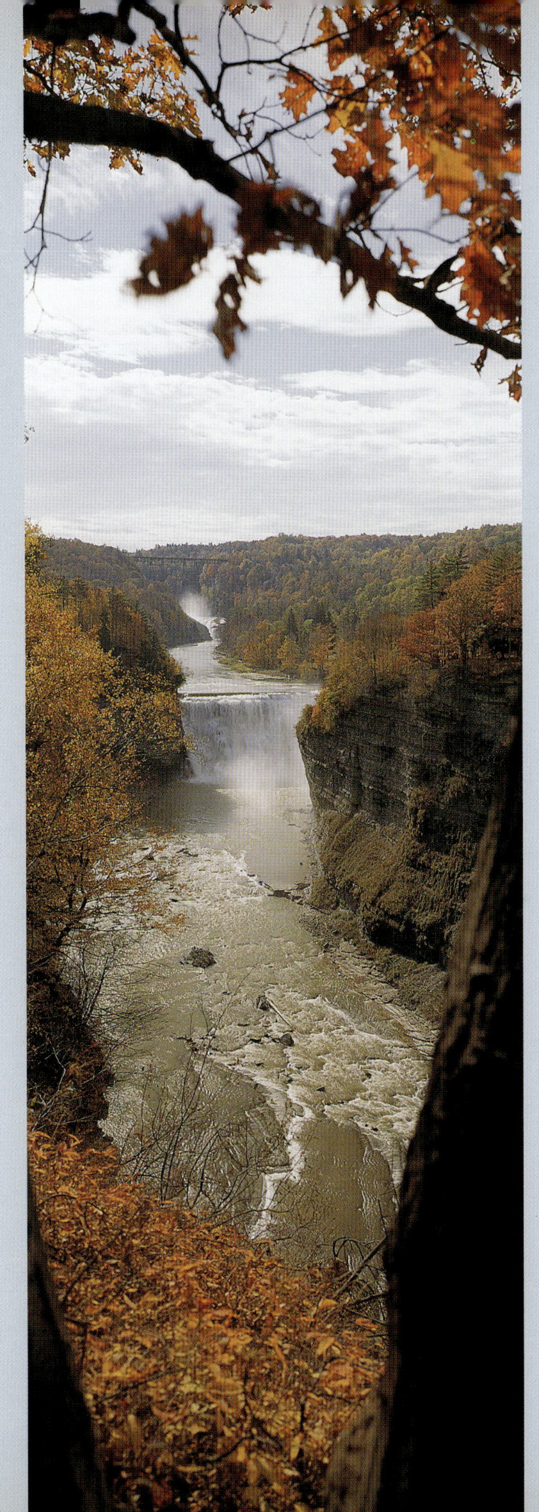

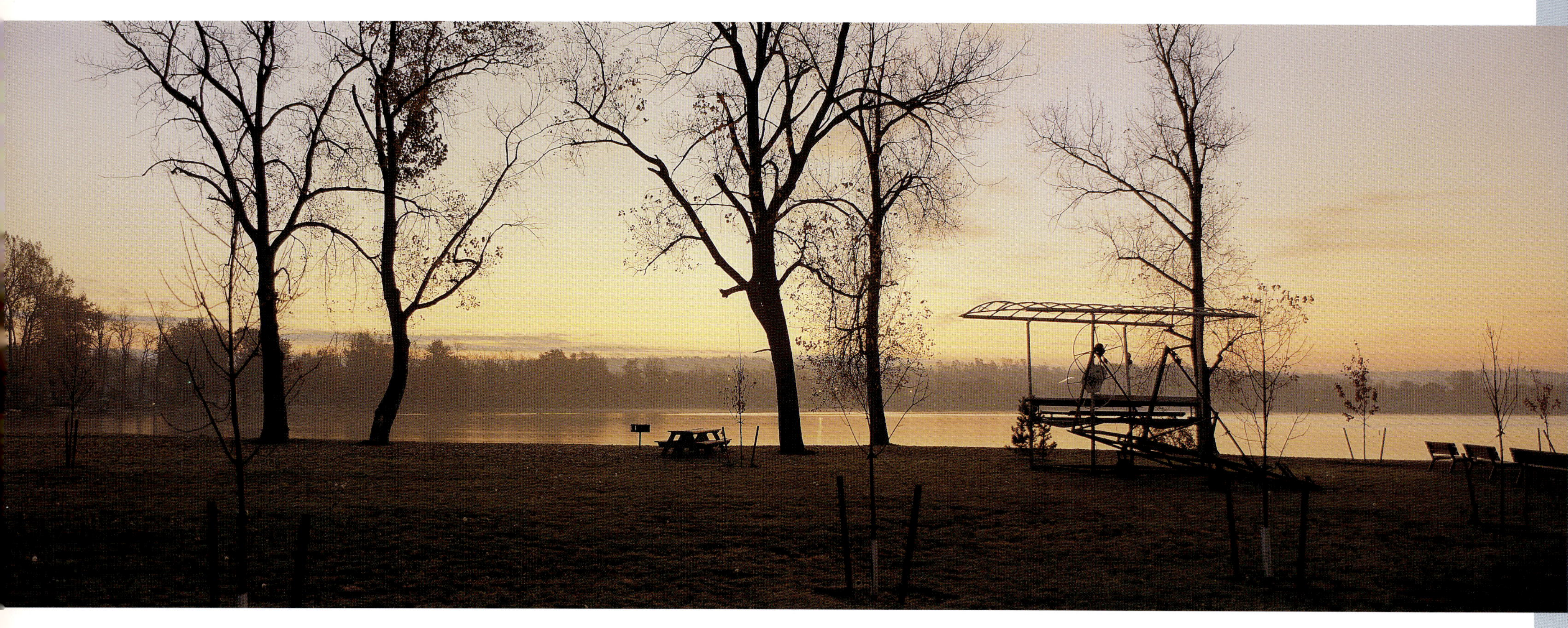

North end of CONESUS LAKE, from
Vitale Park, Lakeville, looking east.

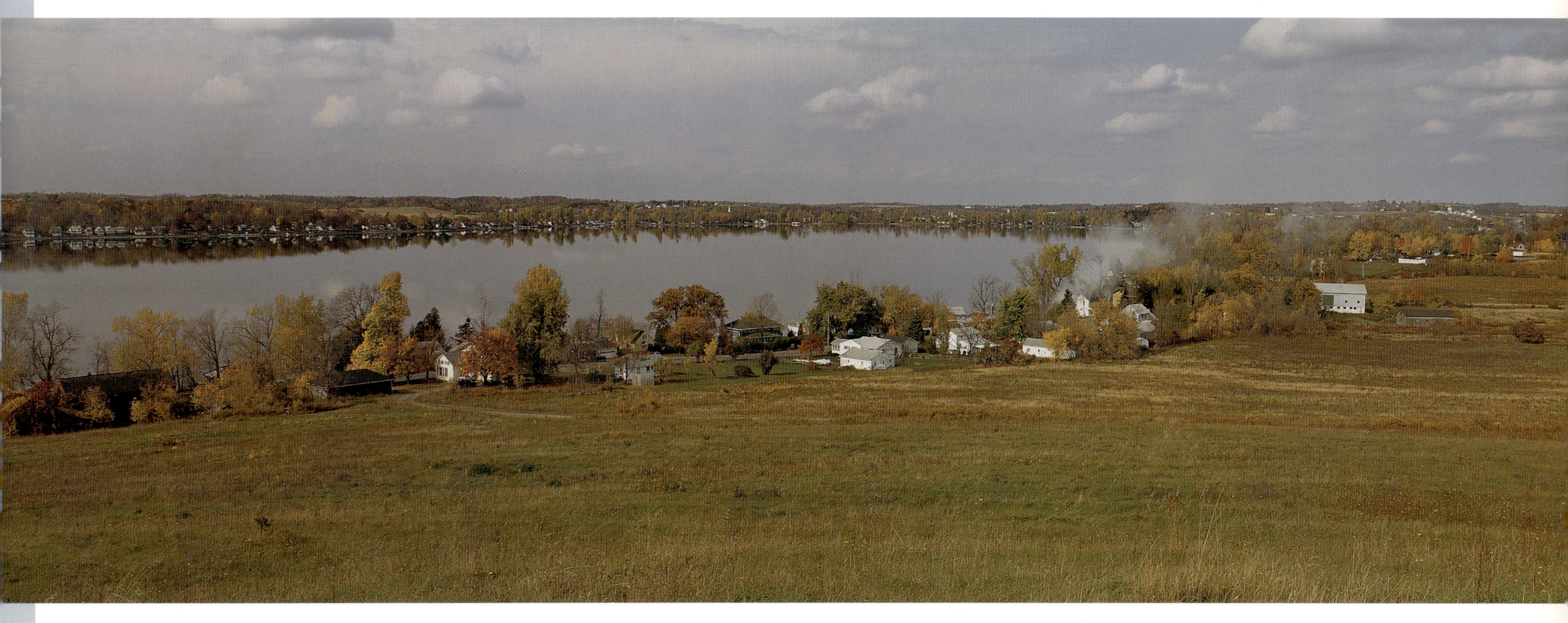

CONESUS LAKE and Lakeville, looking north.

A windless fall day creates an ethereal moment along the hillsides.

3 Hemlock, Canadice, and Honeoye Lakes

HEMLOCK LAKE from north end, looking south.

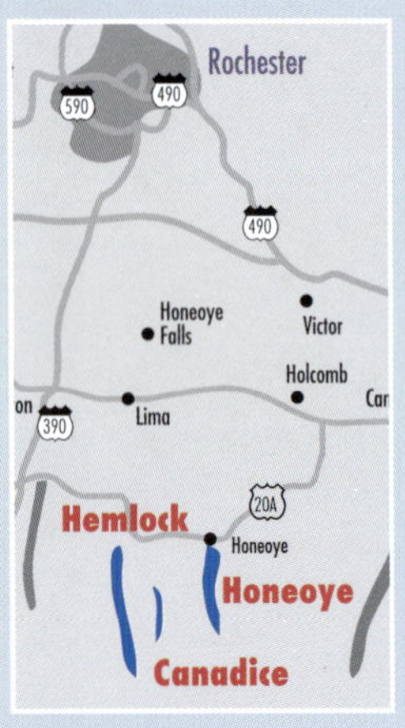

No area in the Finger Lakes region is as pristine as Hemlock and Canadice Lakes, seemingly untouched since creation. Surrounded by the steep Marrowback and Bald Hills and preserved as a drinking water supply, they seem to be thousands of years back in time, before houses, boats, docks, and congestion. Some fishing (limited by permit) is about the only activity. Hemlock Lake itself is eight miles long and 96 feet deep; Canadice, just three miles long and 91 feet deep.

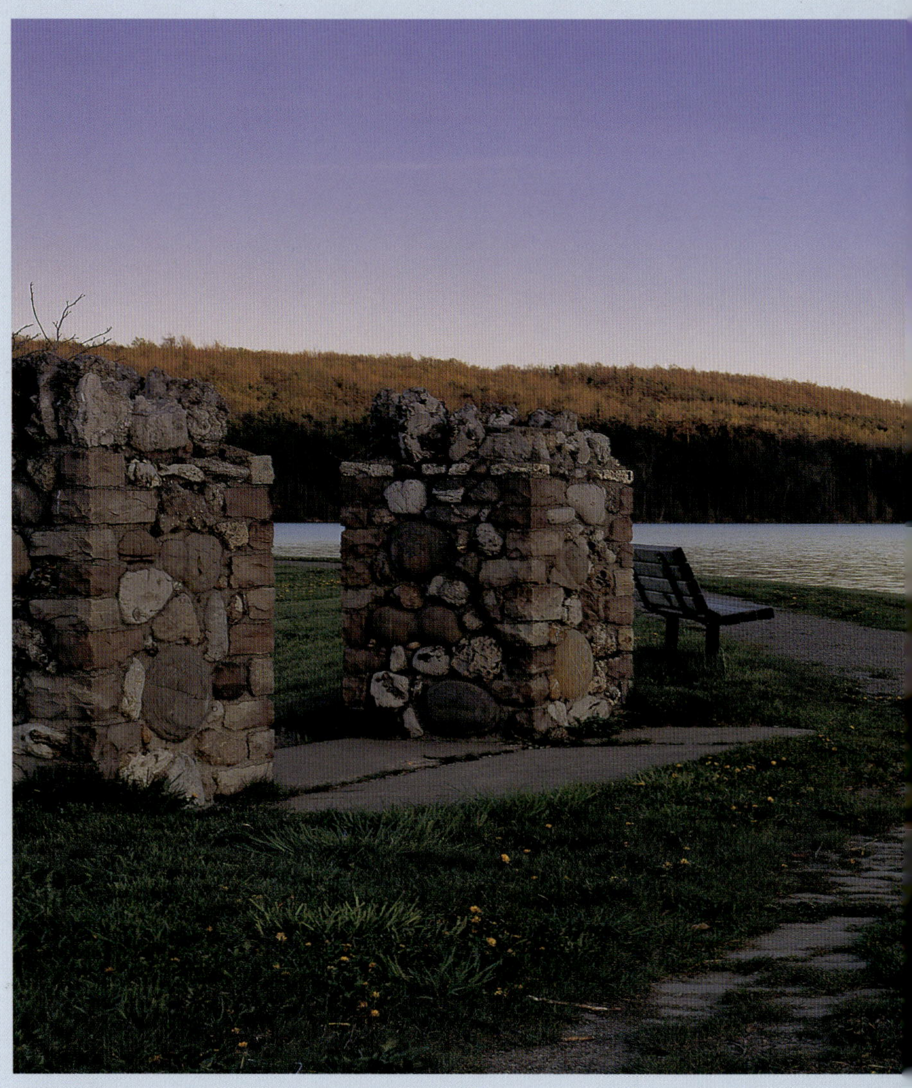

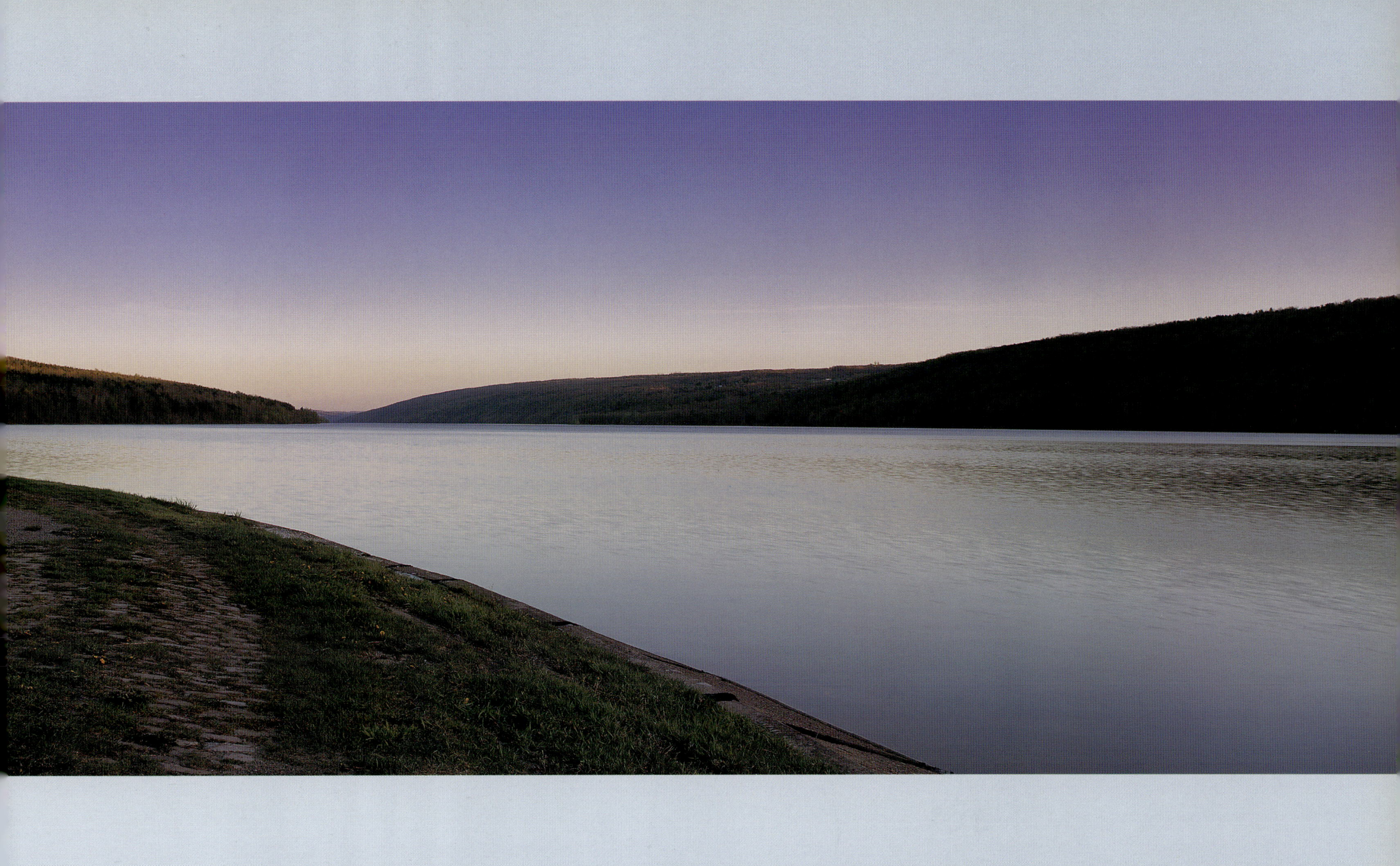

HONEOYE LAKE
from Hollister Park,
looking north.

SEEN from atop Canadice Hill, five-mile-long Honeoye Lake stretches north to Honeoye Village, another ancient Indian site. At just 30 feet deep, the lake is the shallowest of the Finger Lakes and home to bluegills, yellow perch, pickerel, and bass.

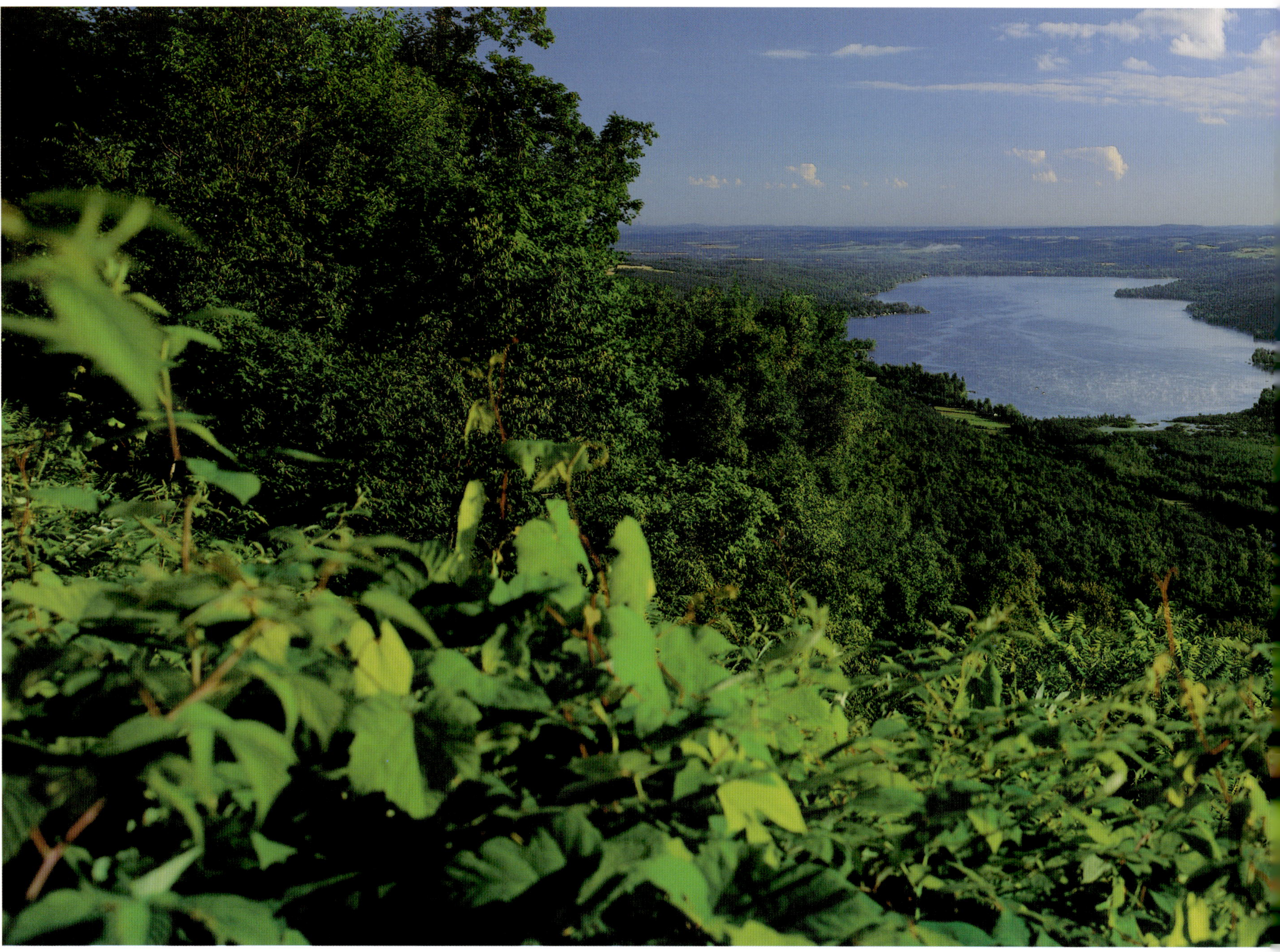

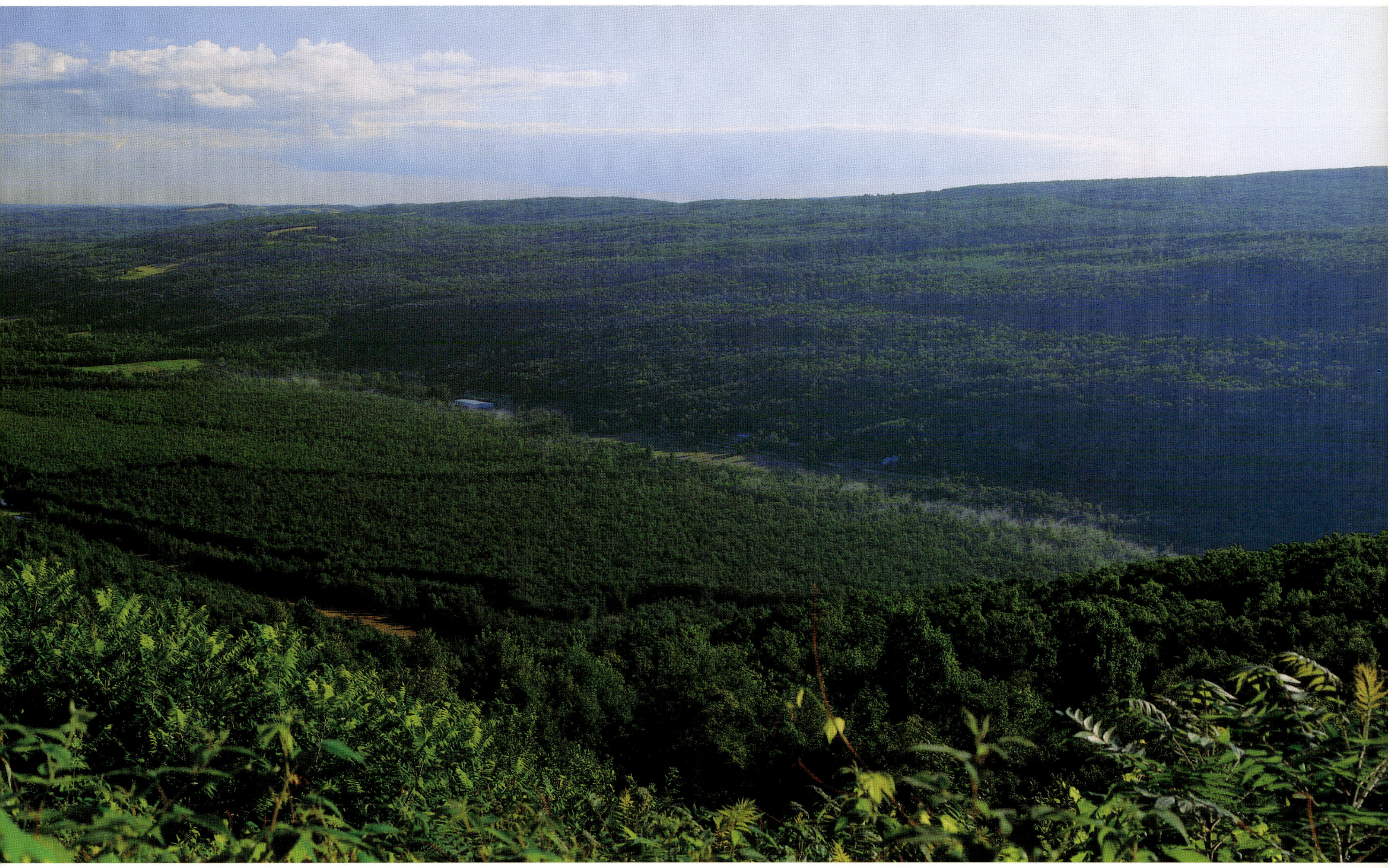

CANADICE LAKE,
looking south.

BALD Hill, on the right, rises steeply to separate Hemlock and Canadice Lakes. Although small, Canadice Lake claims the highest shoreline elevation of all the Finger Lakes—1,099 feet.

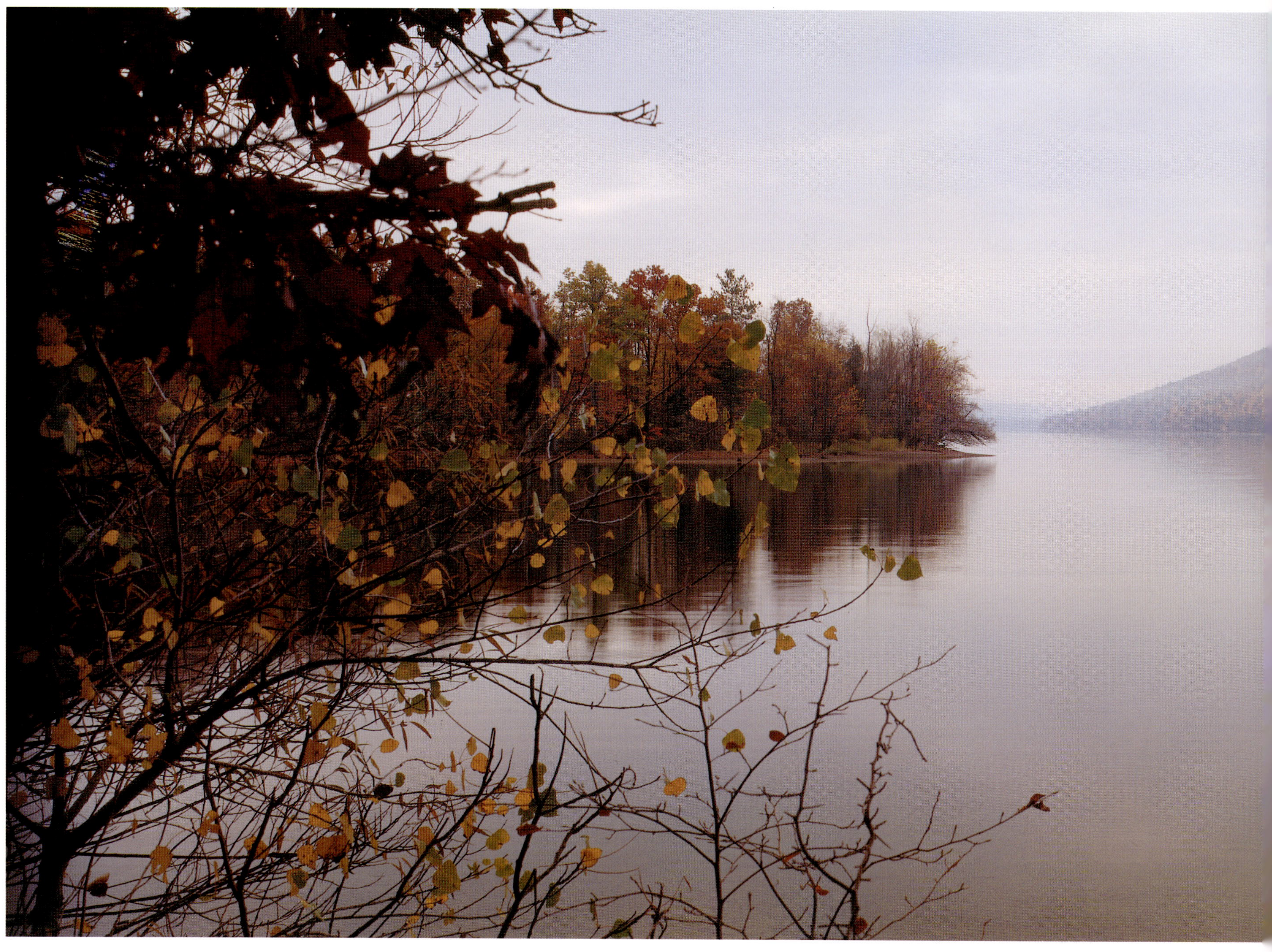

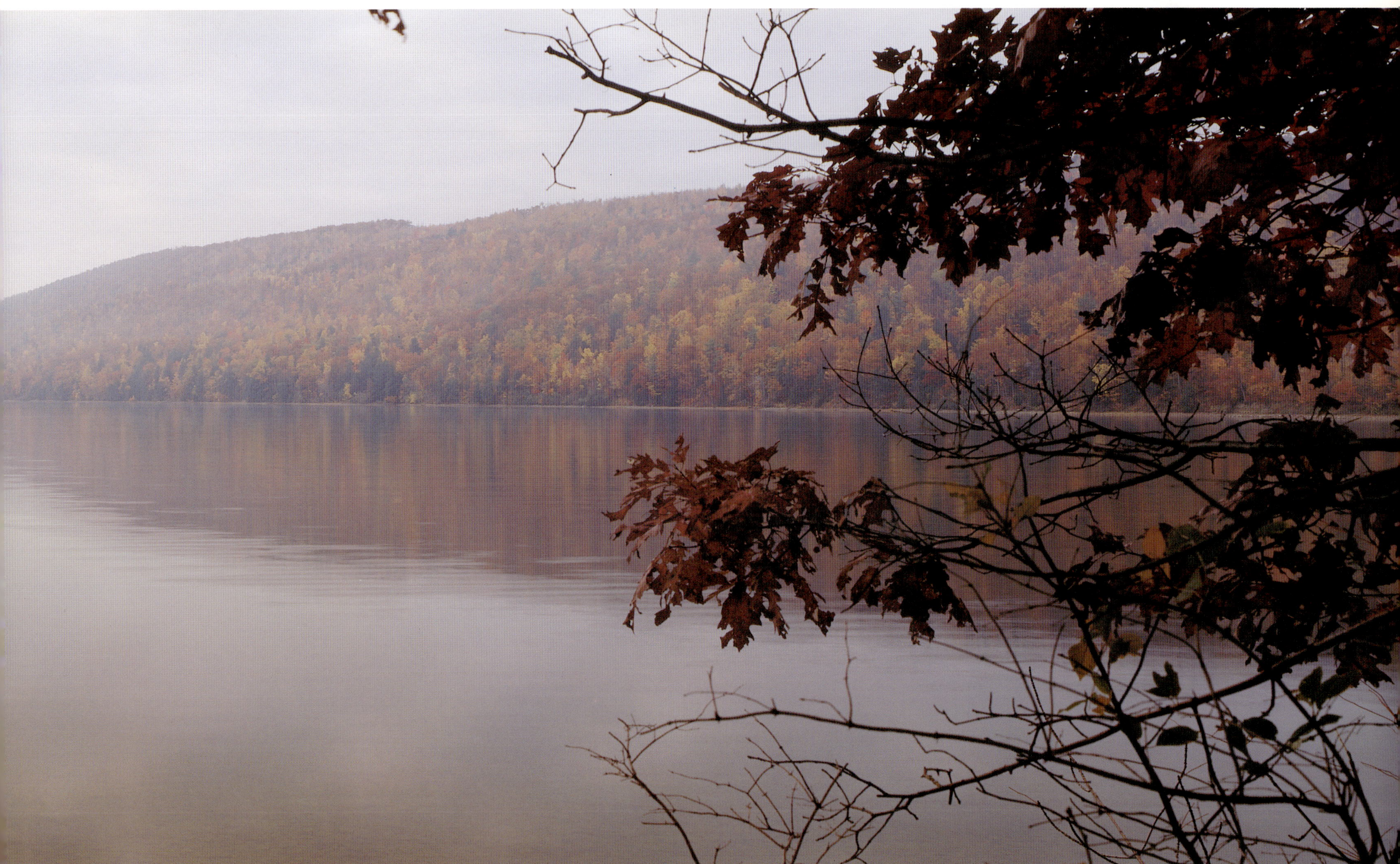

4 Canandaigua Lake

CANANDAIGUA LAKE, from Naples Road, looking northeast.

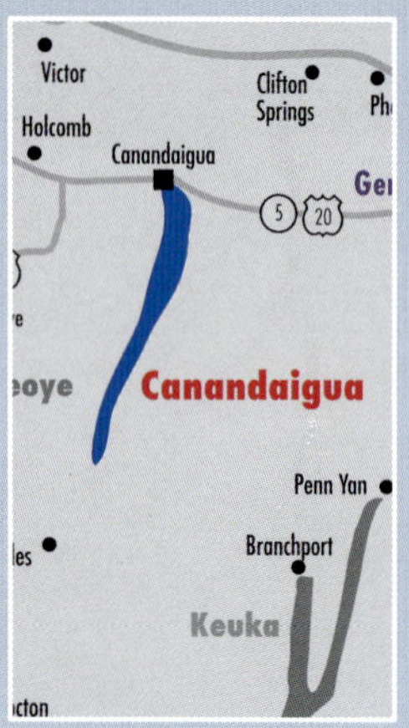

Long ago, the Seneca Indians knew "Kanandarque" as the Chosen Spot. They built longhouses, thrived on corn, beans, and squash, and established the Seneca Nation. Today, the city of Canandaigua flourishes near this site on the north end of the lake. The lake itself is 16 miles long, reaches depths of 262 feet, and is famous for rainbow, brown, and lake trout.

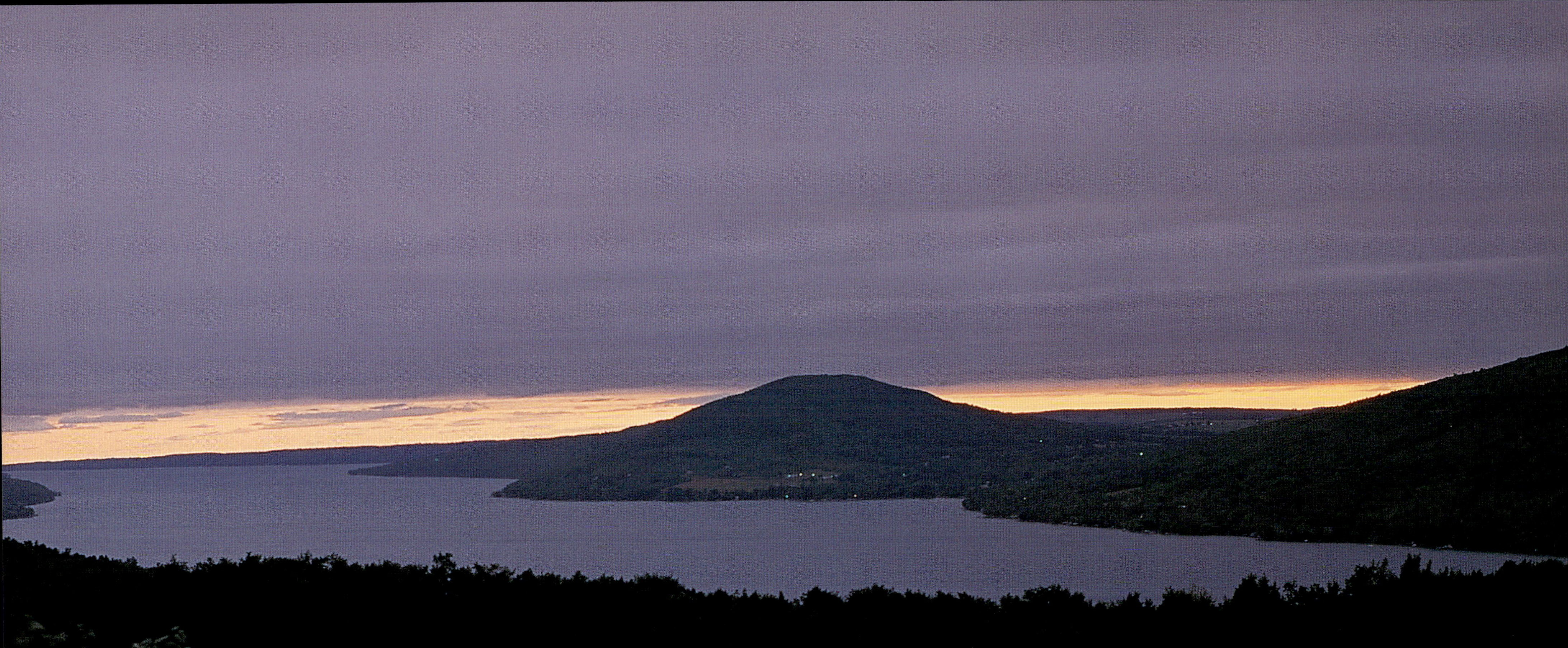

CANANDAIGUA LAKE, from City Pier, looking south.

The city of Canandaigua is known for its thoroughbred race track, the stunning Sonnenberg Gardens, and handsome old homes.

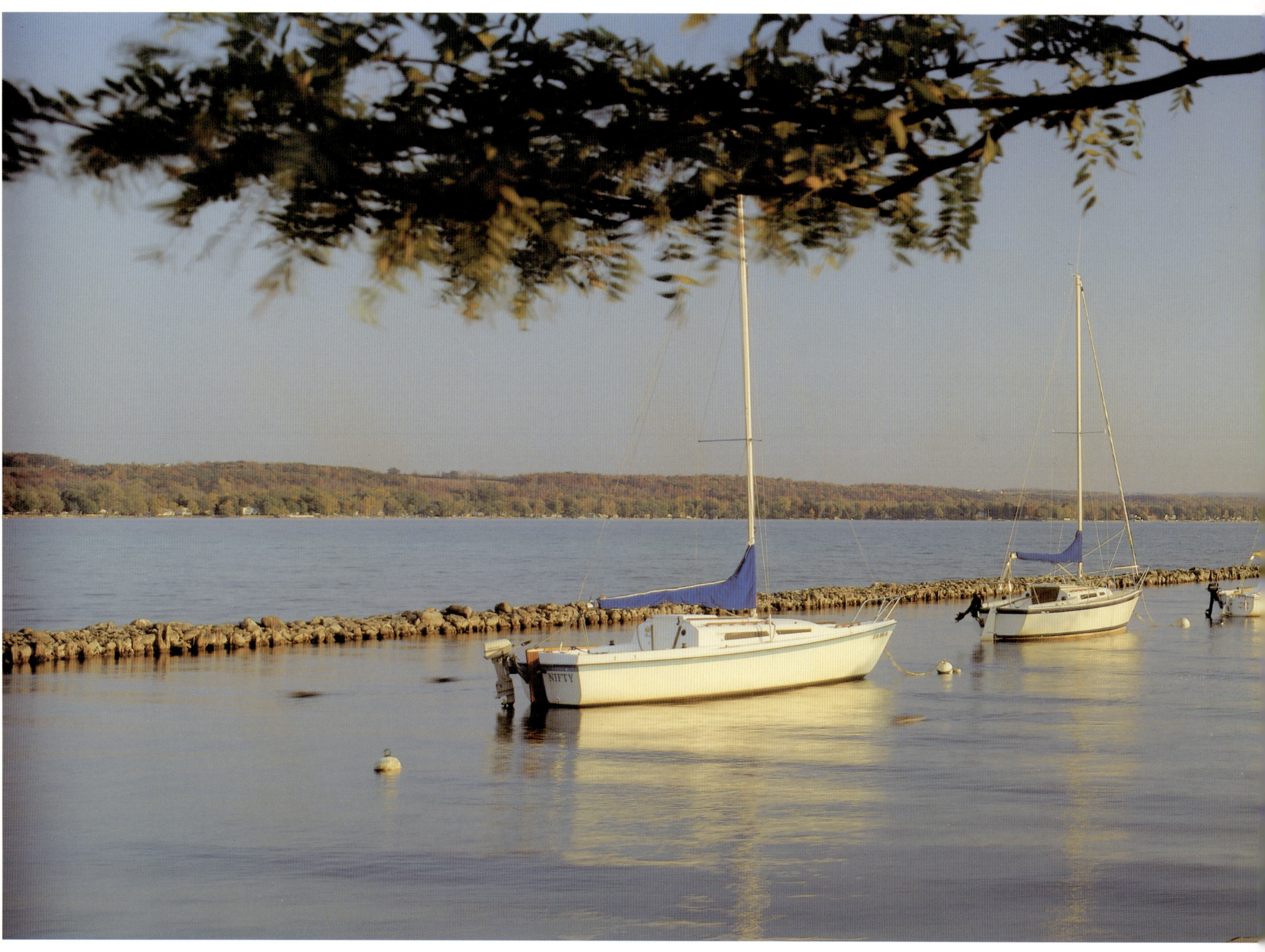

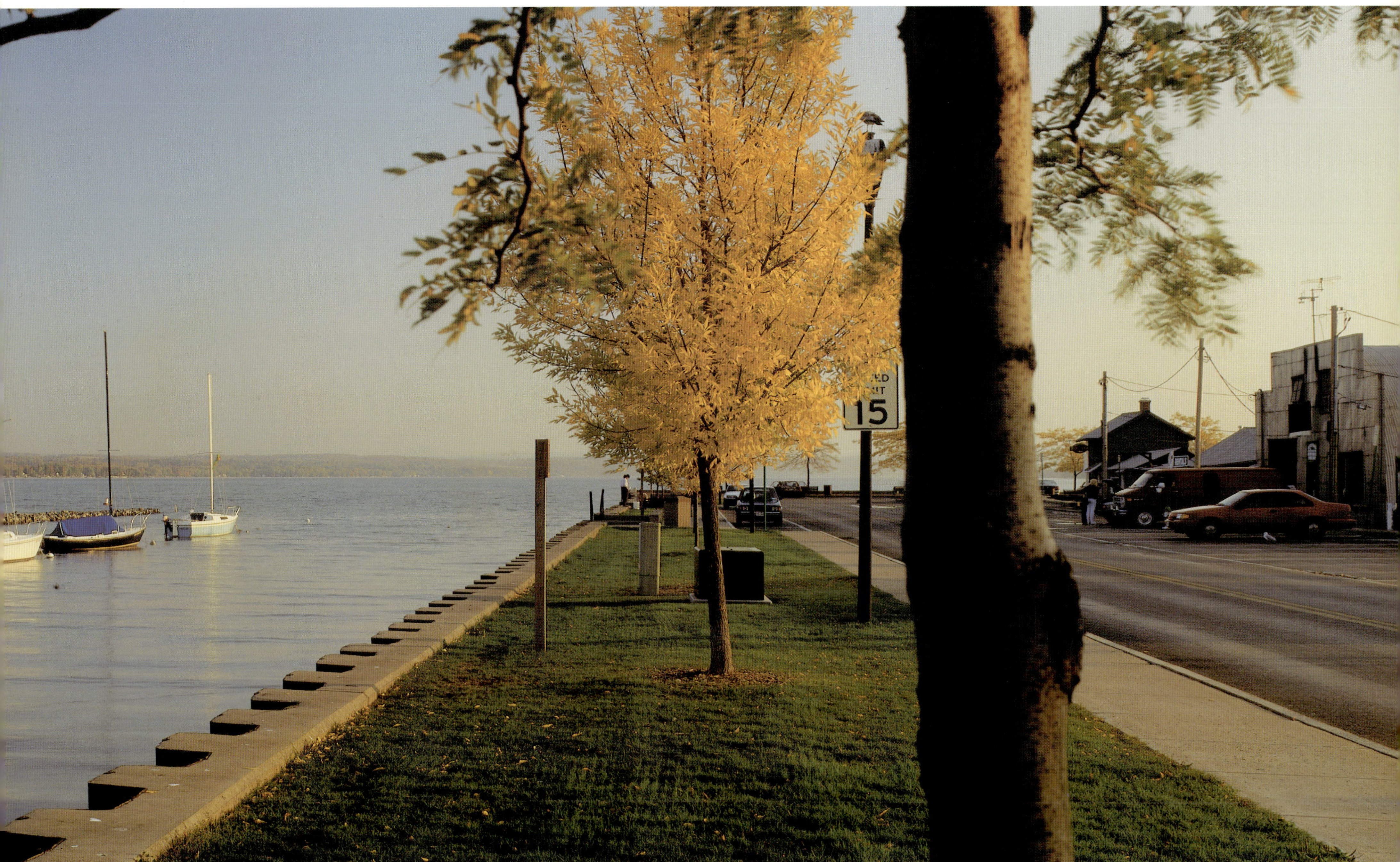
15

CANANDAIGUA LAKE, from Canandaigua Yacht Club, looking east.

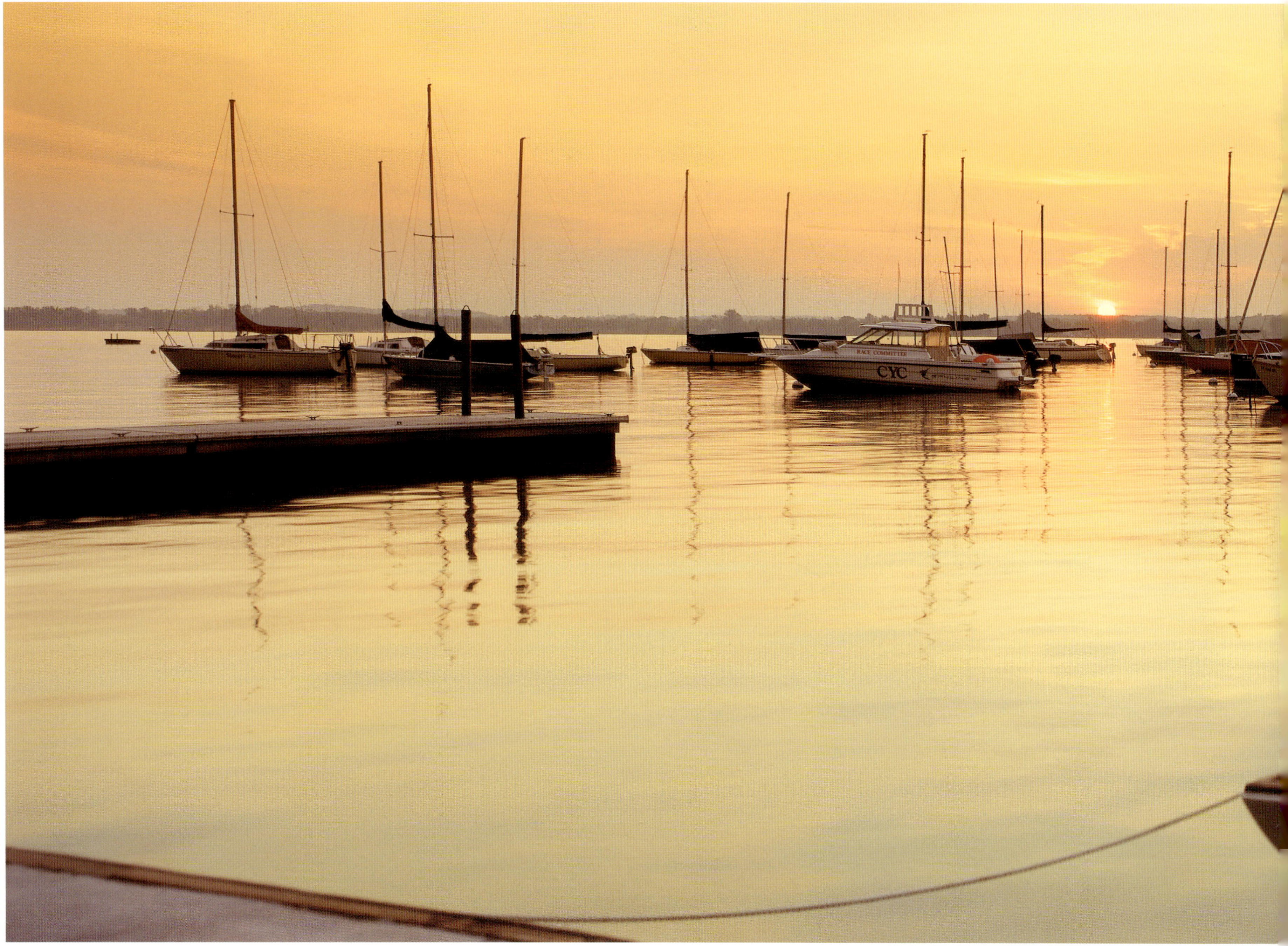

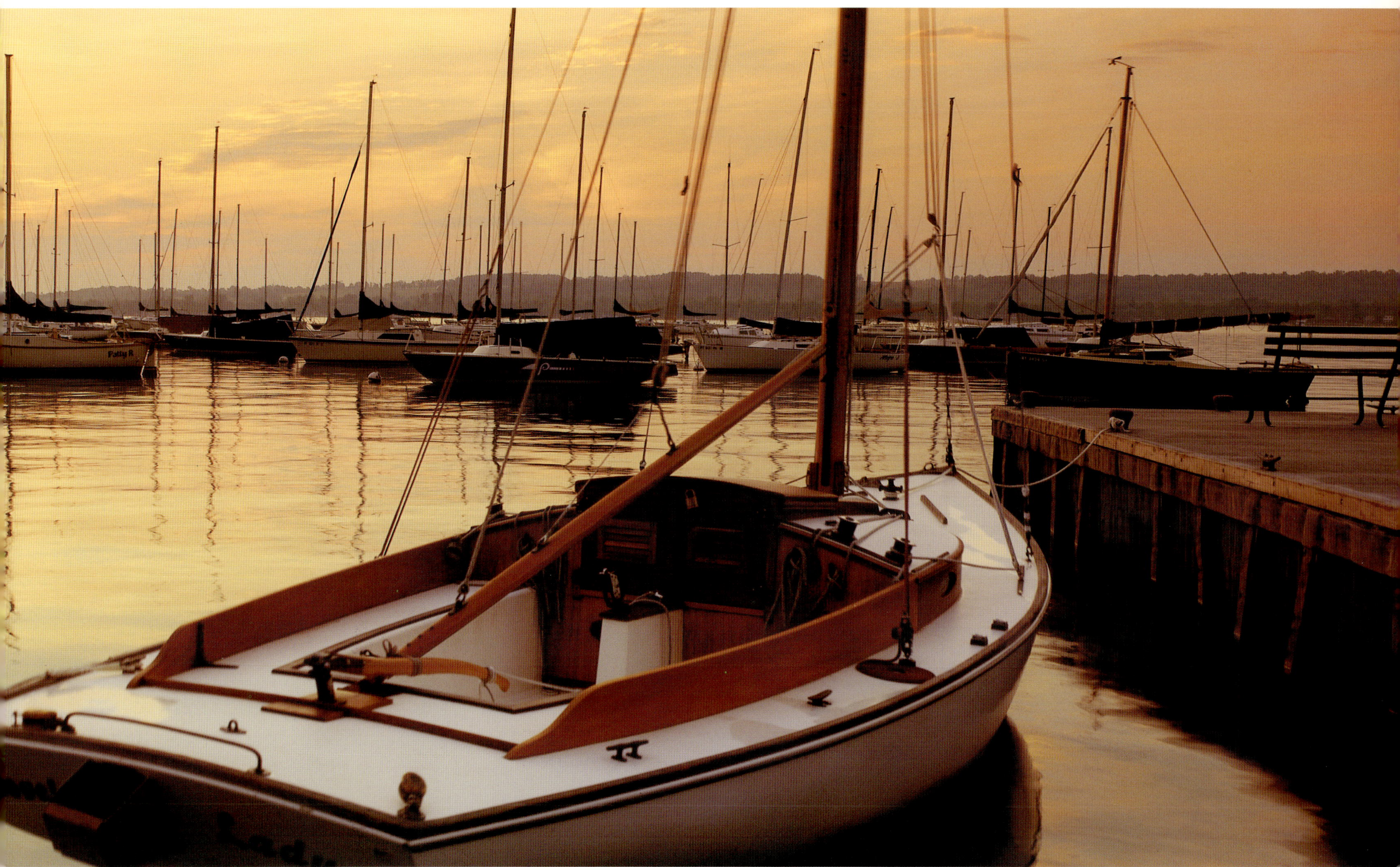

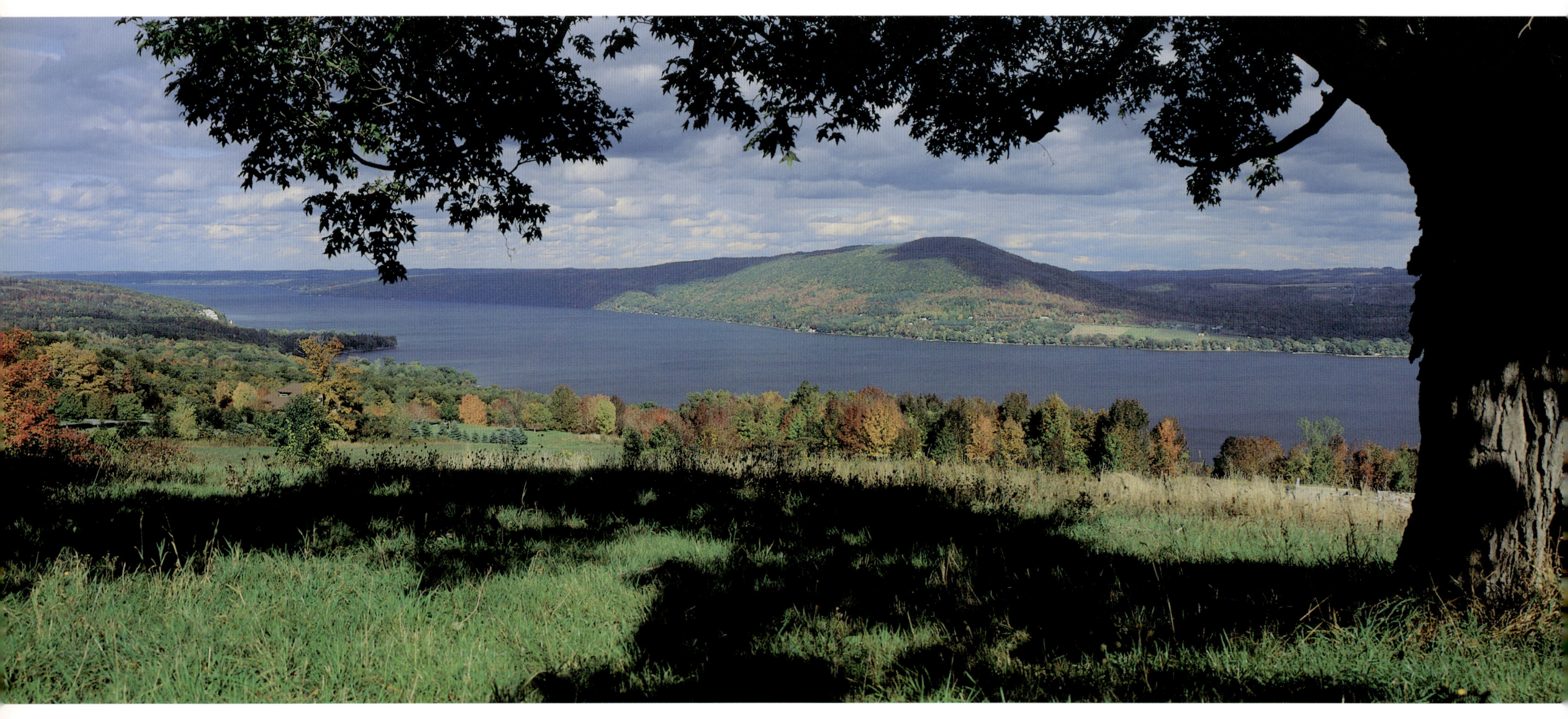

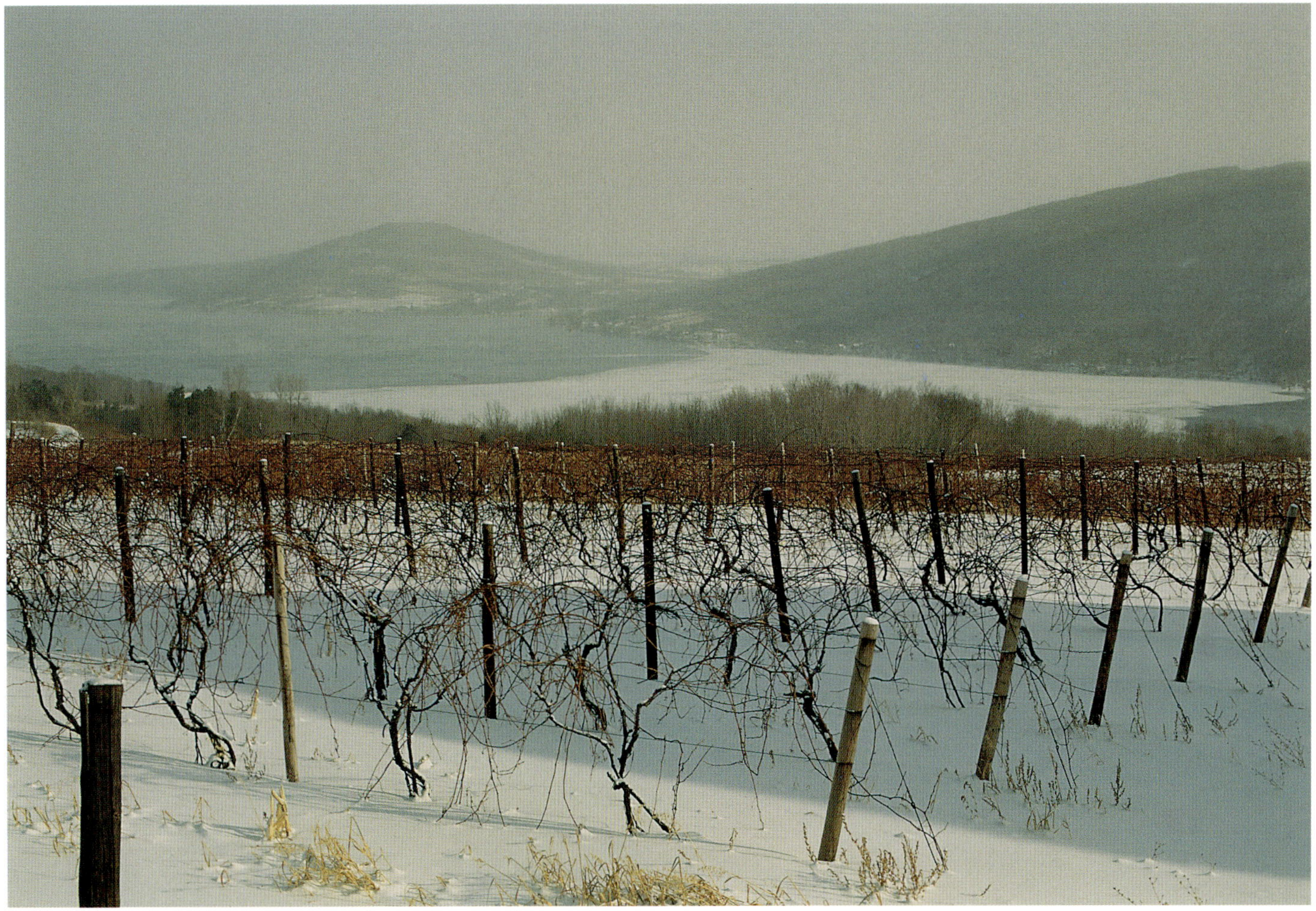

Far left:
CANANDAIGUA LAKE and Bare Hill, looking east.

BARE Hill, rising across the lake, is the most recognizable land form on Canandaigua Lake. According to Indian legend, the Seneca people emerged from the earth at this spot.

Left:
CANANDAIGUA LAKE, South Hill, Vine Valley, and Bare Hill from Naples Road, looking northeast.

5 Keuka Lake

KEUKA LAKE, from Camp Cory south of Penn Yan, looking southwest.

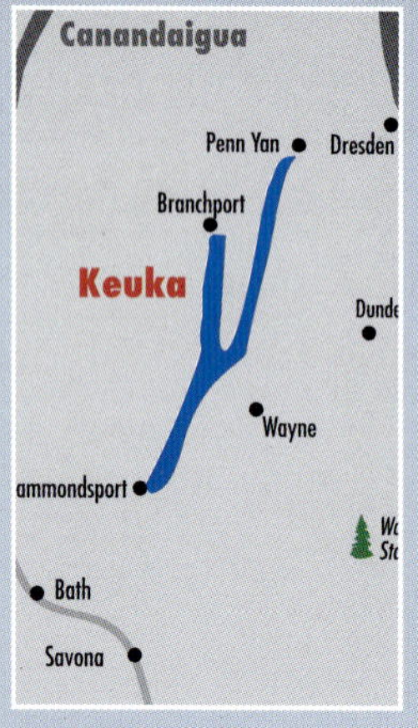

With its distinctive "Y" shape, Keuka Lake is probably the most easily recognized of all the Finger Lakes. Its longest stretch, from Hammondsport to Penn Yan, is 22 miles. The west branch, from Bluff Point (at the tip of the Y's tongue) to Branchport, is eight miles long on its own. Keuka is 187 feet deep, known for wild lake trout, bass, and landlocked salmon. Nearly a dozen wineries ring the lake, adding a European flavor to the area. Route 54A, on the west shore, has been designated one of the most scenic drives in the state of New York.

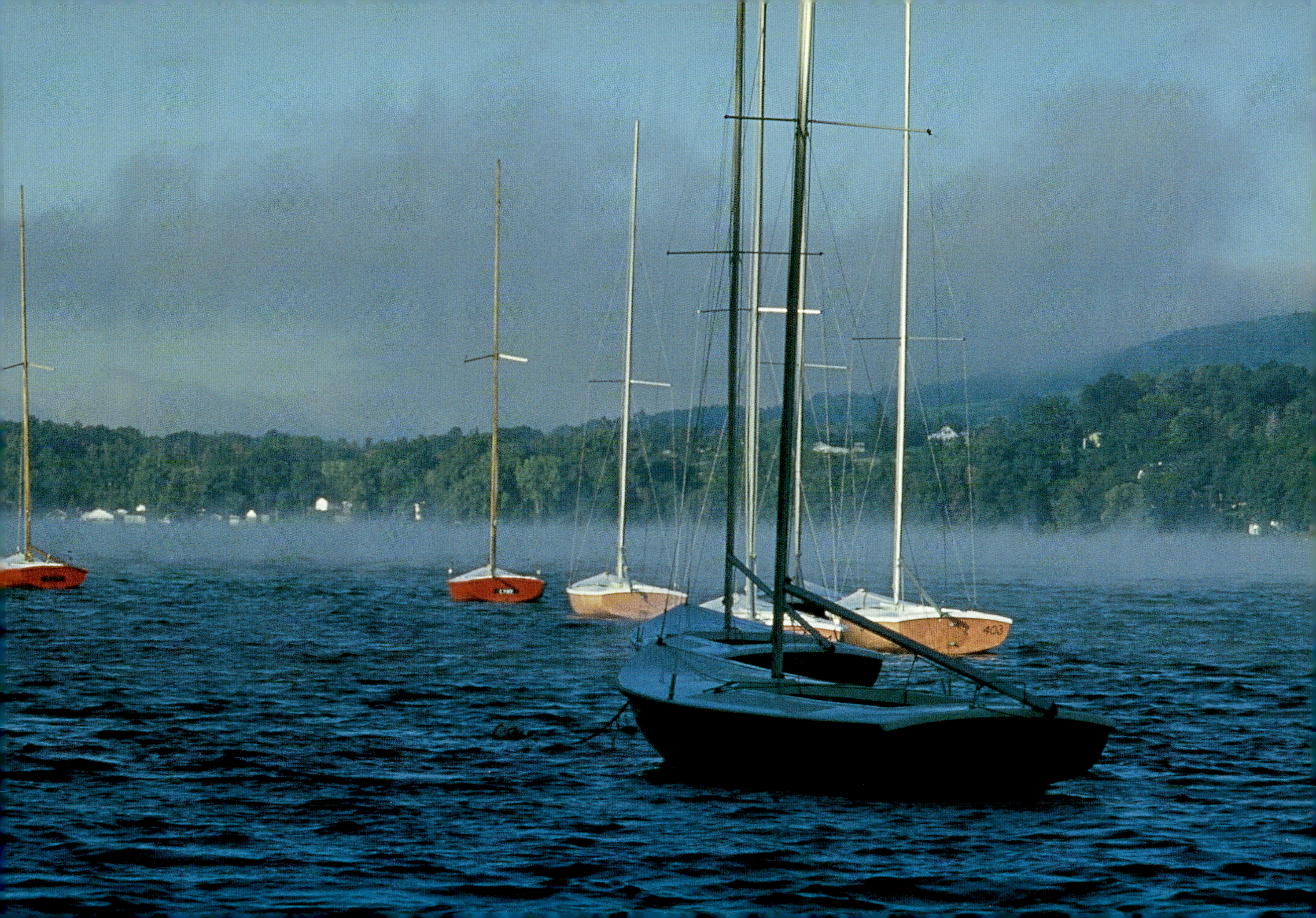
403

KEUKA LAKE,
West Branch from
Esperanza.

ONE of the finest views of Keuka Lake is from the steps of the Esperanza Mansion, near Branchport. Completed in 1838, the mansion took over ten years to build and is now on the National Historic Register. The builders created its stately pillars by laying bricks around the trunks of trees, then applying stucco, made with sand from the end of Bluff Point.

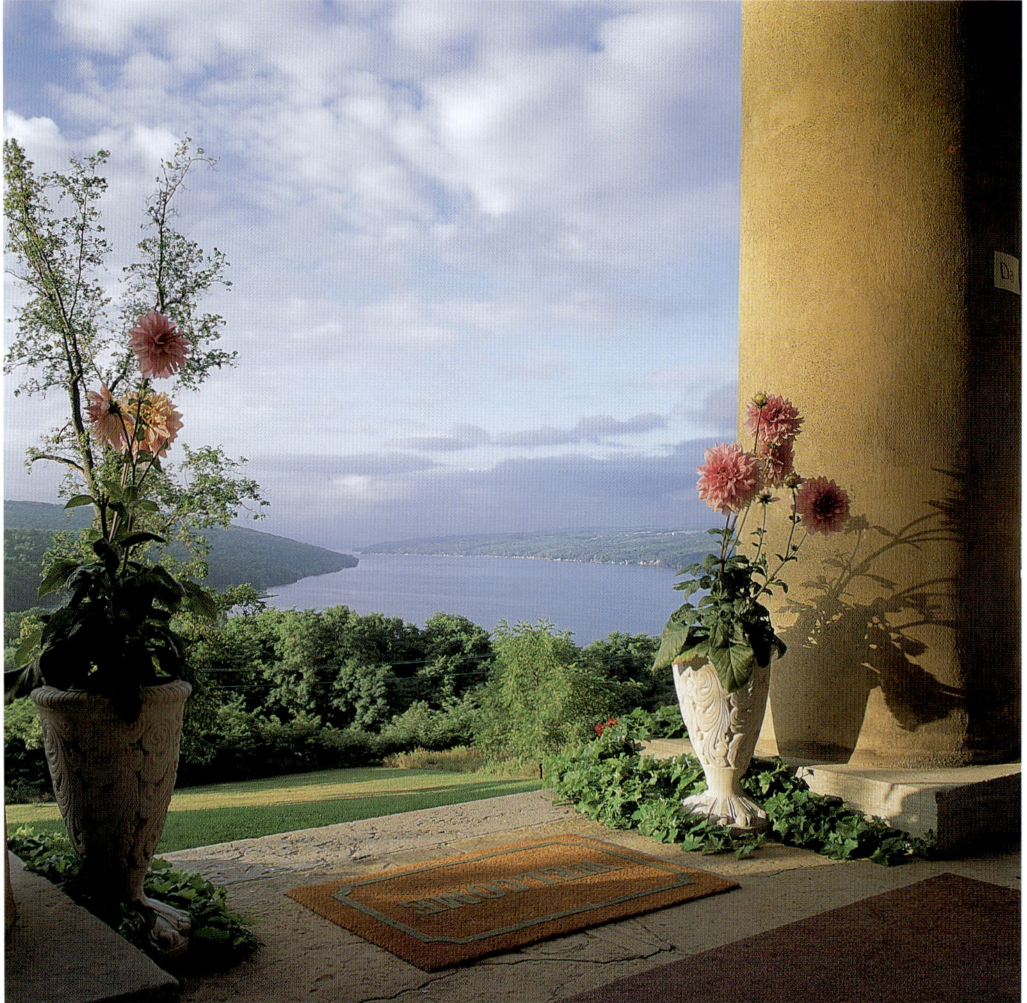

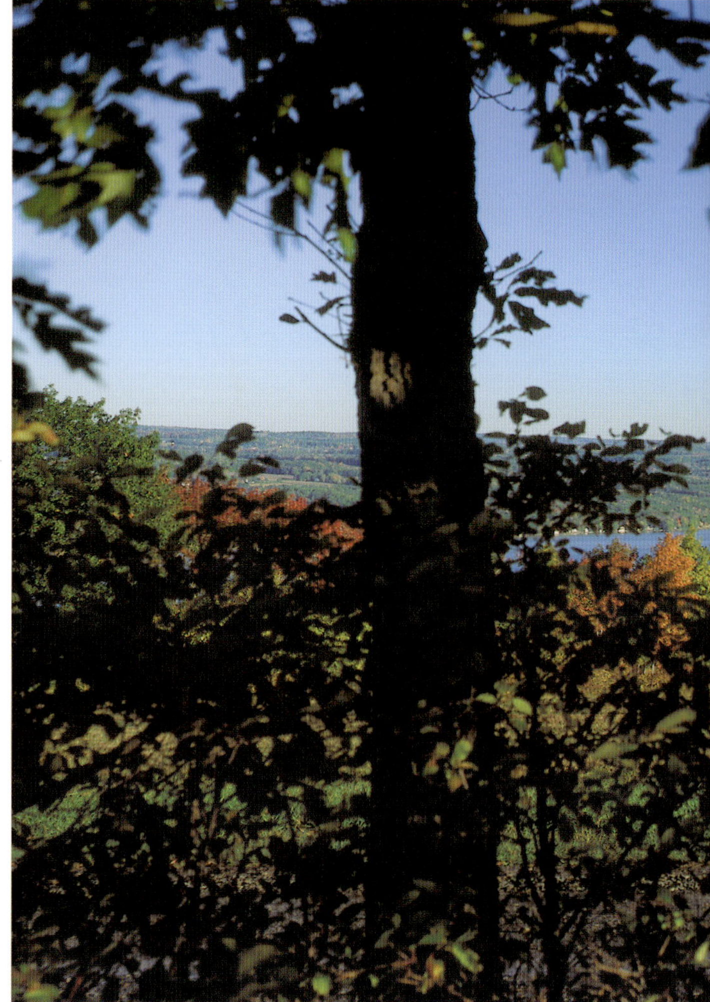

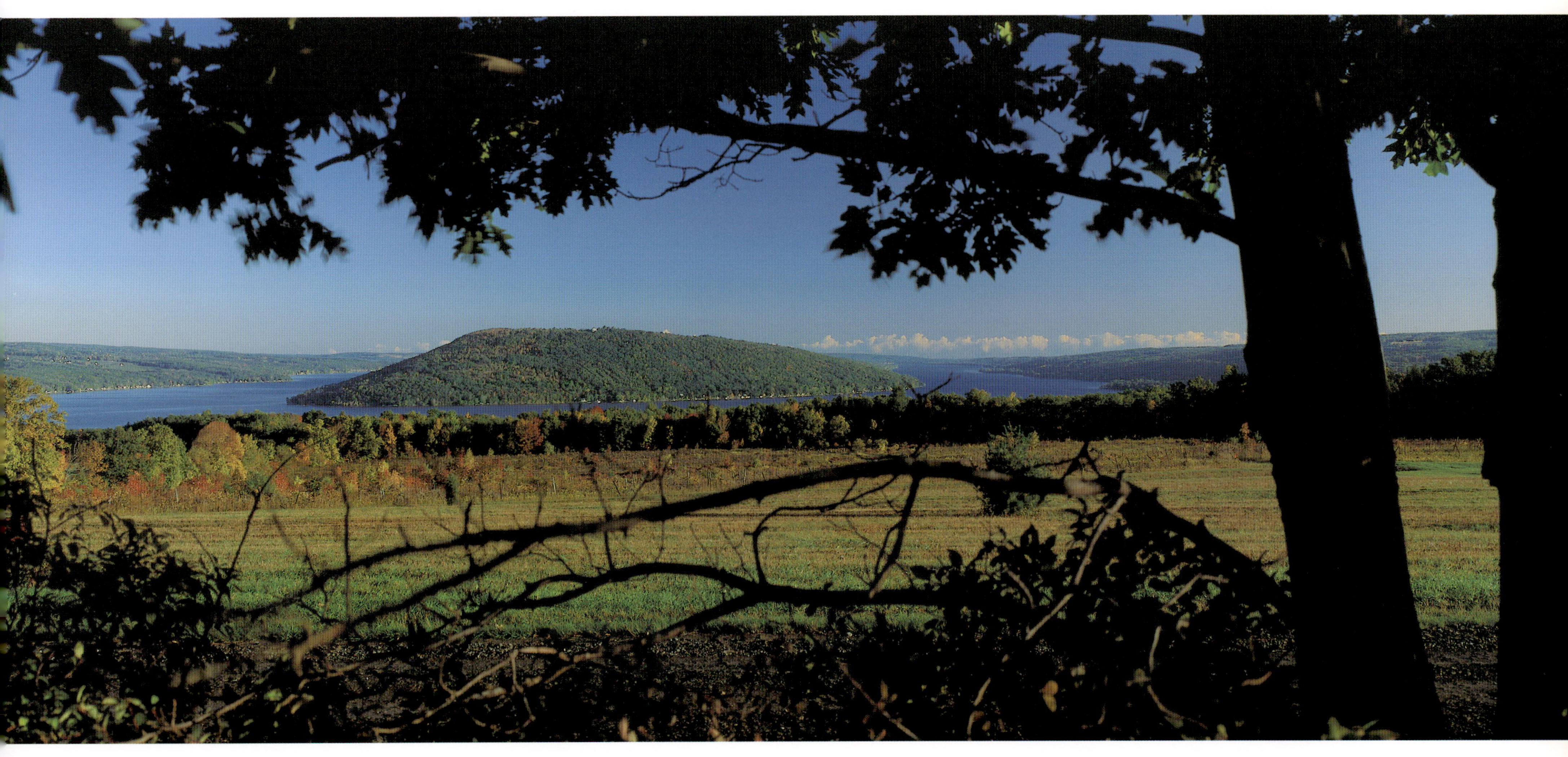

KEUKA LAKE, Bluff Point from Silsbee Road, looking north.

RISING nearly 700 feet above the water's edge, where the east and west branches of Keuka meet, Bluff Point is frequently mistaken for an island. The village of Penn Yan clusters around the tip of the eastern branch and the hamlet of Branchport around the western branch. Near the summit of Bluff Point is the Wagner mansion, with Garrett Chapel just down the slope to the right.

KEUKA LAKE, from Bluff Point, looking south.

THE long stem of the "Y" is seen here from the top of Bluff Point. The village of Hammondsport lies just around the bend of shoreline on the west (center right). The first Finger Lakes–made wines began to flow from vineyards on the western hillsides around 1830.

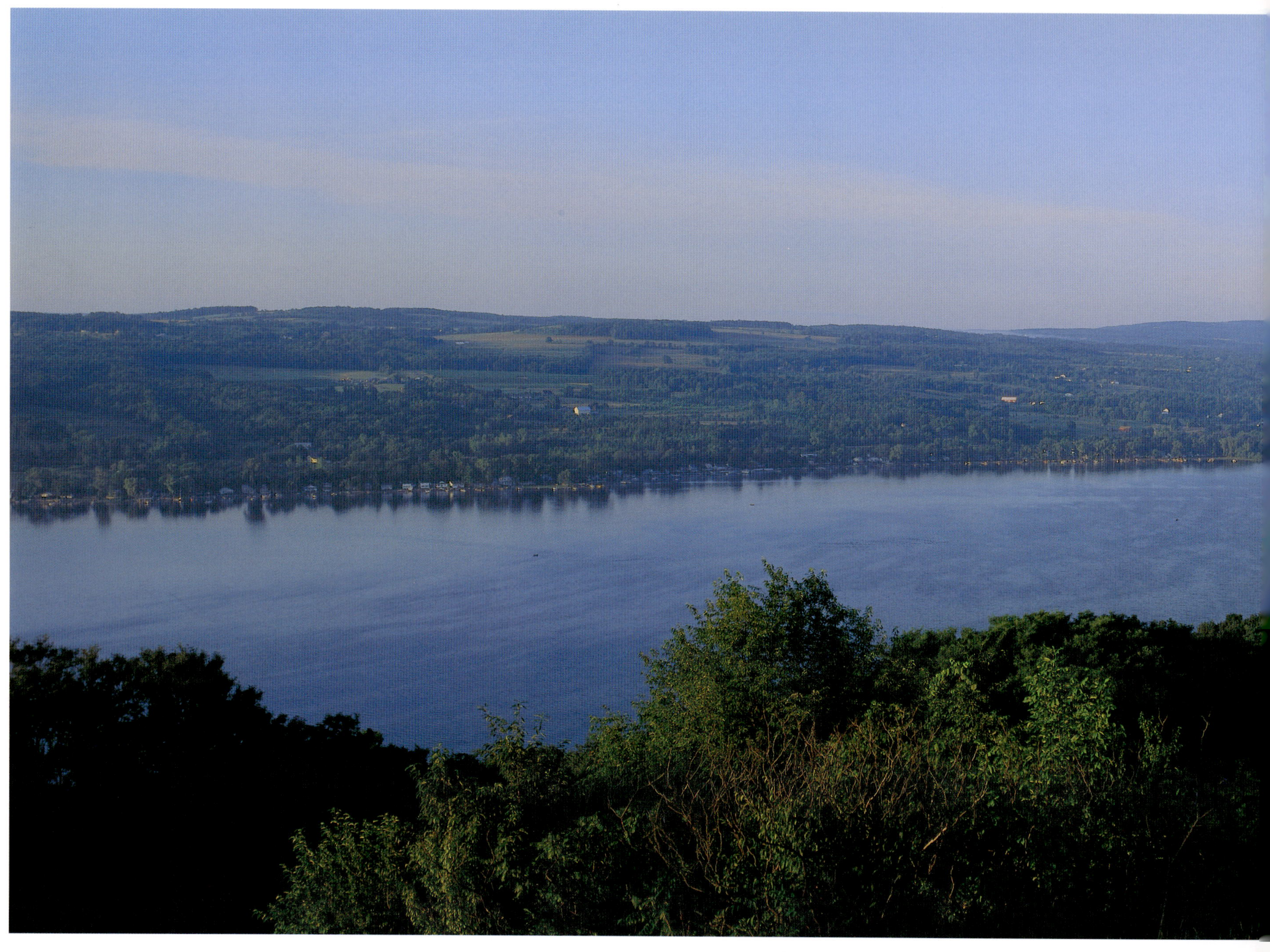

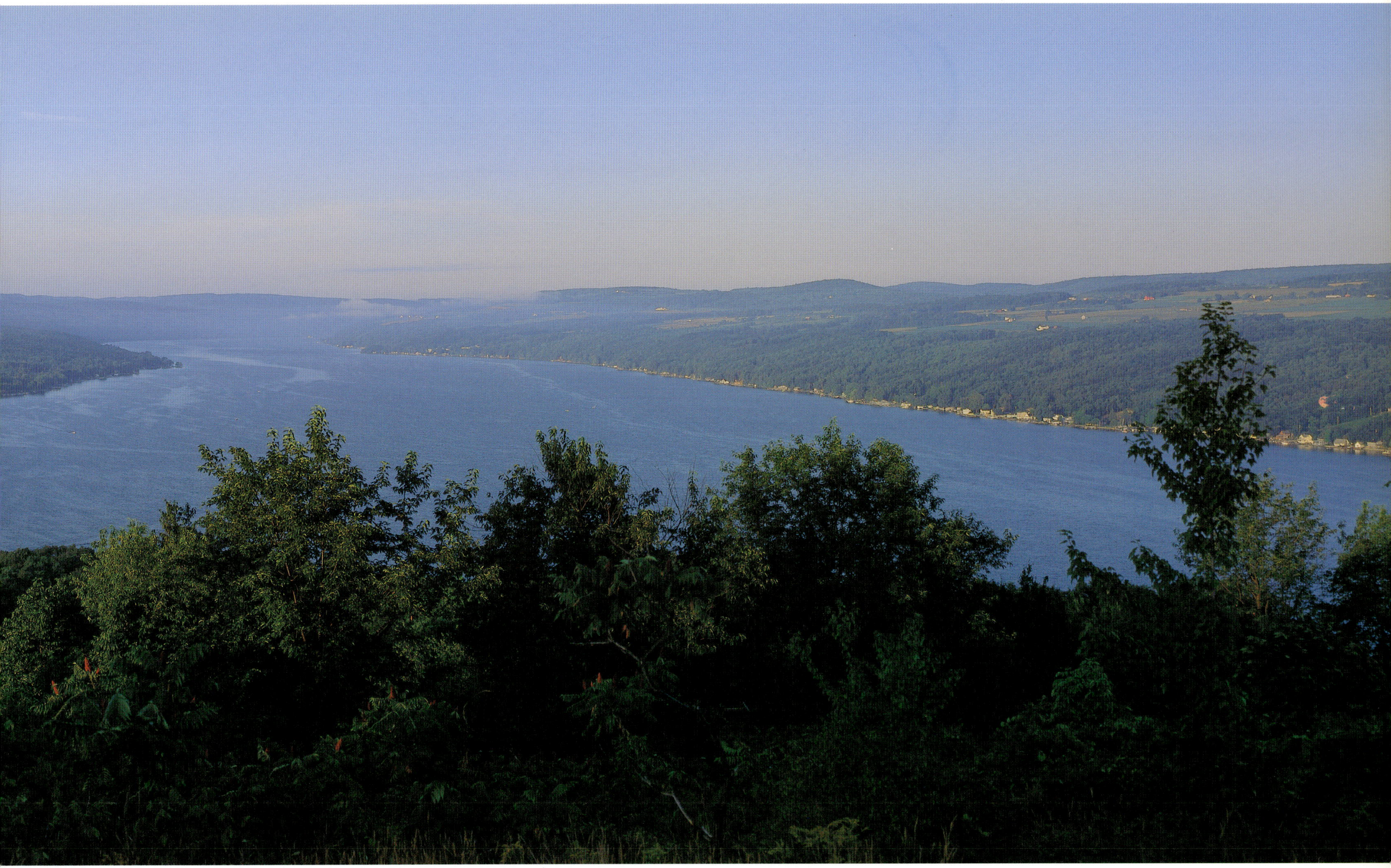

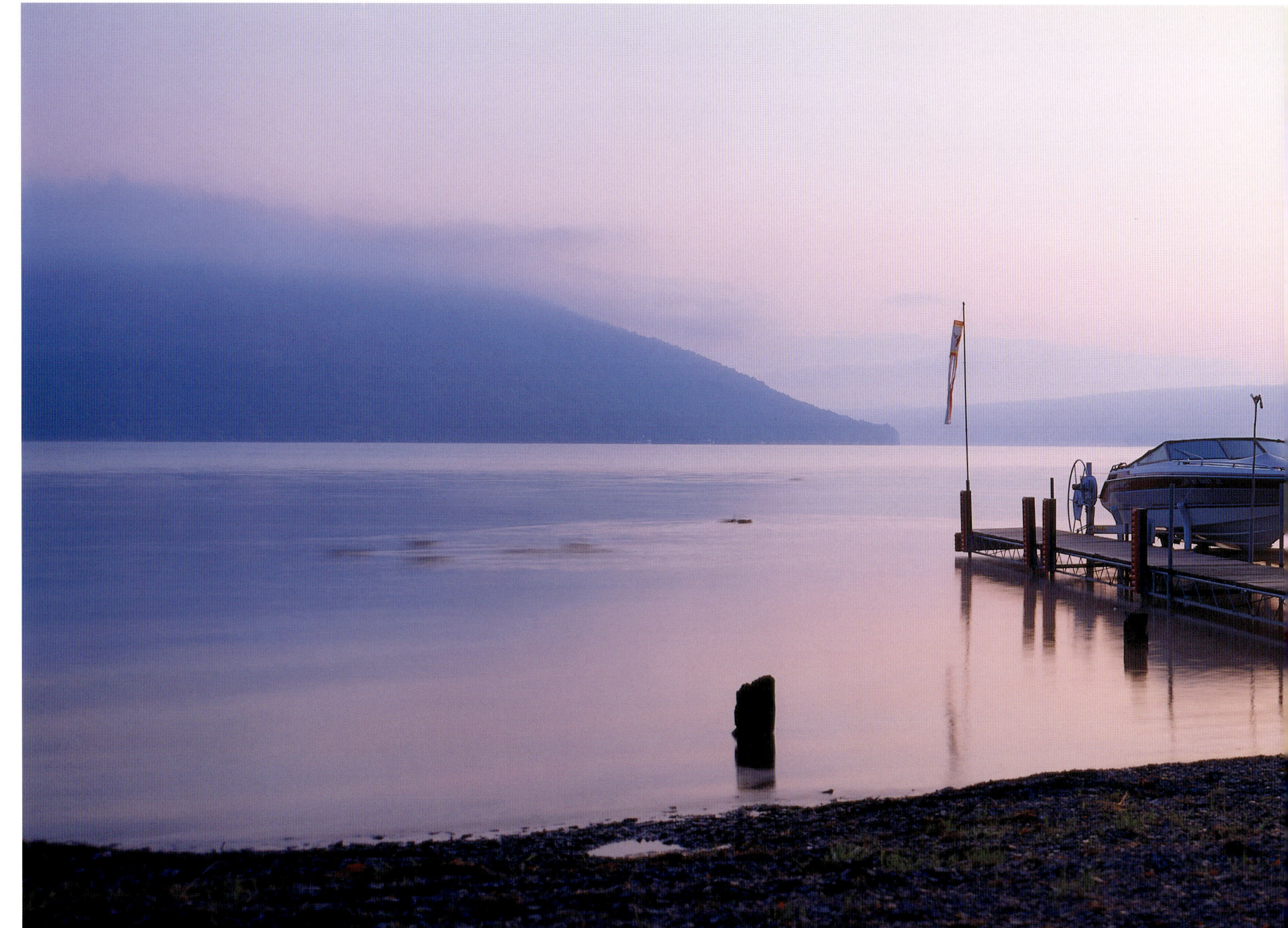

KEUKA LAKE, from Marlena Point, looking northeast.

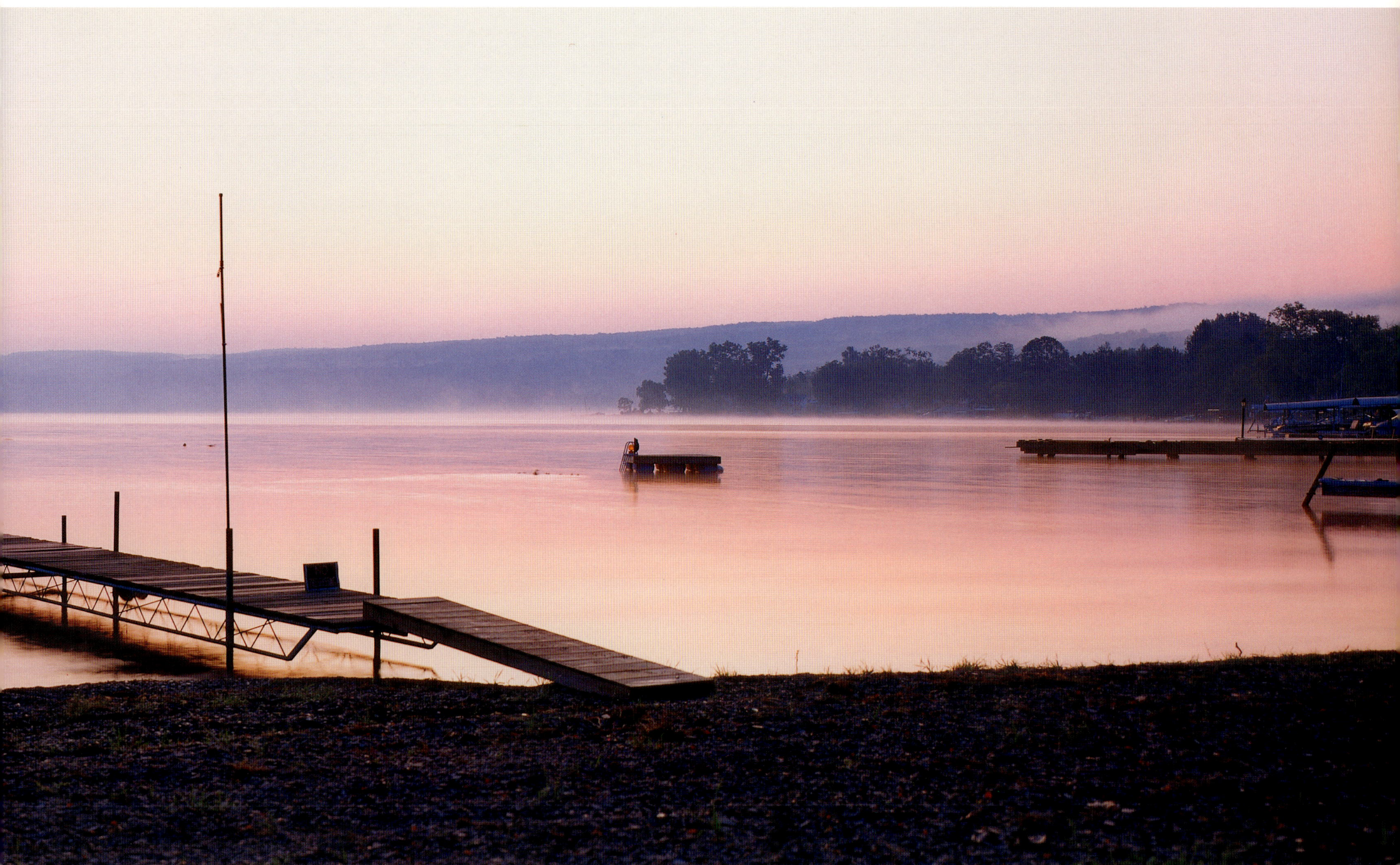

KEUKA LAKE, from Hammondsport, looking north.

EARLY morning fog rolls off the lake toward the quiet village of Hammondsport. At the southern tip of Keuka Lake, Hammondsport is the birthplace of the wine industry in New York State and has been called the champagne center of America.

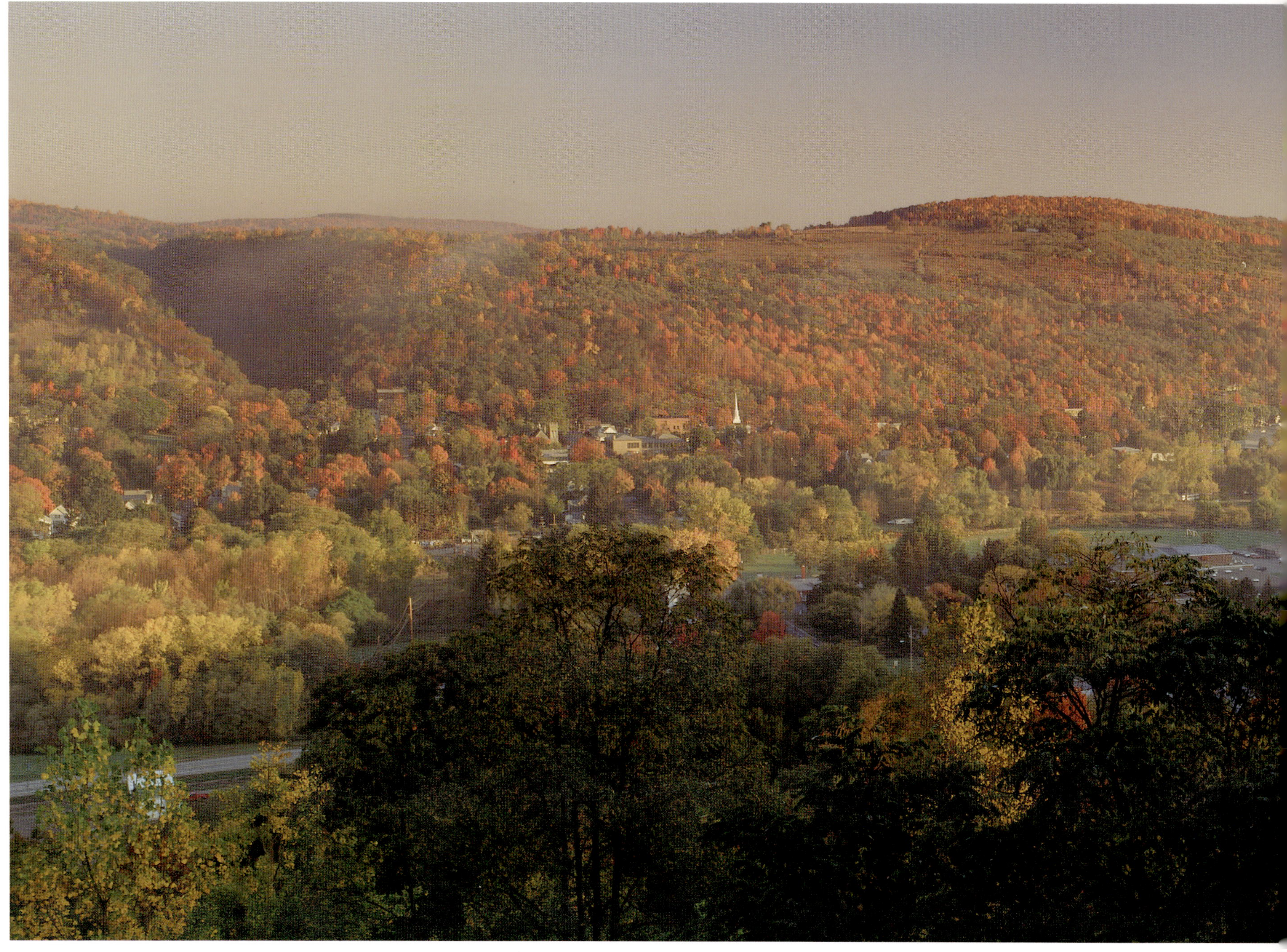

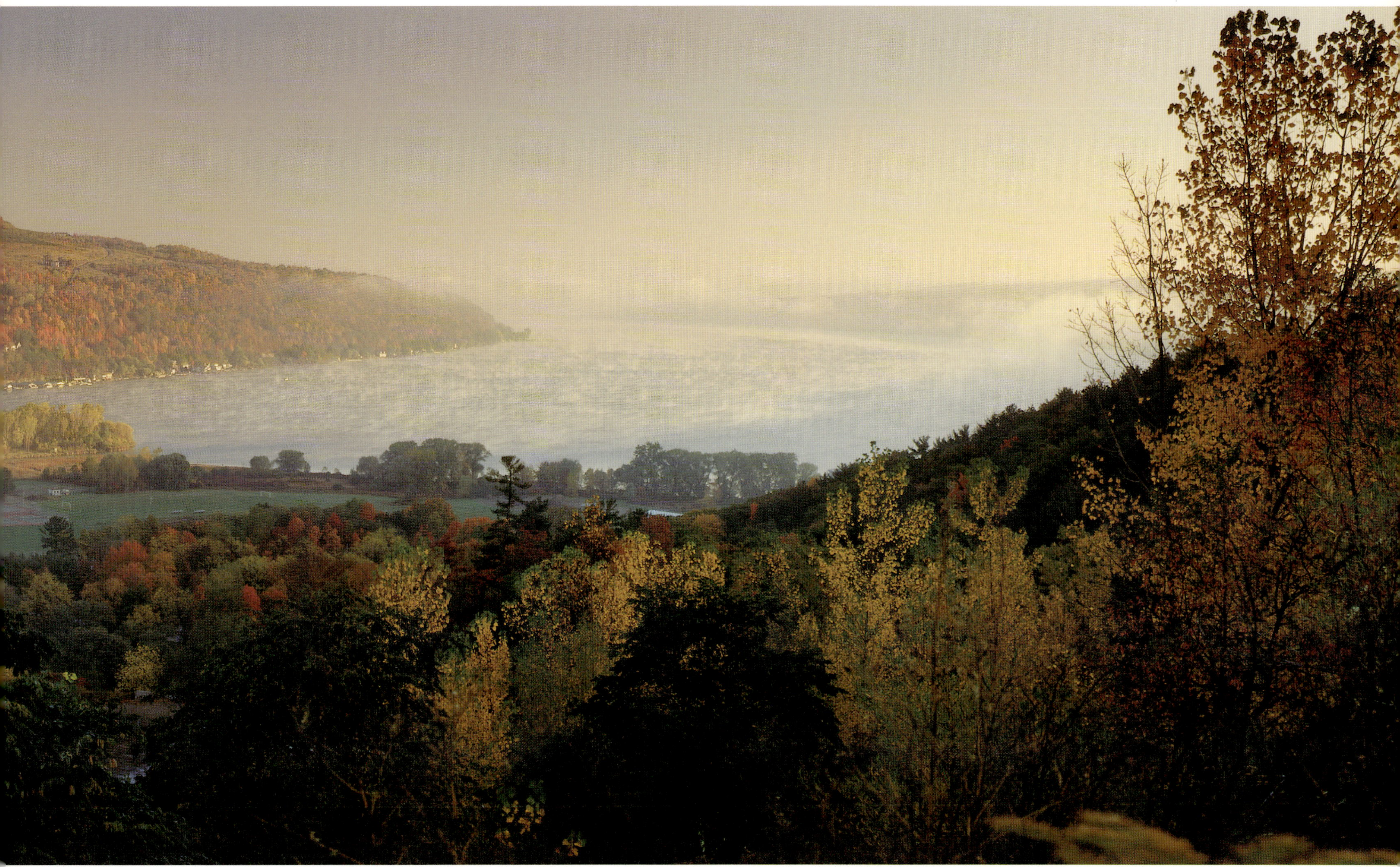

KEUKA LAKE and Hammondsport, looking southwest.

TINY Hammondsport was the home of Glenn Hammond Curtiss, aviator and inventor. In 1907, Curtiss rode his eight-cylinder motorcycle at 136.4 miles per hour. In 1908, he made the first officially witnessed flight of one kilometer in America, earning him pilot's license Number One.

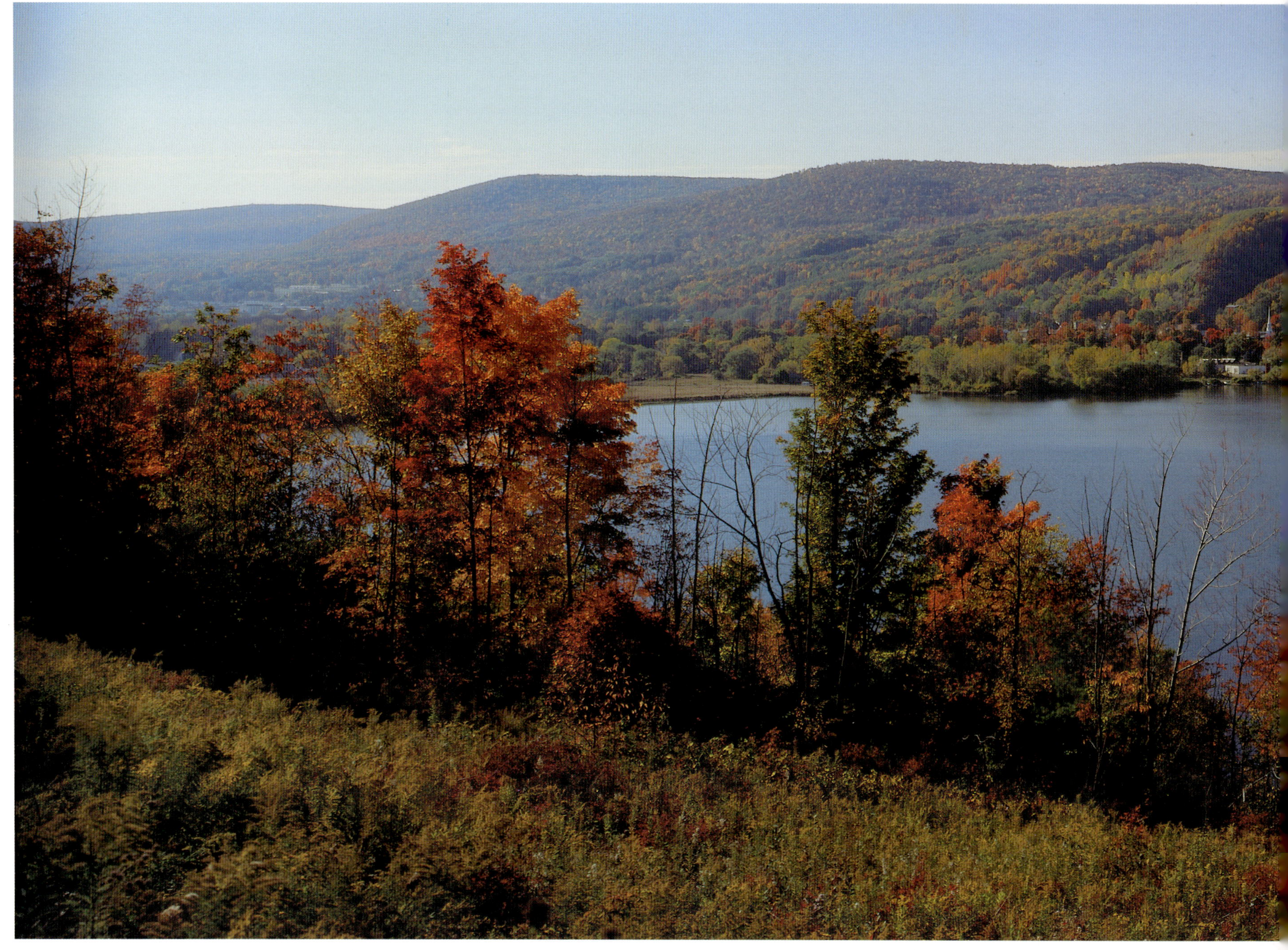

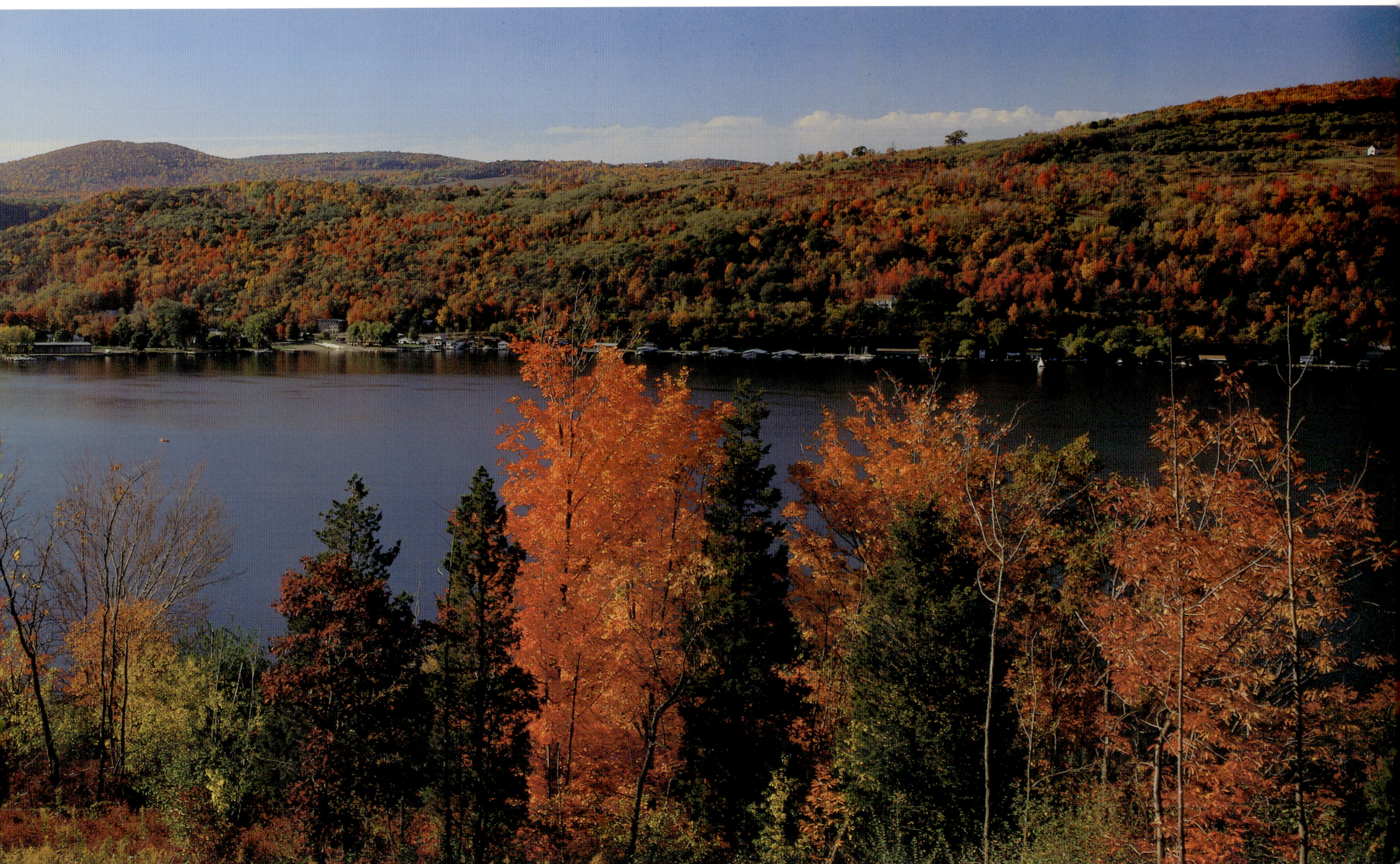

KEUKA LAKE Outlet, near Penn Yan.

THE Keuka Lake Outlet flows east from Keuka Lake at Penn Yan to meet Seneca Lake at the tiny community of Dresden. Keuka is the only Finger Lake whose water flows into that of another Finger Lake. A railroad bed paralleling the Outlet became the foundation of the Keuka Outlet Trail, a six-mile linear park that meanders past abandoned mills and their now-unleashed waterfalls.

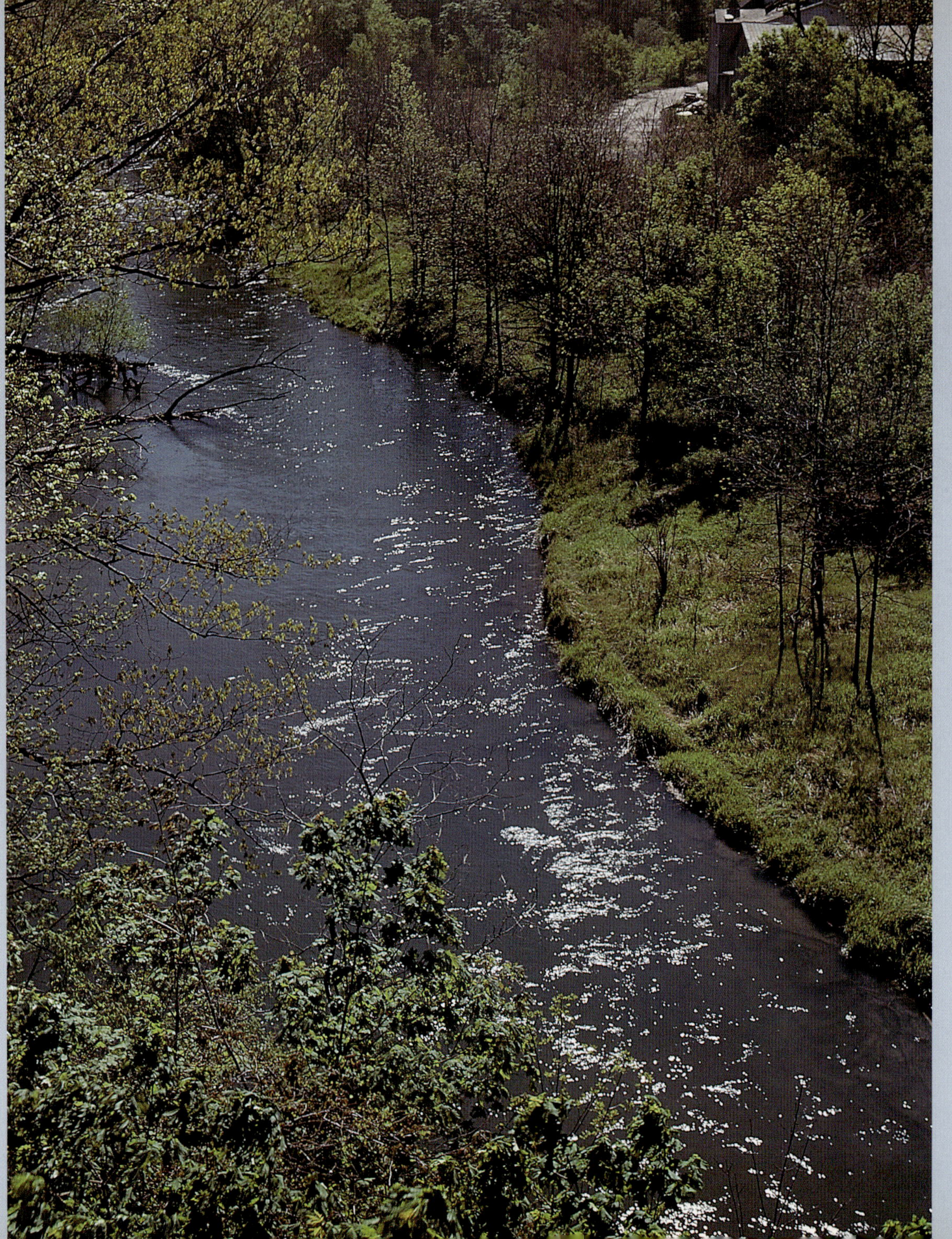

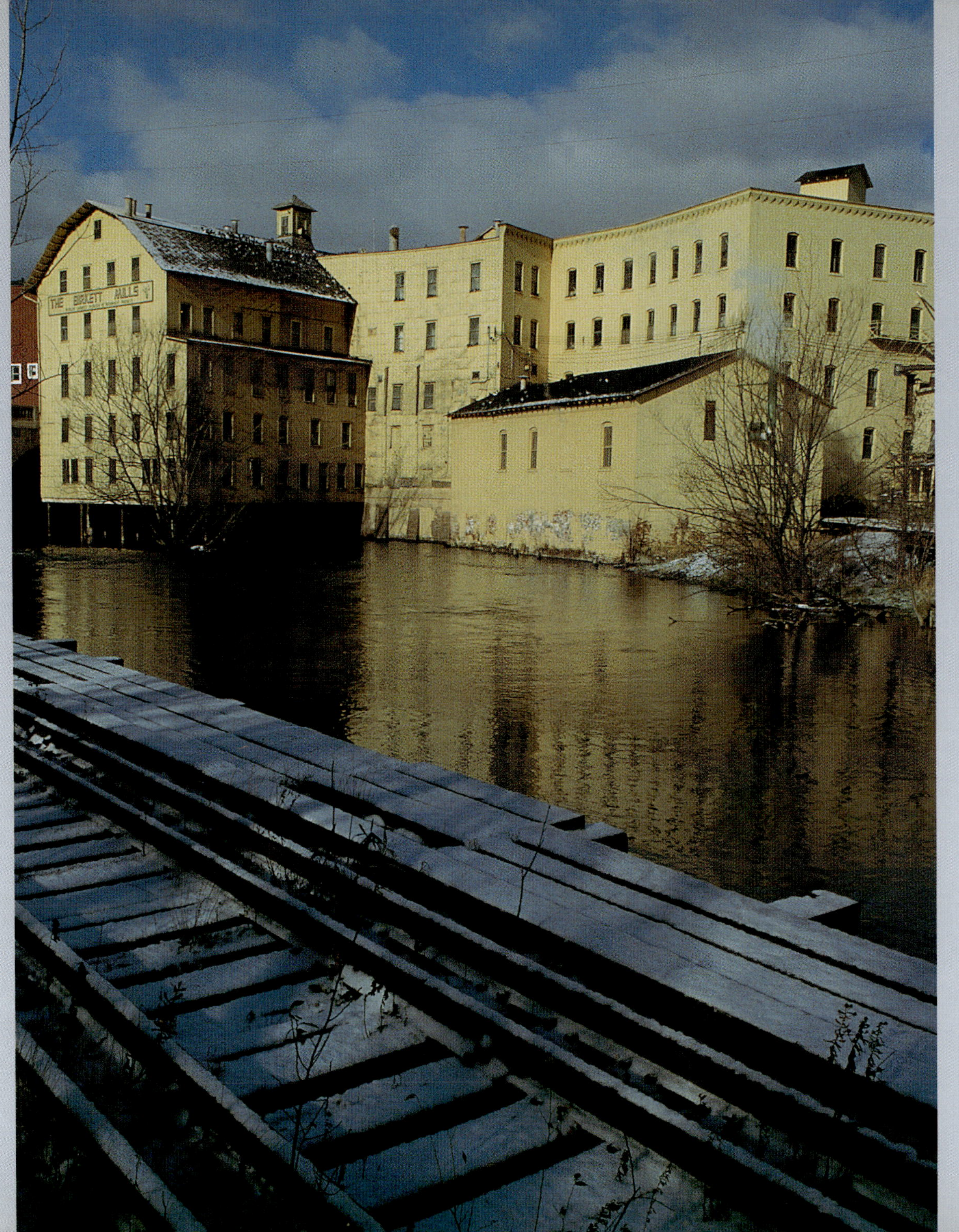

The Birkett Mills,
PENN YAN.

AT the northern end of the east branch of Keuka Lake lies the village of Penn Yan, named for early Pennsylvania and Yankee settlers. The village has been ranked in the top 100 small U.S. towns, and is home to the Birkett Mills, the world's largest manufacturer of buckwheat products.

6 Seneca Lake

SENECA LAKE from Chateau Lafayette Reneau Winery, looking west.

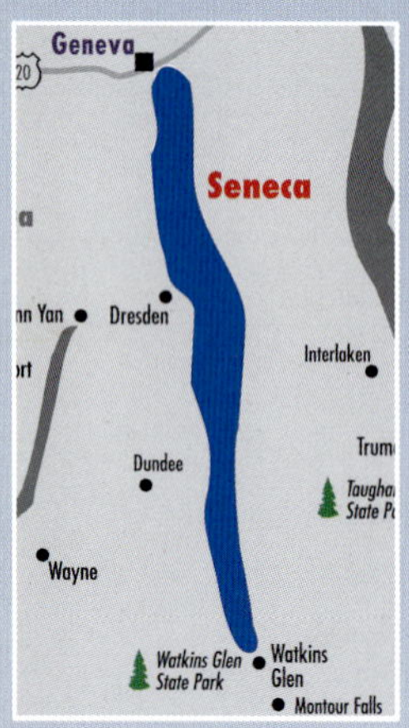

Few lakes in the world—and none in the Finger Lakes—are deeper than Seneca Lake. At 632 feet, its bed actually dips below sea level. Legend suggests that the lake emits strange grumbling sounds, sometimes called the "Death Drums" of the Seneca Indians.

More than 20 wineries have been established on the hillsides around the lake, and the city of Geneva lies at the north end. At the south is the village of Watkins Glen, former site of the American Grand Prix auto race.

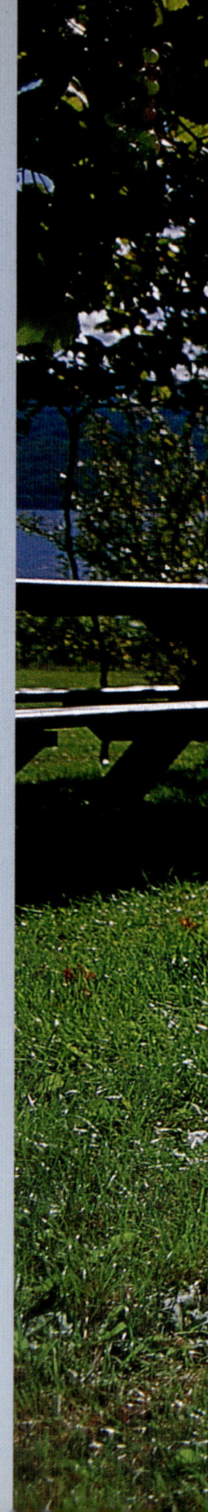

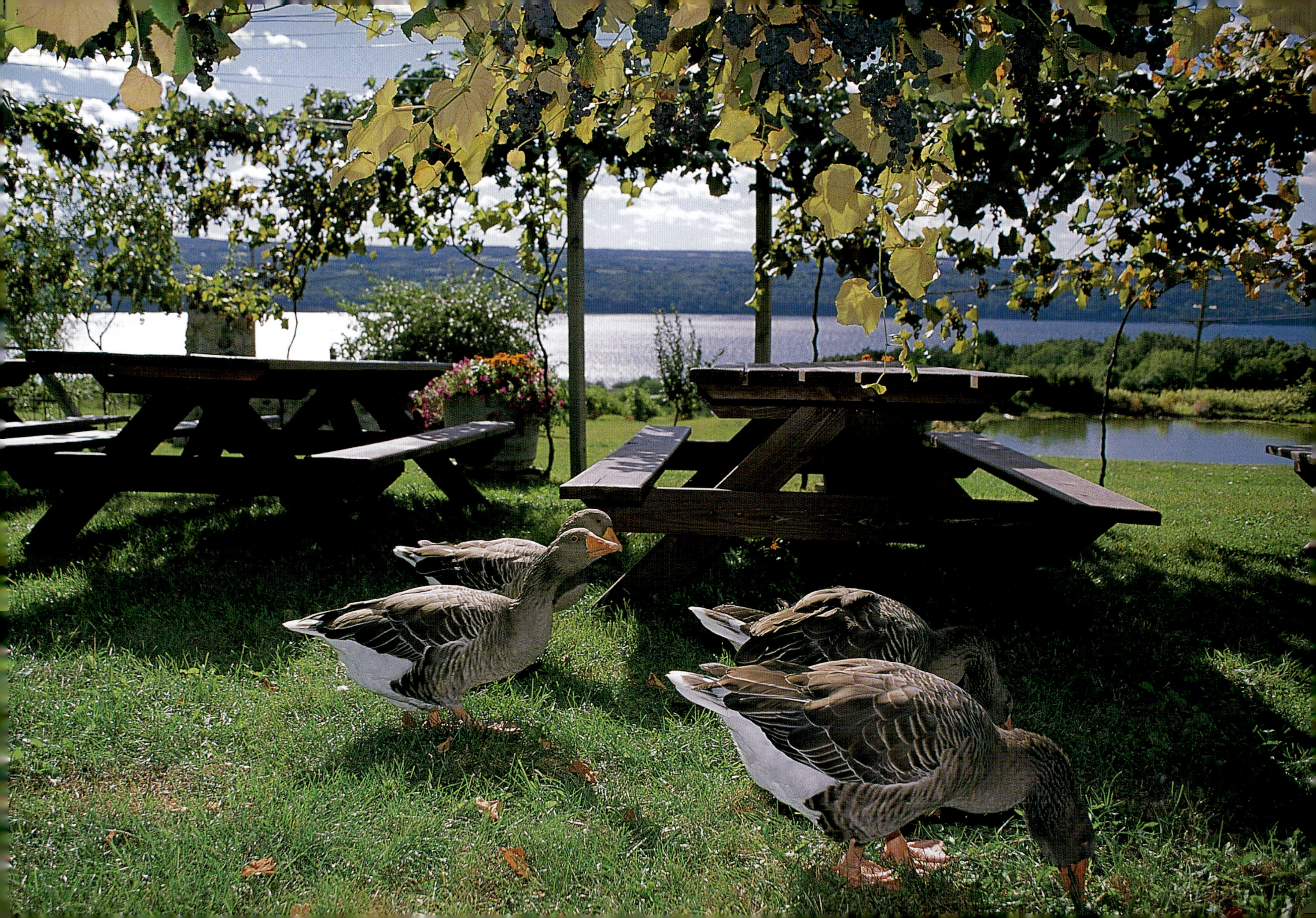

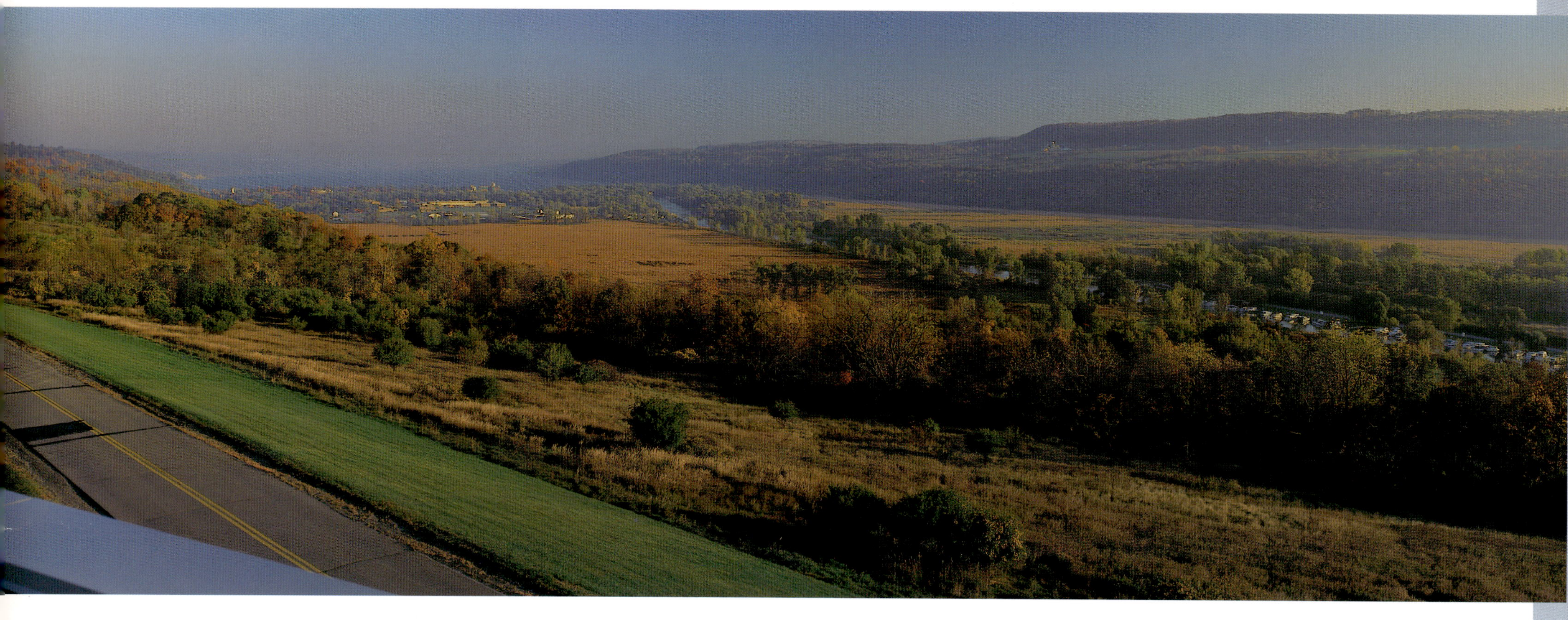

Above: SENECA LAKE and Catharine Creek from Montour Falls, looking north.

Right: SENECA LAKE from Satterly Hill, Burdett, looking southwest.

FROM Belle Cornell Drive, high above the village of Montour Falls, the view takes in Seneca Lake and, on its shore, Watkins Glen. Catharine Creek, to the right, is one of New York State's most famous trout streams. Today, the creek connects Montour Falls with Seneca Lake but at one time, the Chemung Canal followed its course to link Seneca Lake with Elmira.

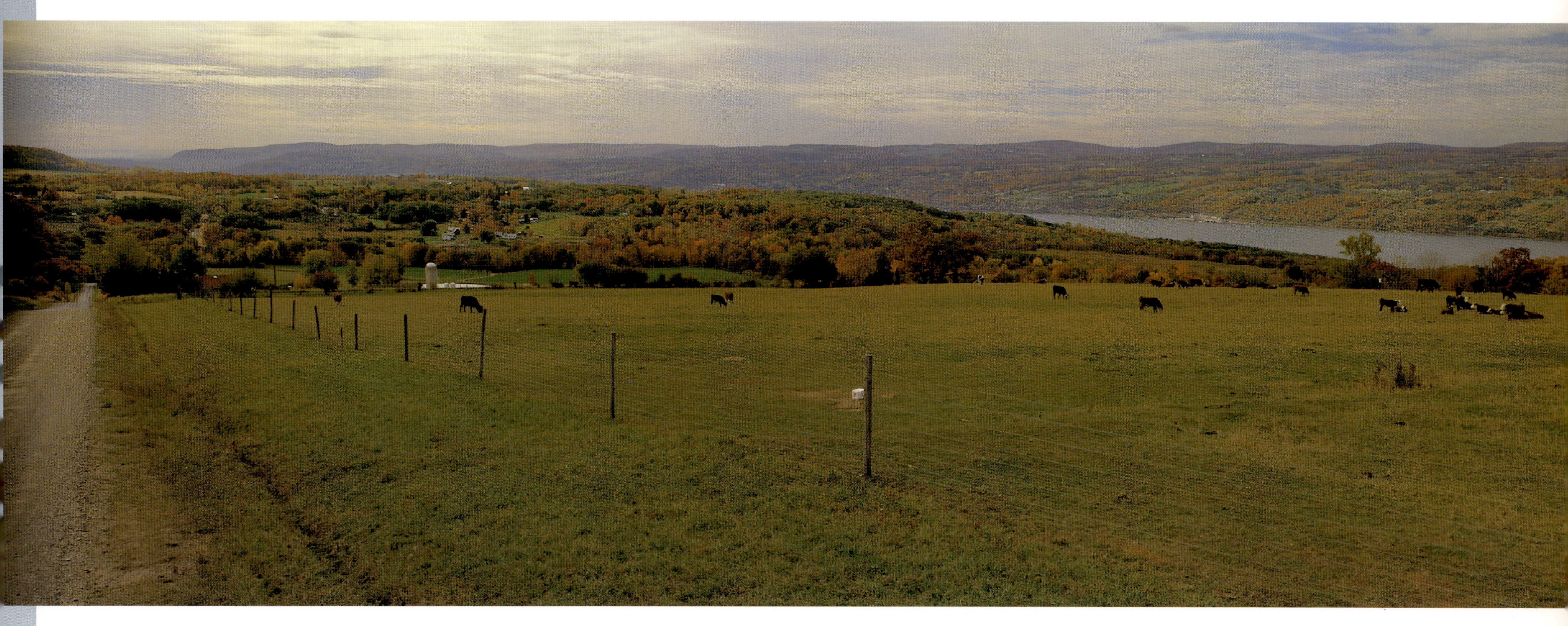

Overleaf:
CAVERN CASCADE,
Watkins Glen State Park.

FOR over 12,000 years, Glen Creek has tumbled down this steep valley, creating the gorge now known as Watkins Glen State Park. First opened in 1863, the park is the oldest state park in New York and one of the oldest public parks in America. Nineteen glistening waterfalls dot the mile and a half of its gorge trail. Those who walk it delight in ducking behind this Cavern Cascade.

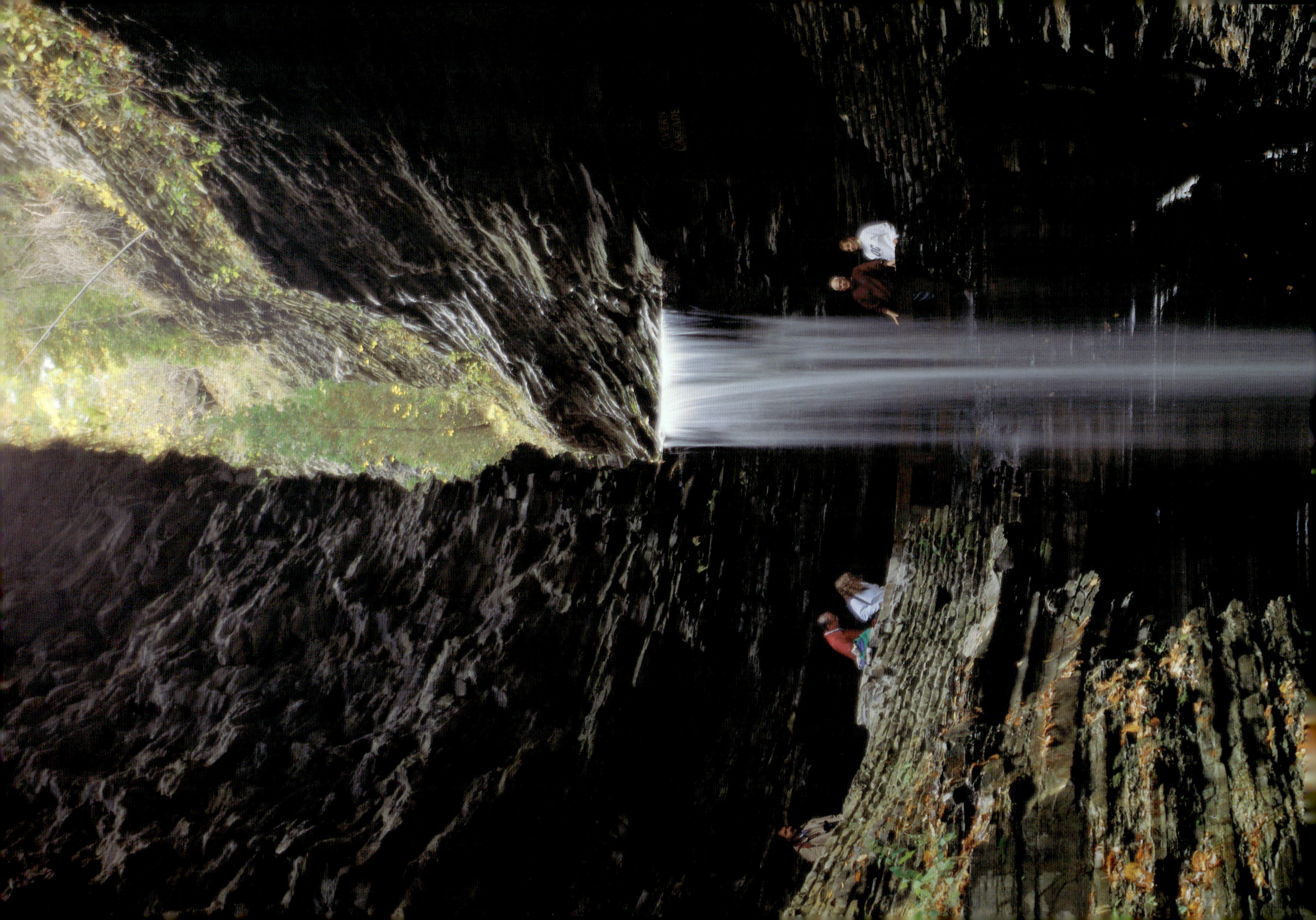

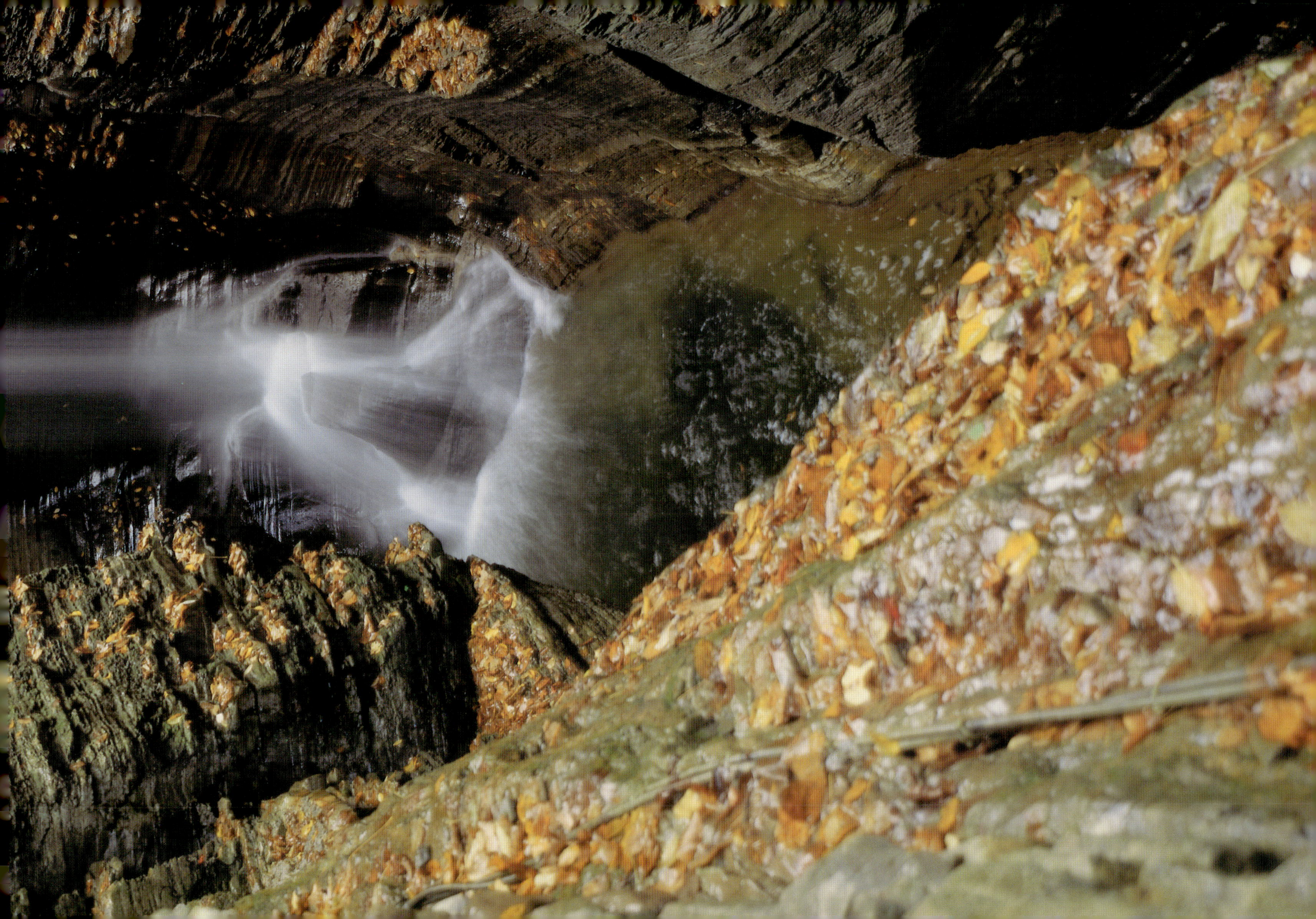

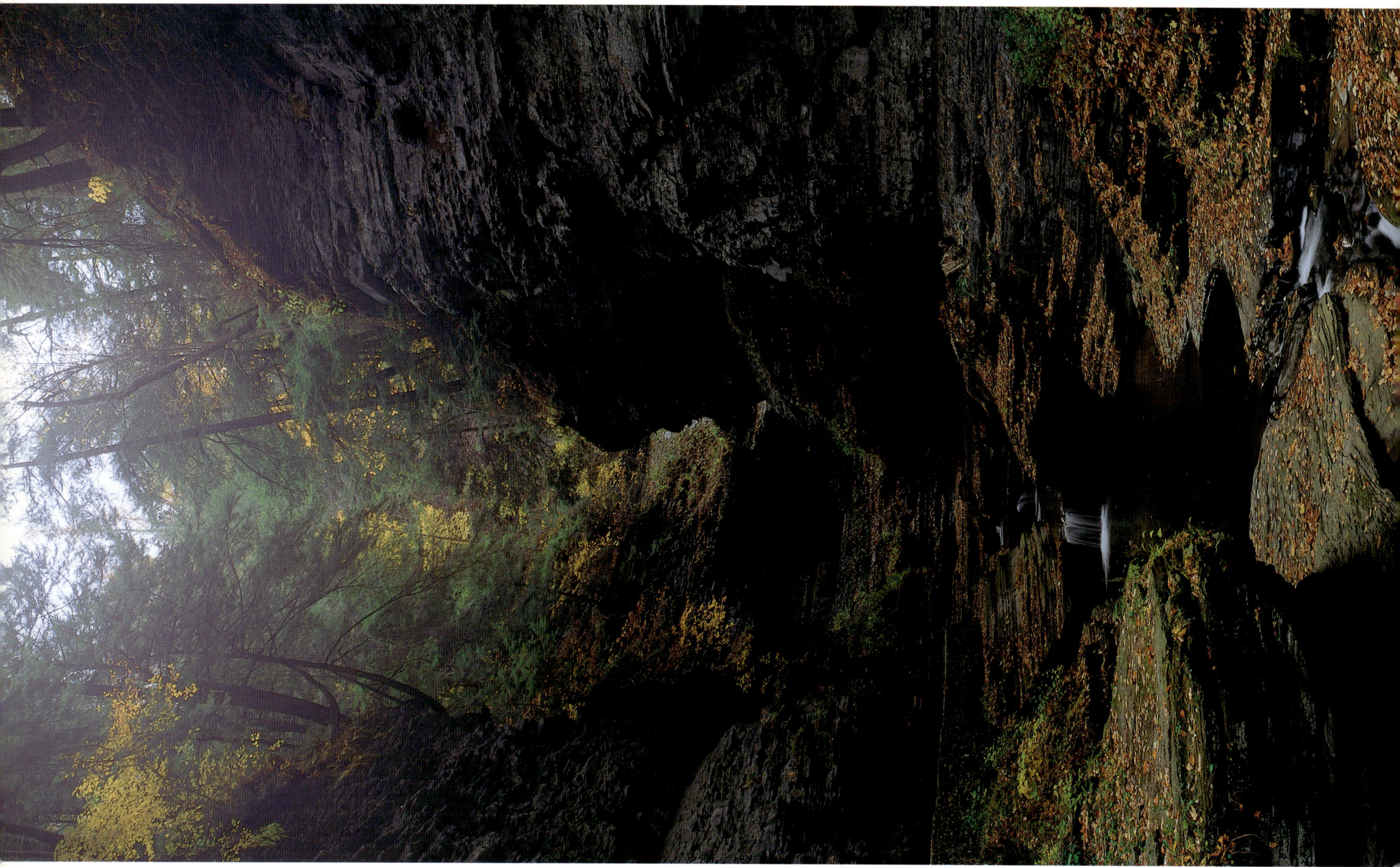

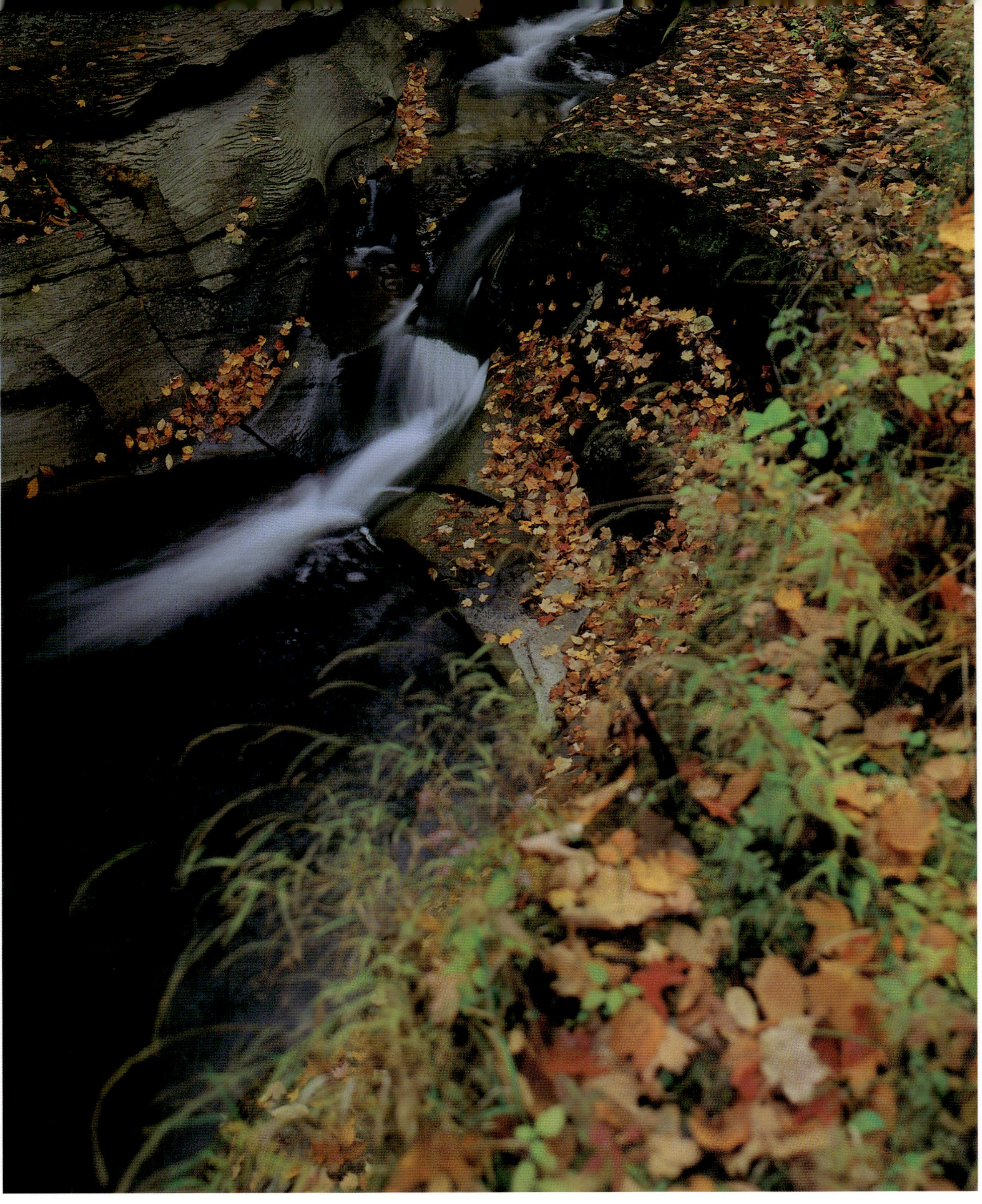

GLEN OF POOLS, Watkins Glen State Park.

Along the creek bed are many "plunge pools" or "pot holes," formed by water pounding at the base of ancient waterfalls.

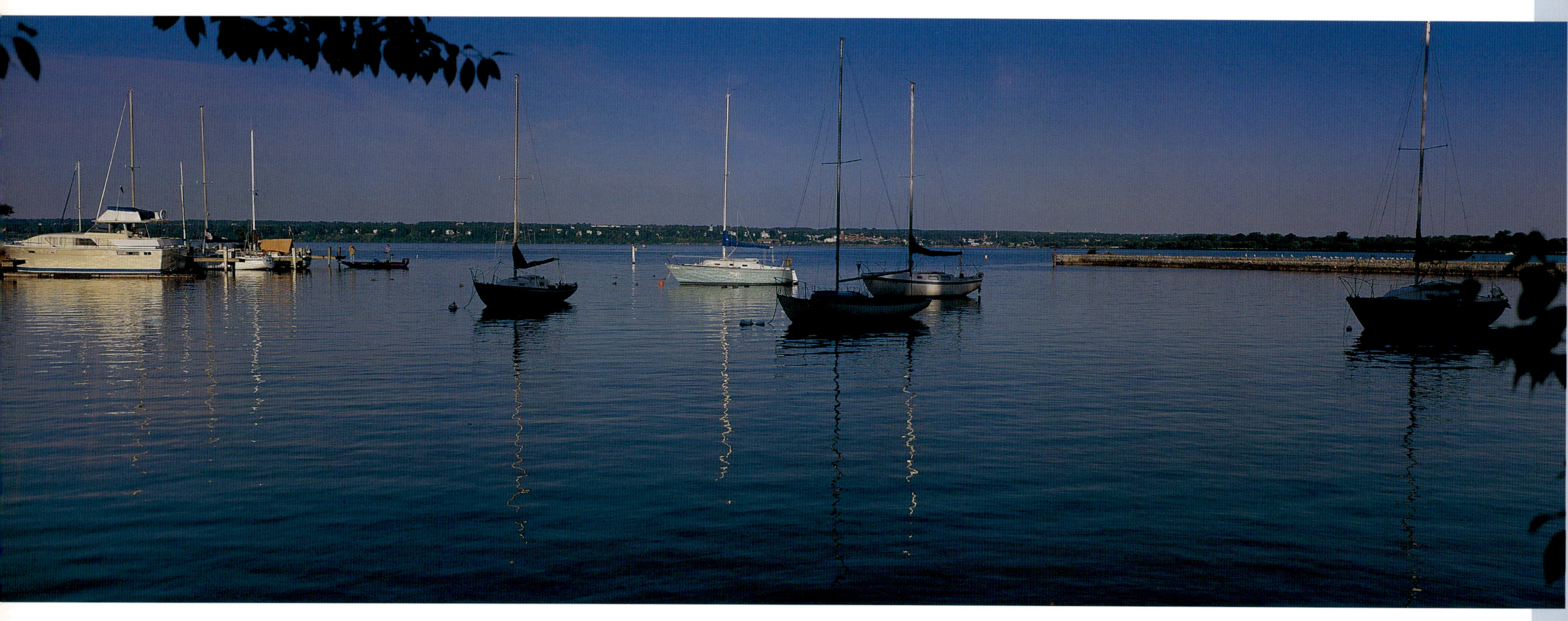

SENECA LAKE and Geneva, looking west.

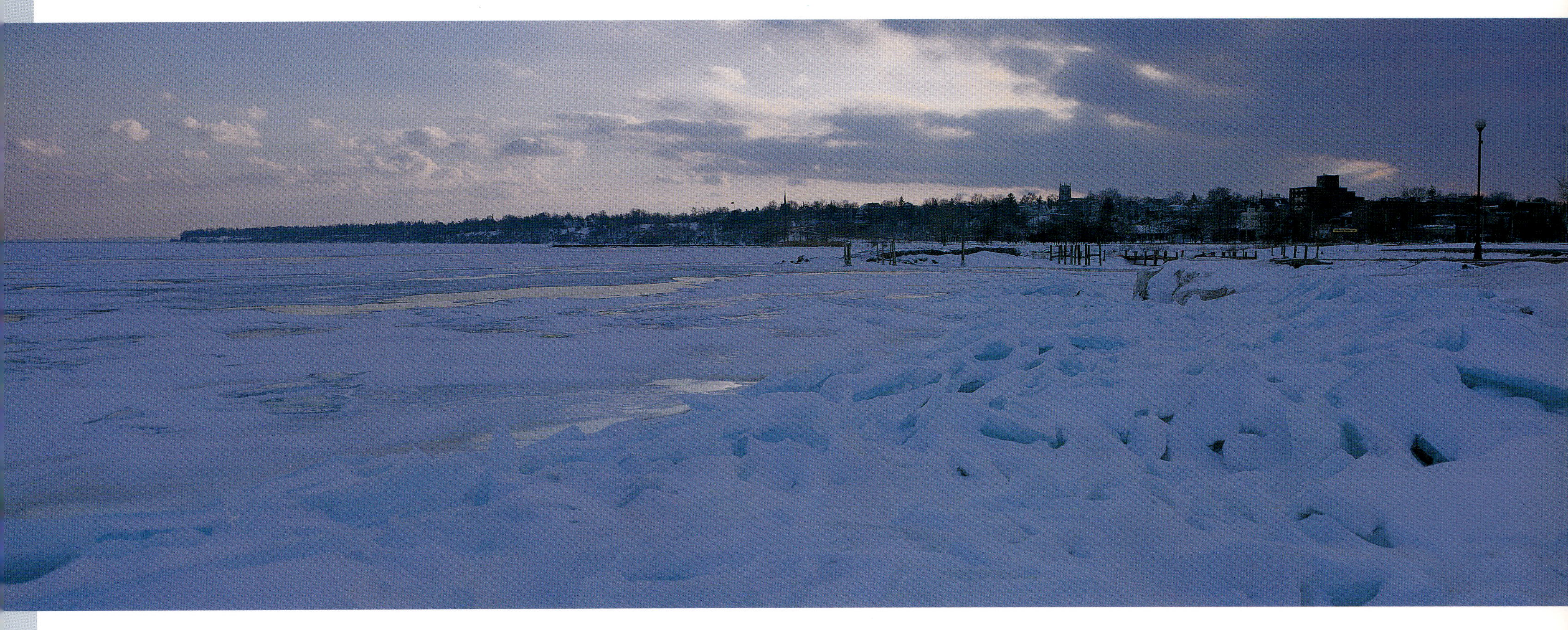

SENECA LAKE and Geneva, looking southwest.

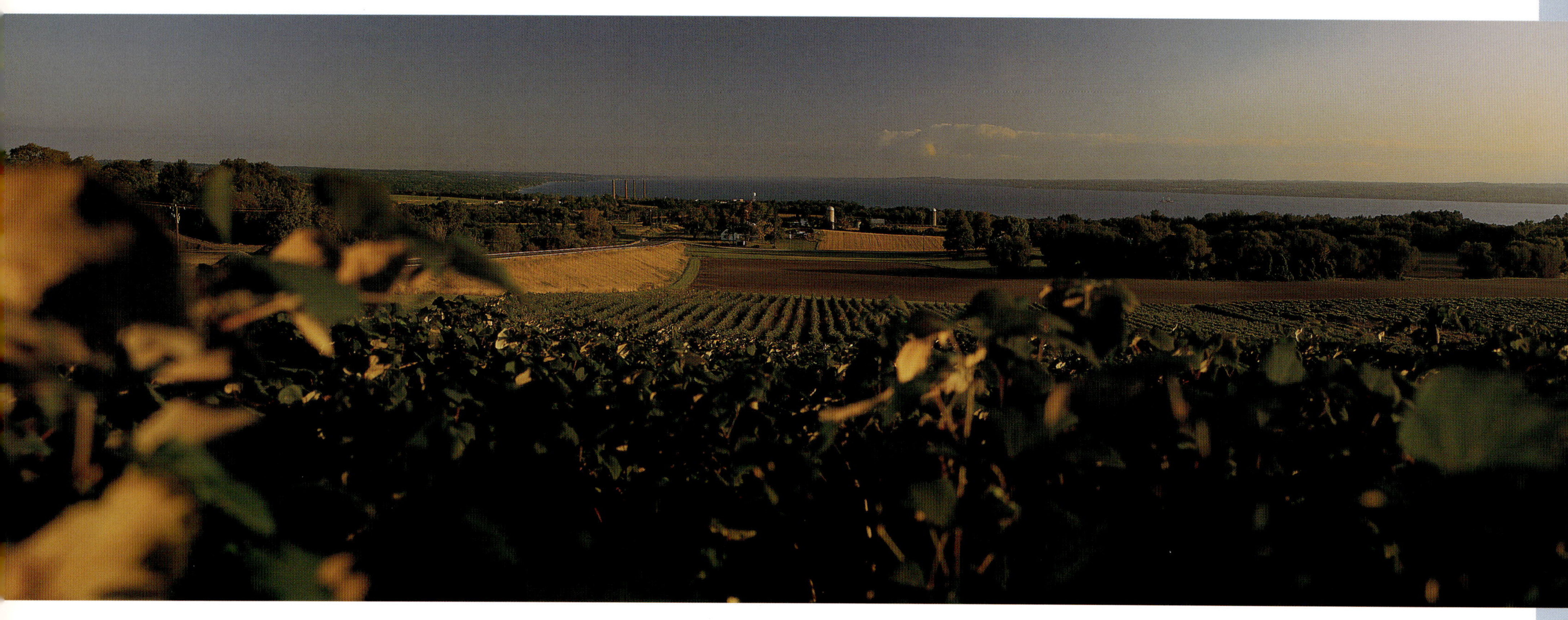

SENECA LAKE and Dresden, looking north

ONE of the widest stretches of water in the Finger Lakes is at Dresden, where agriculture and industry share a tremendous view. Sleepy Dresden is the birthplace of 19th century lecturer and lawyer Robert Ingersoll, known as "the Great Agnostic." The factory in the distance is Greenidge Station, a New York State Electric power plant.

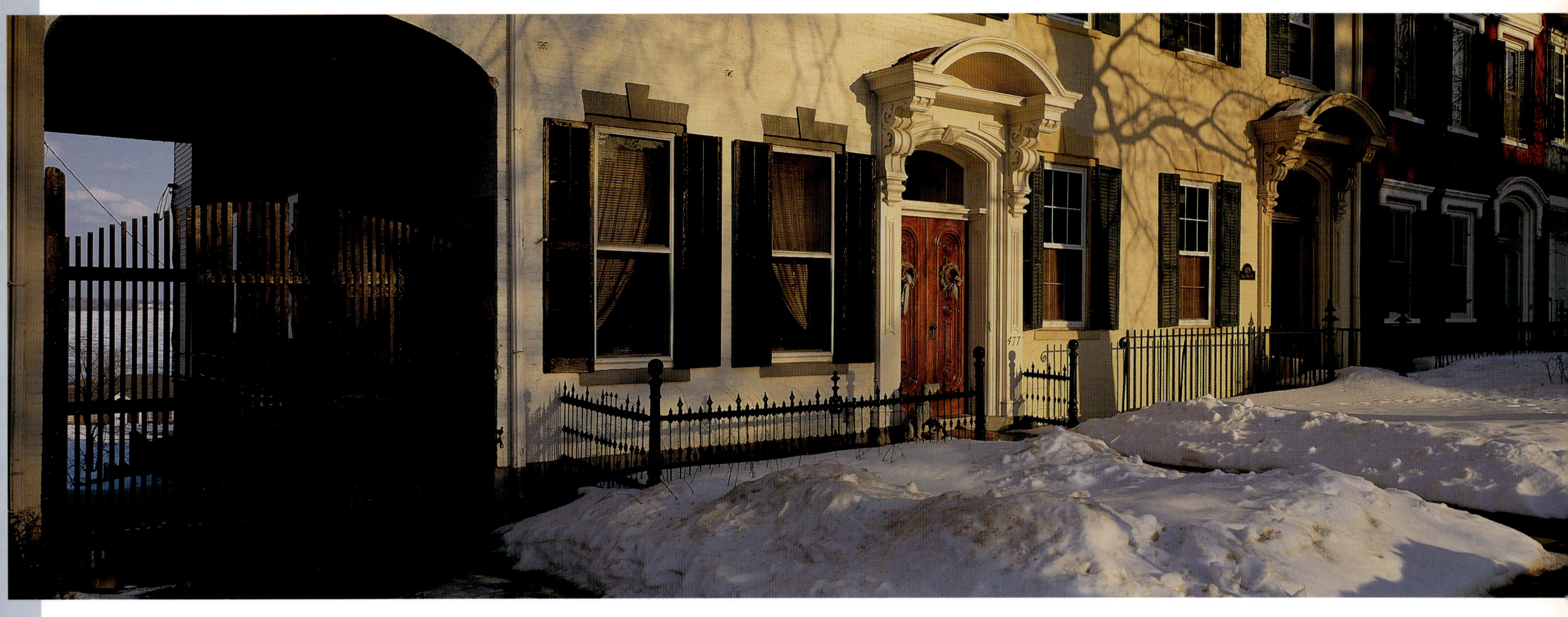

GENEVA, South Main Street.

CENTURY-old trees and stately homes line South Main Street in Geneva, one of the largest cities in the region and home to Hobart and William Smith Colleges. During World War II and the Korean War, thousands of servicemen trained at nearby Sampson, first a naval base, then an Air Force training base, and now an expansive state park.

SENECA LAKE at Watkins Glen, looking southeast.

Sunrise warms the pier and Franklin Street (right) as Seneca Harbor Park silently awaits the activity of daytime.

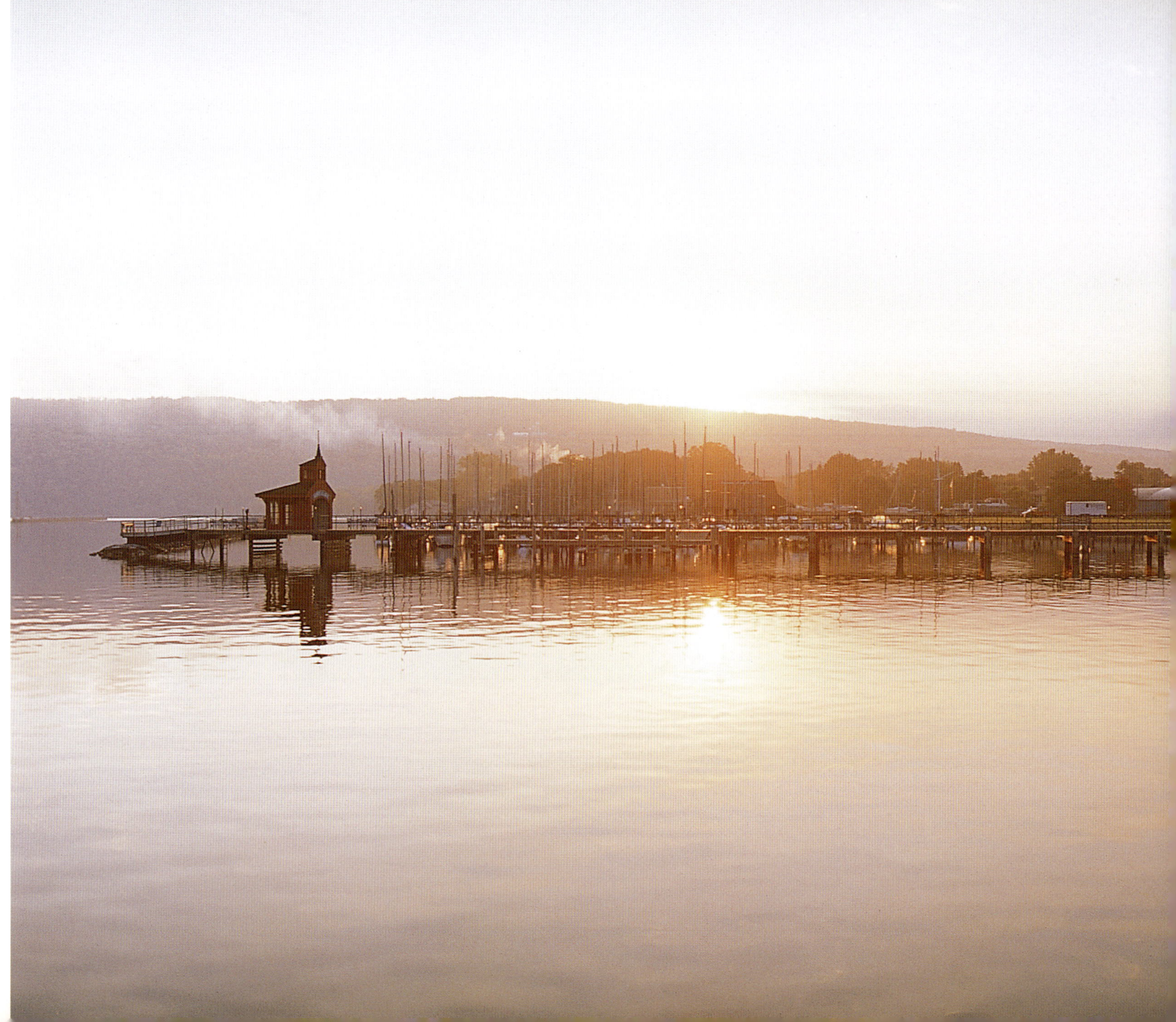

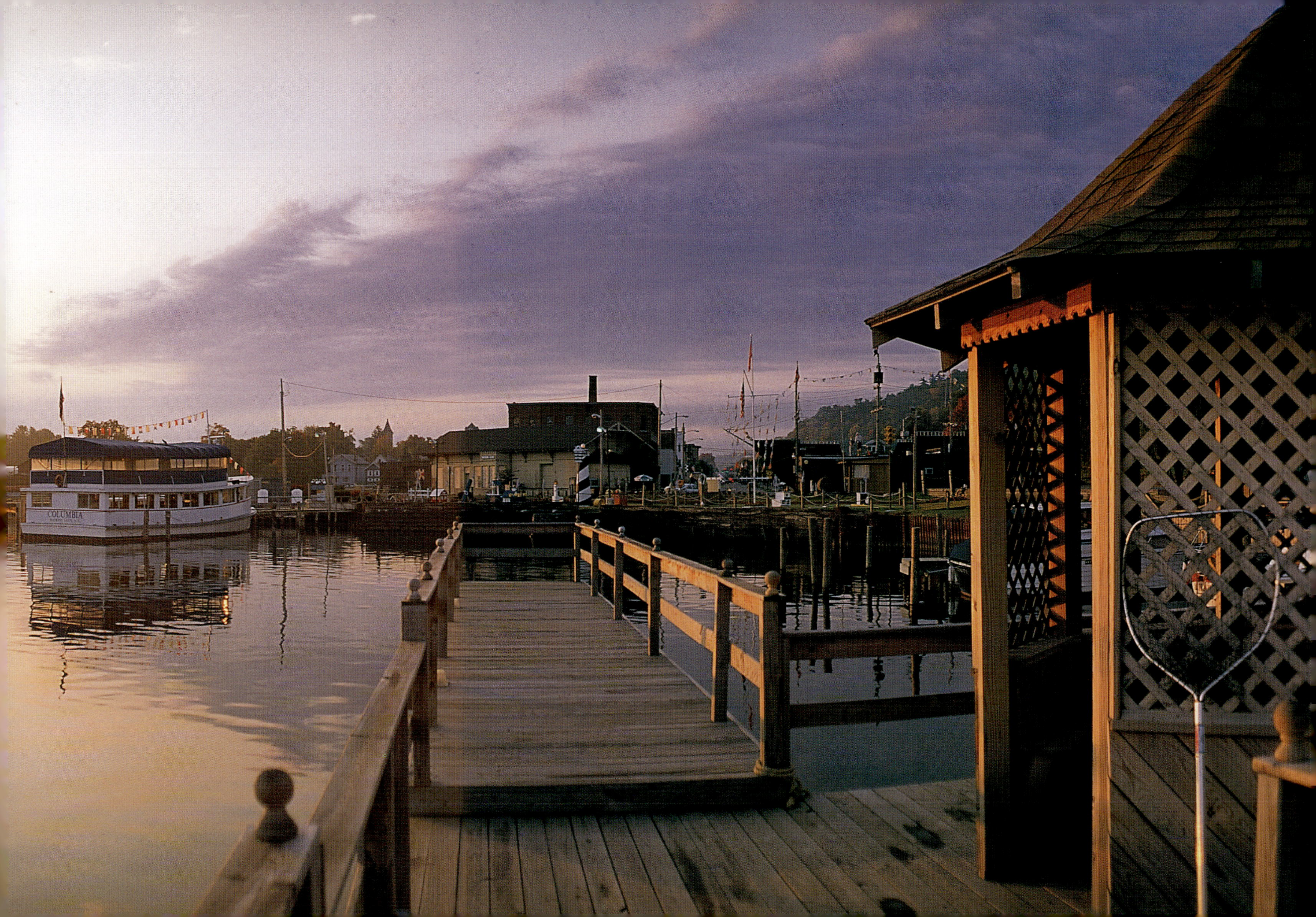
COLUMBIA

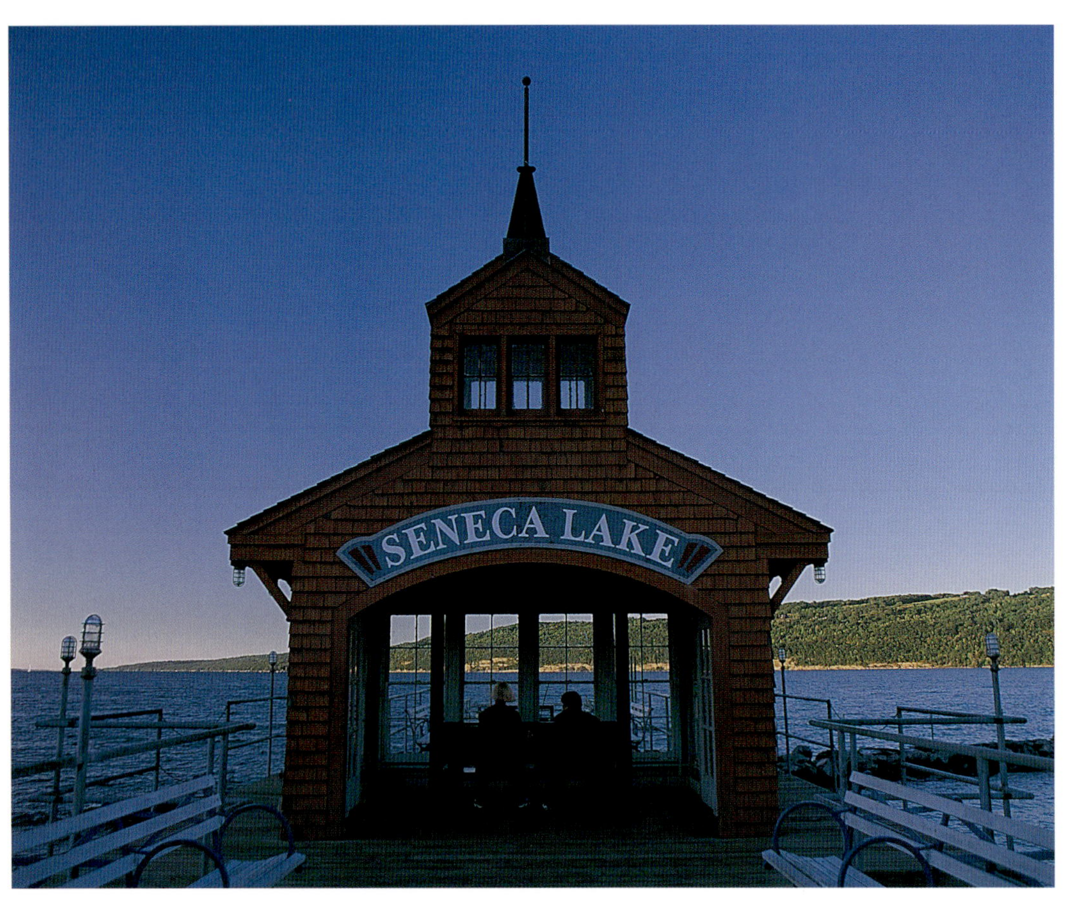

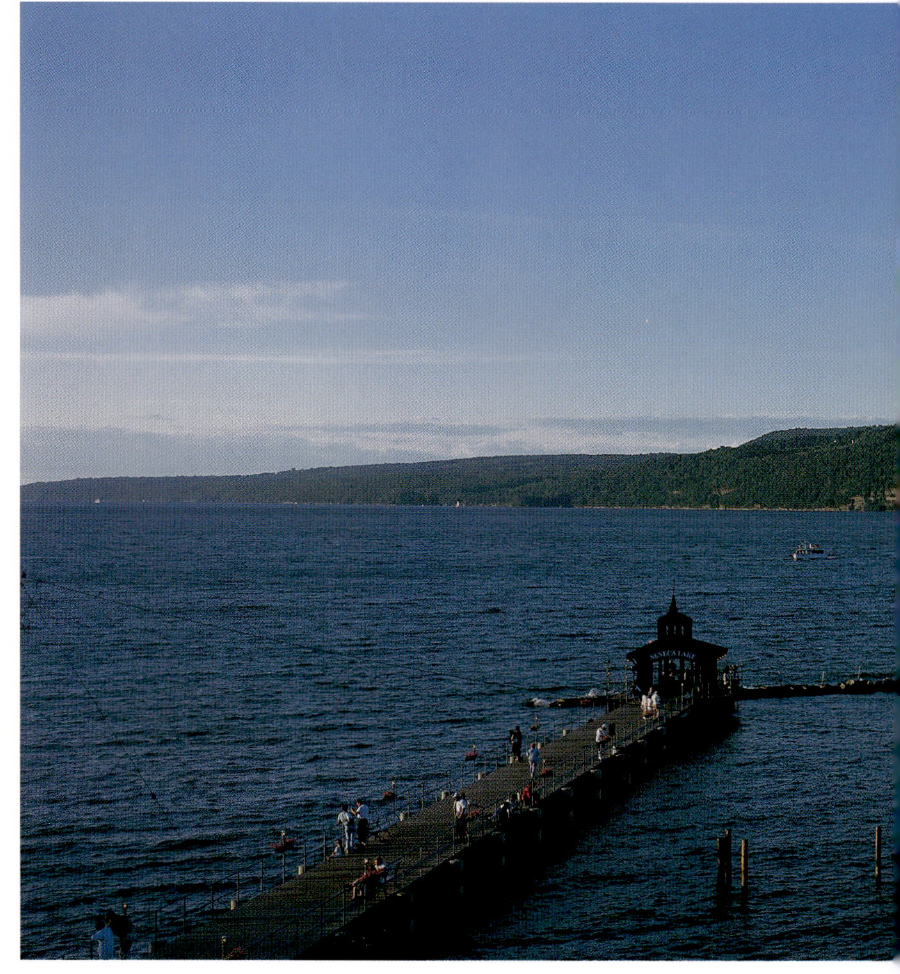

SENECA HARBOR PARK at Watkins Glen.

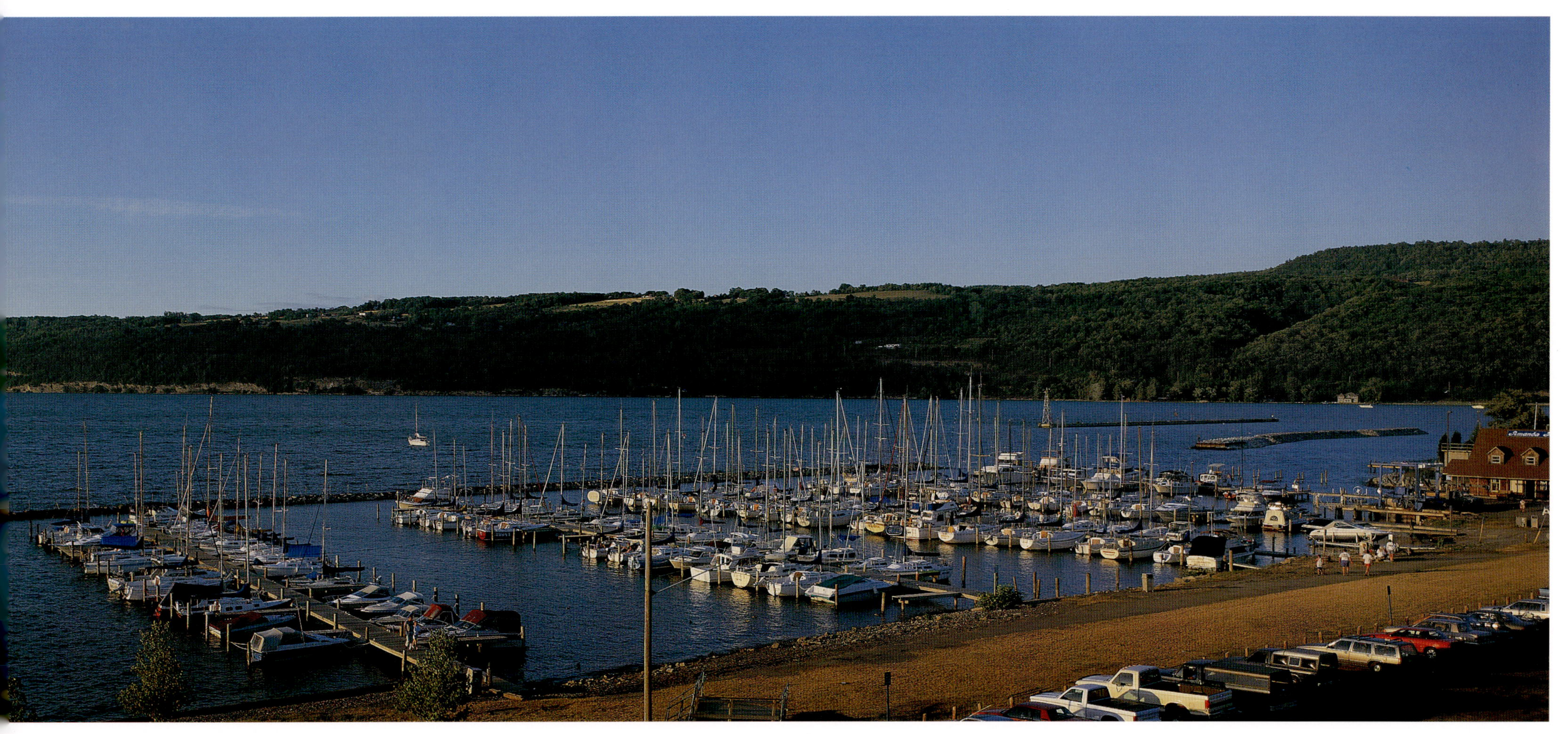

SENECA LAKE at Watkins Glen, looking northeast.

AT the southern end of Seneca Lake is the village of Watkins Glen, known as "the home of American road racing" for the auto races run every summer on its famous track. Inhabited for centuries by the Seneca tribe of the Iroquois nation, the area was settled by Revolutionary War veterans in the late 1700s. Watkins Glen's main avenue, Franklin Street, runs north past charming turn-of-the-century buildings to Seneca Harbor Park, with its 300-foot pier, award-winning gazebo, dinner cruises, and over 160 protected boat slips.

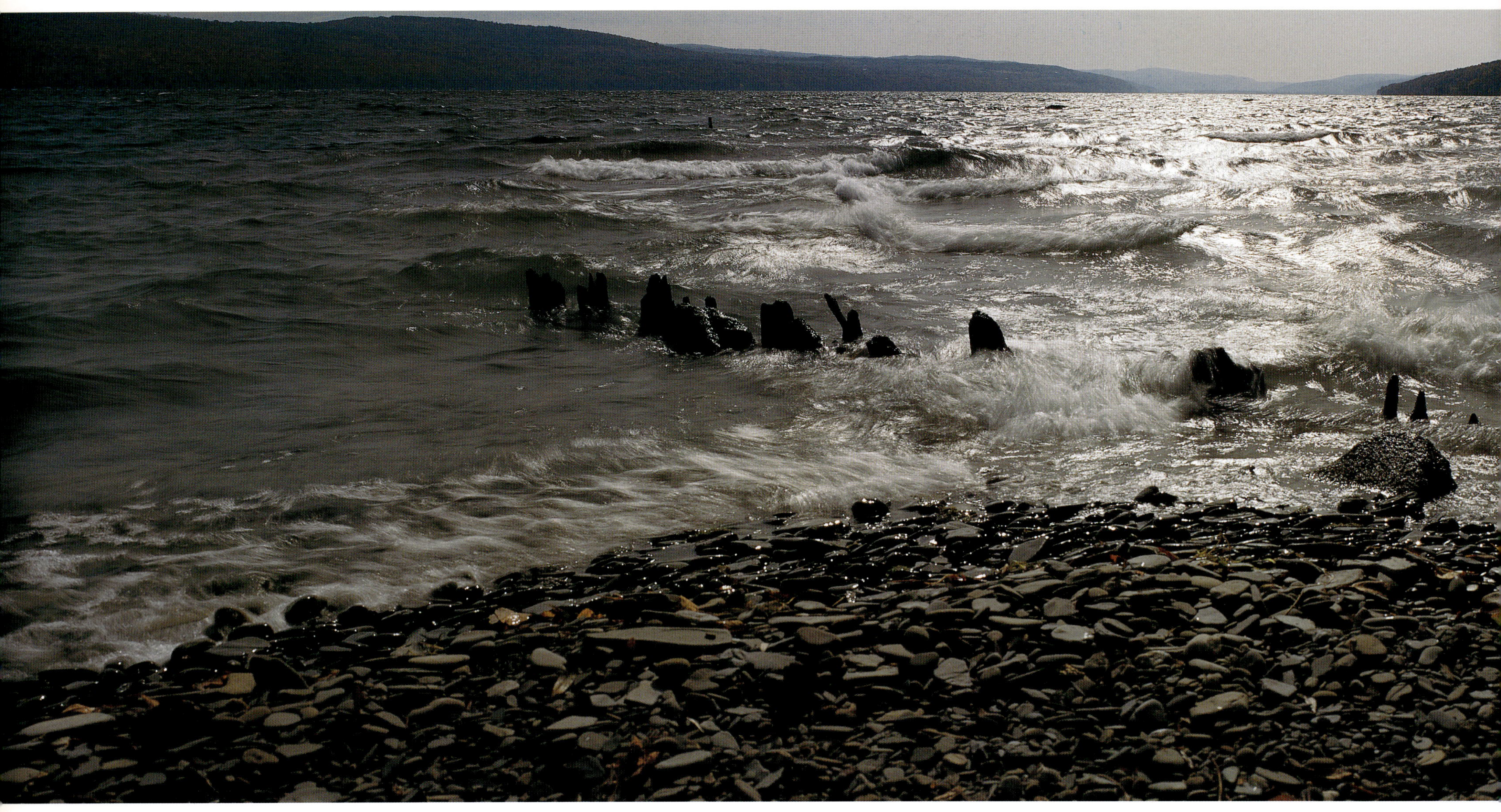

SENECA LAKE from Glenora Point, looking south.

Watkins Glen lies in the distance as wild weather whips Seneca Lake into a fury along the shore at Glenora Point.

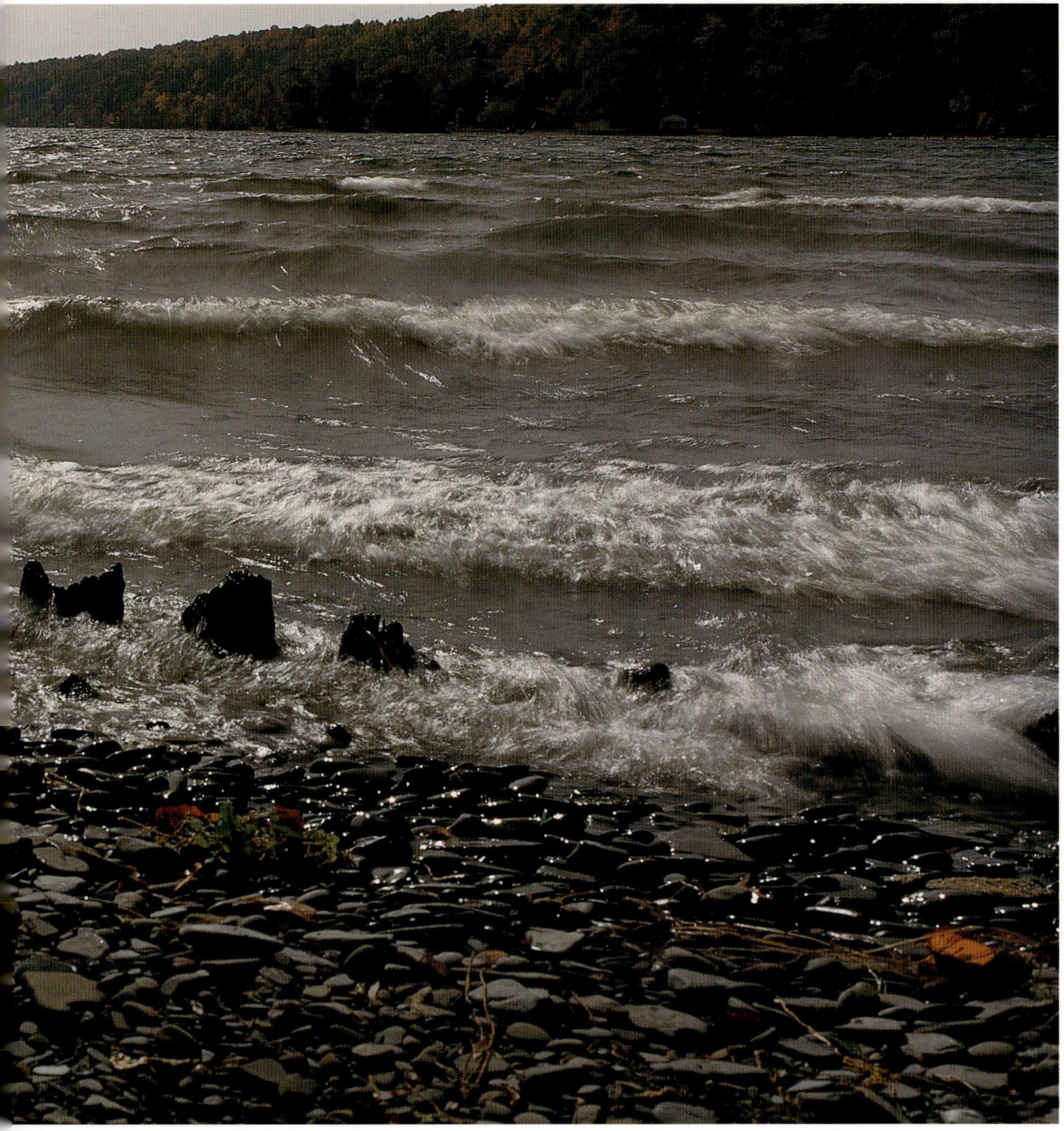

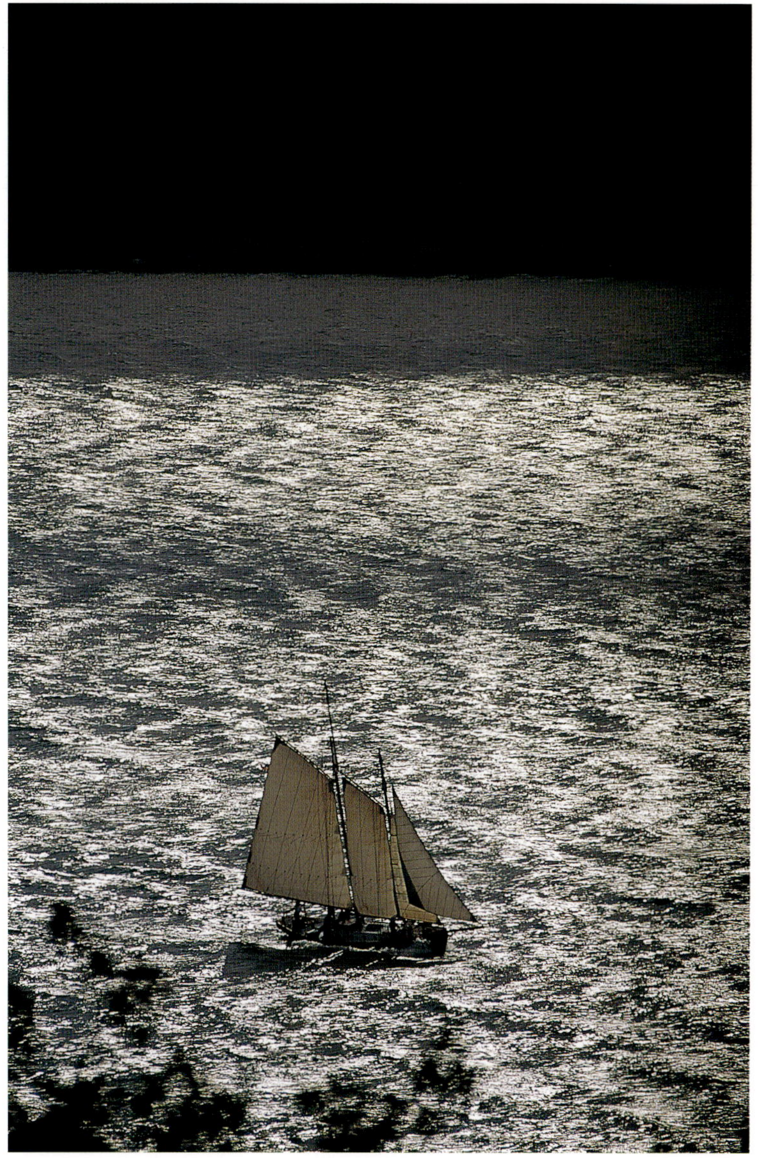

SENECA LAKE near Watkins Glen, looking west.

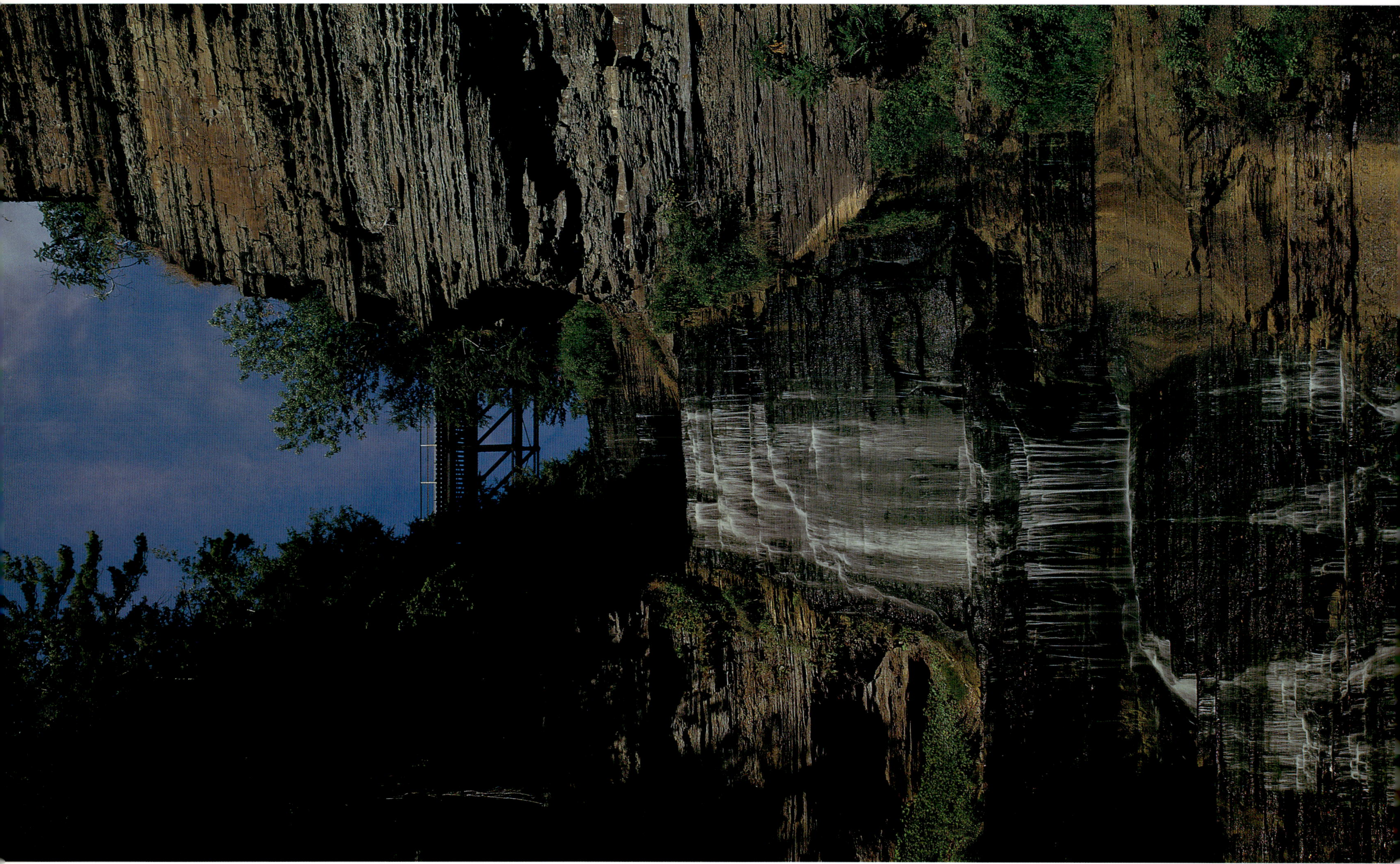

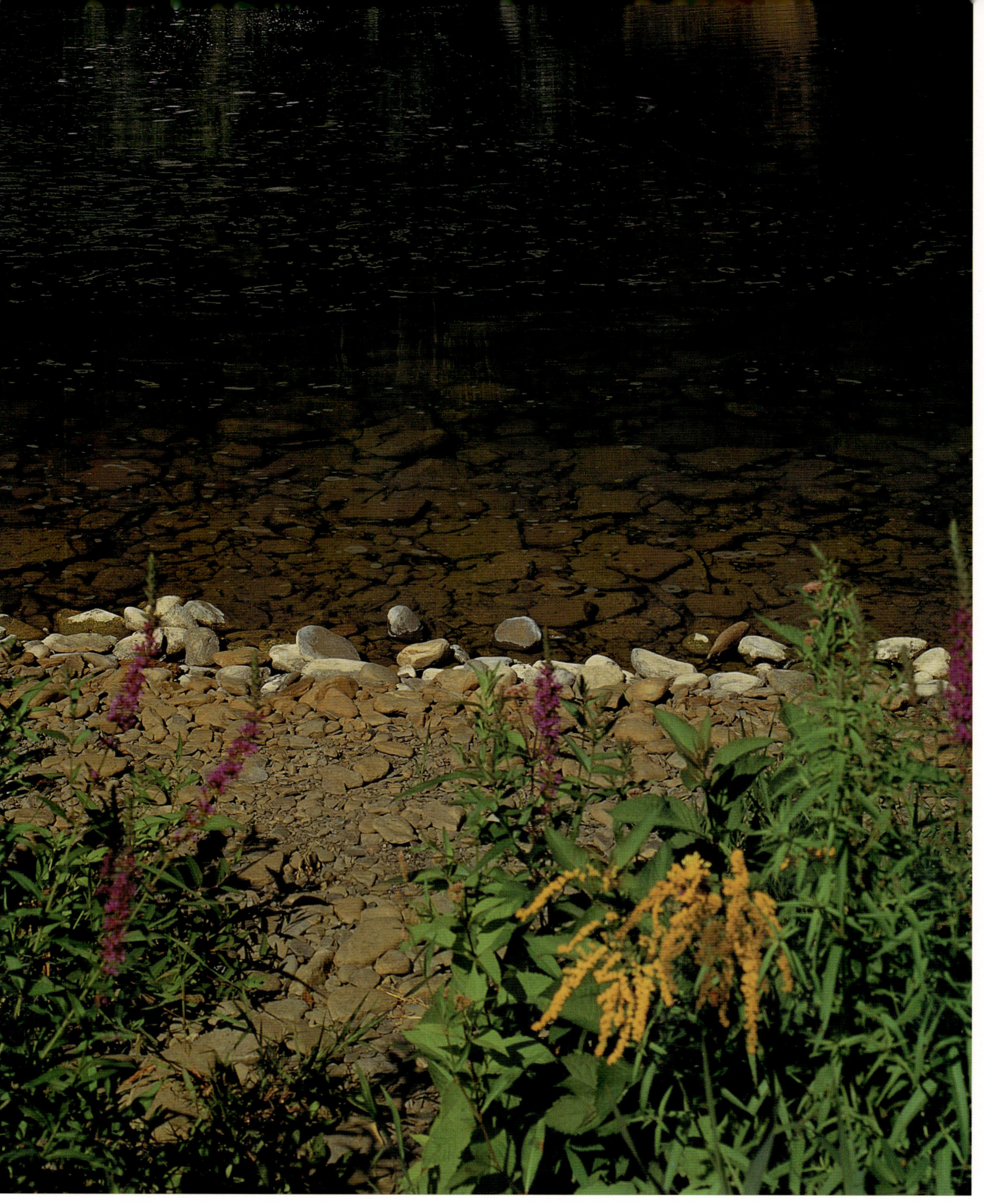

GLENORA FALLS.

Colorful lichens cling to the rock where Glenora Falls makes its final plunge near Seneca Lake.

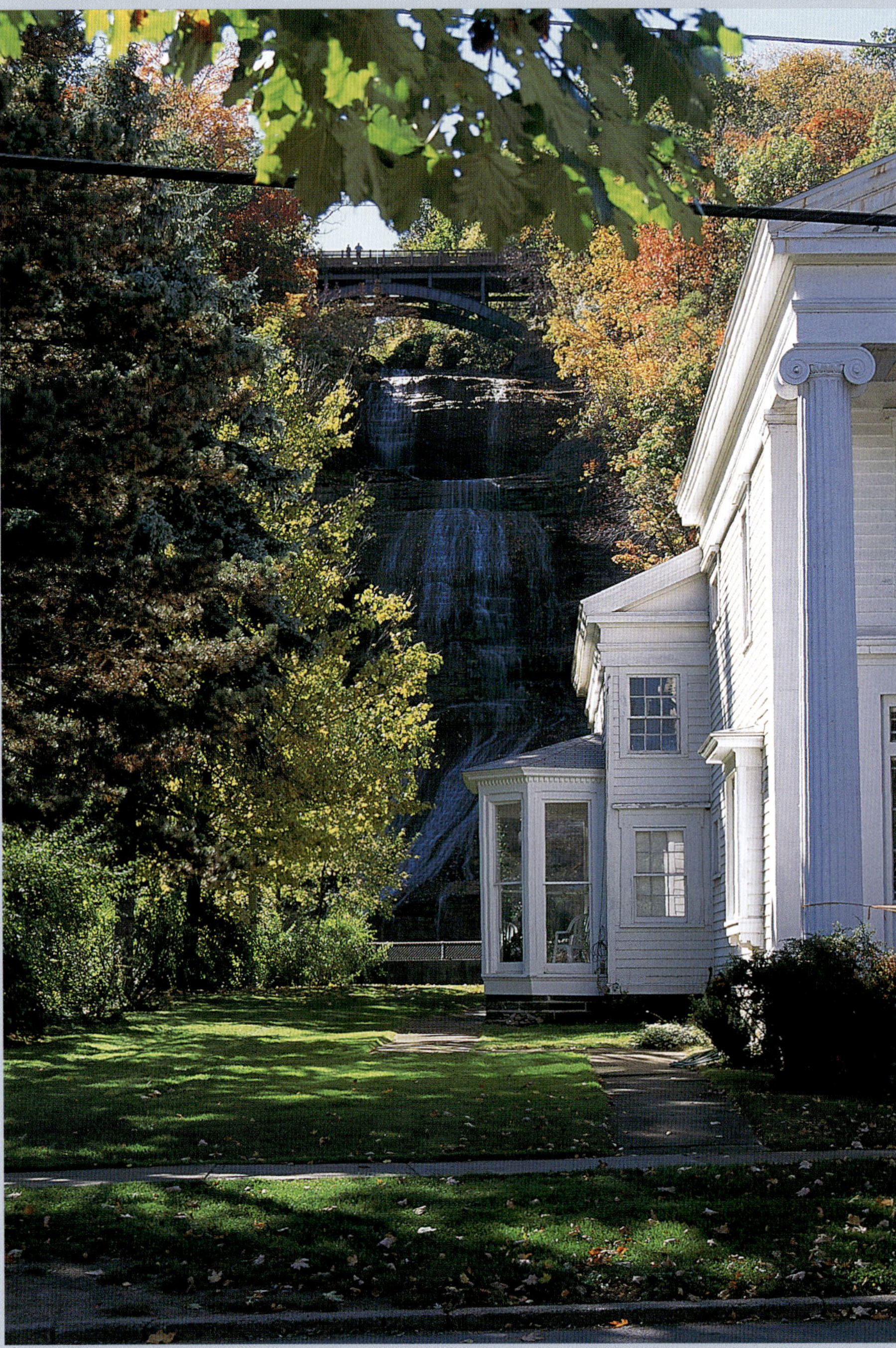

Left:
SHE-QUA-GA FALLS, village of Montour Falls.

Right:
SENECA LAKE from Hector, looking west.

North of Watkins Glen along the east side of Seneca Lake, a cluster of vineyards and fine wineries dot the hillsides near Hector and Valois.

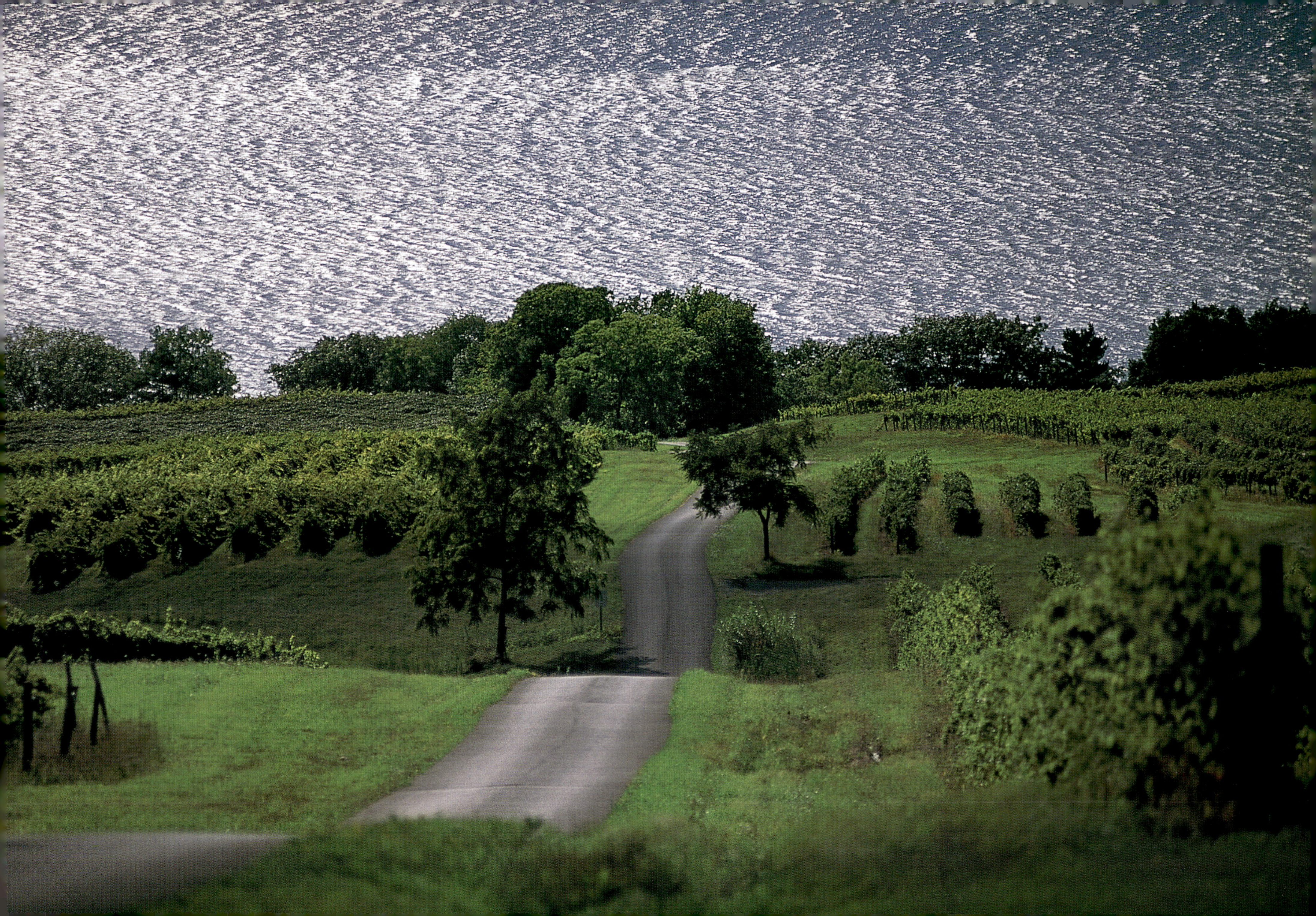

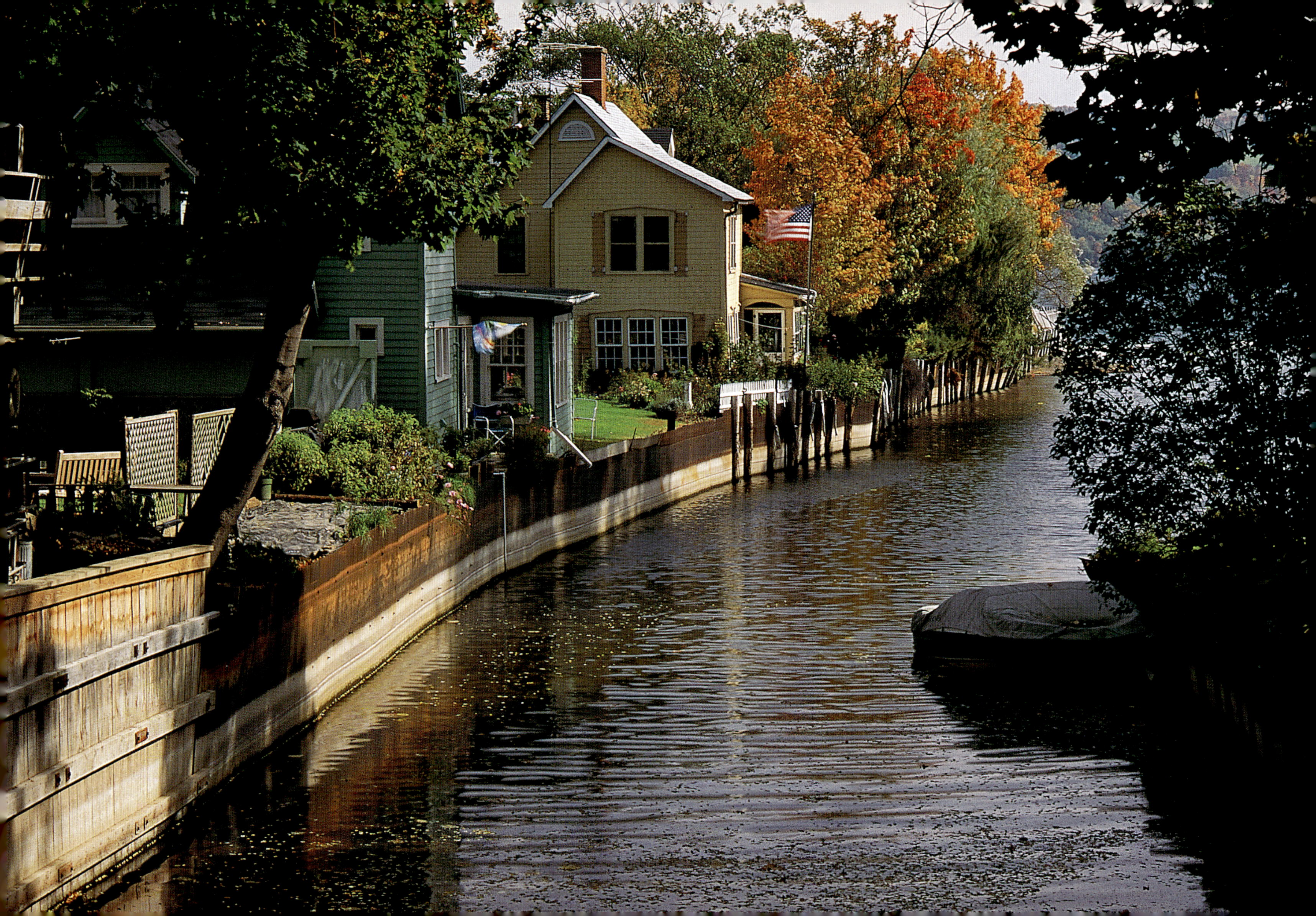

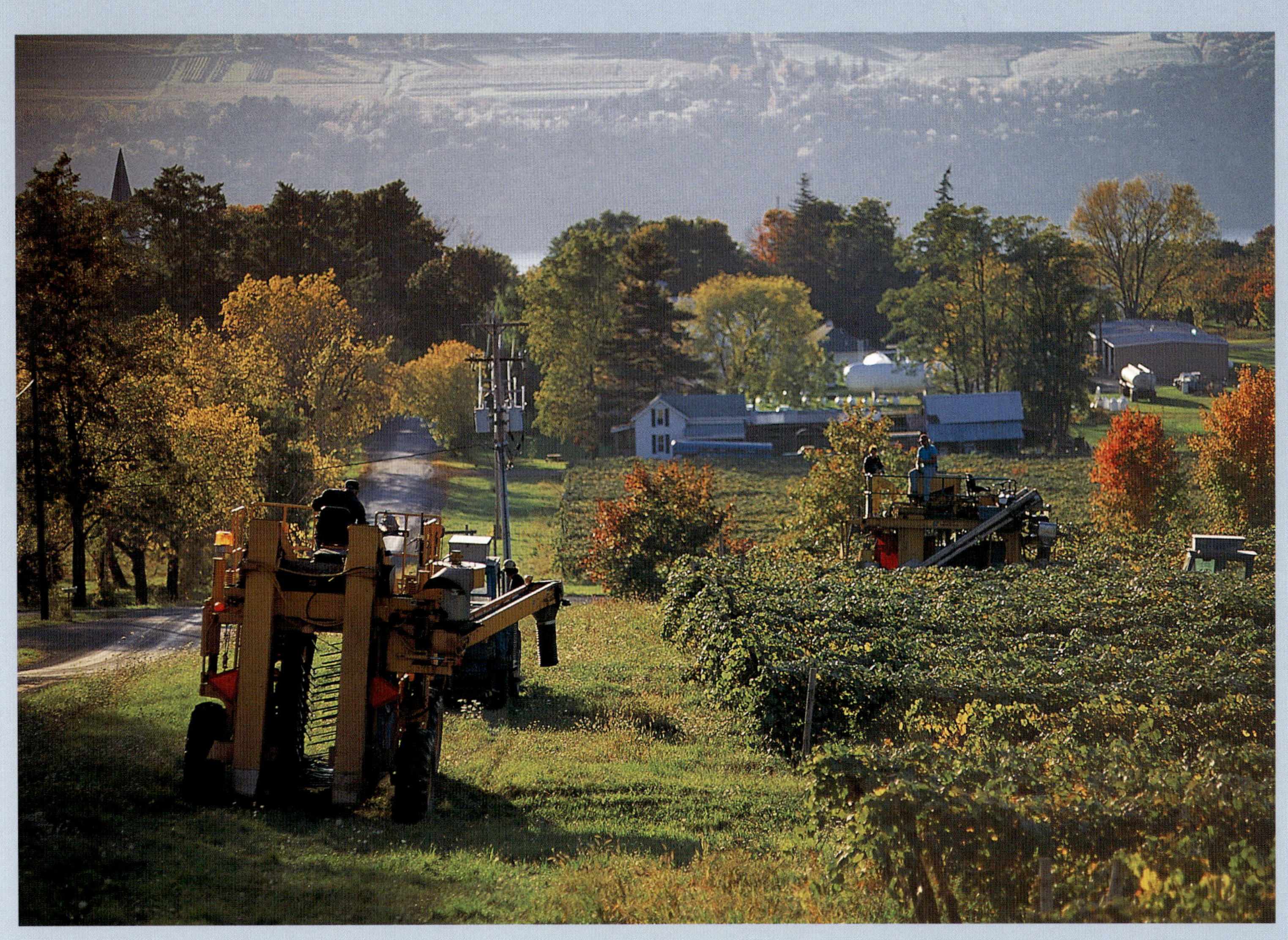

Far left:
SENECA LAKE at Glenora Point, looking east.

After tumbling over Glenora Falls, the water in Big Stream meanders past cottages before emptying into the lake.

Left:
SENECA LAKE from Hector.

Mechanical harvesters await refueling as their crews work well into a fall evening, trying to collect the last of the year's harvest.

7 Cayuga Lake

CAYUGA LAKE
near Union Springs,
looking west.

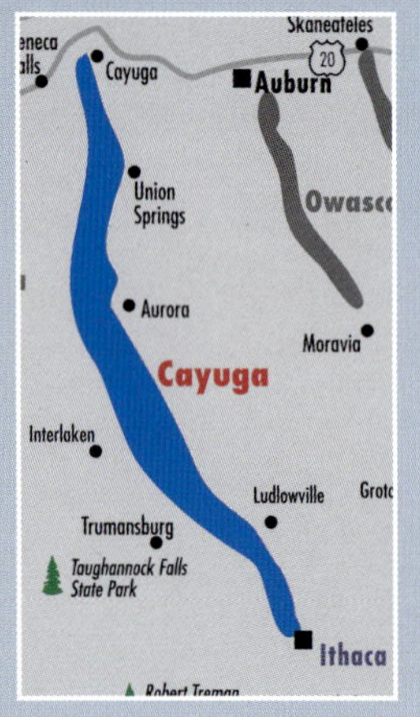

Cayuga Lake is the longest Finger Lake, stretching nearly 40 miles from the village of Seneca Falls in the north to the city of Ithaca in the south. More than 3 ½ miles wide near Aurora, it reaches a depth of 474 feet (93 feet below sea level!) and lies at the lowest elevation of all the Finger Lakes.

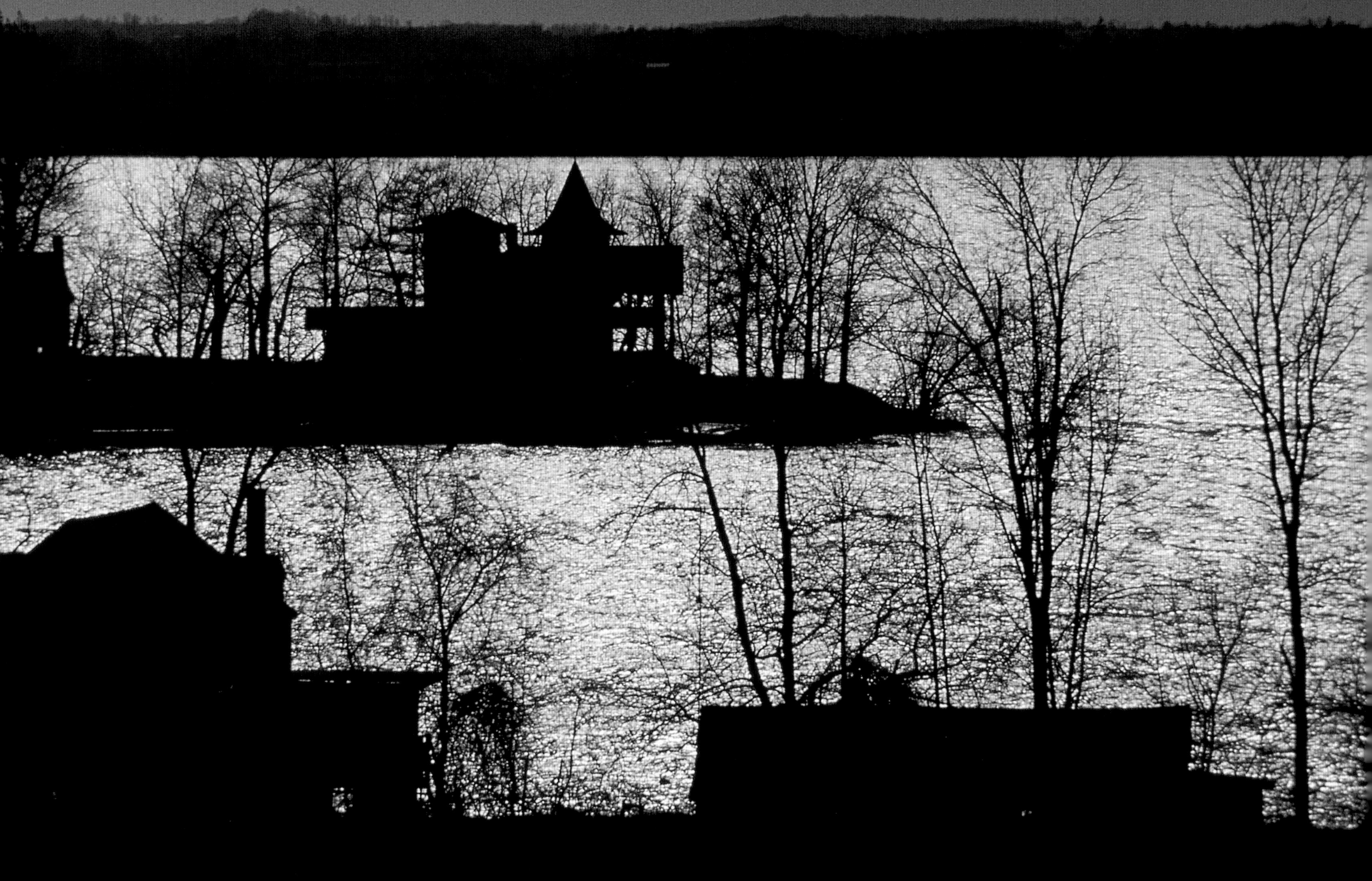

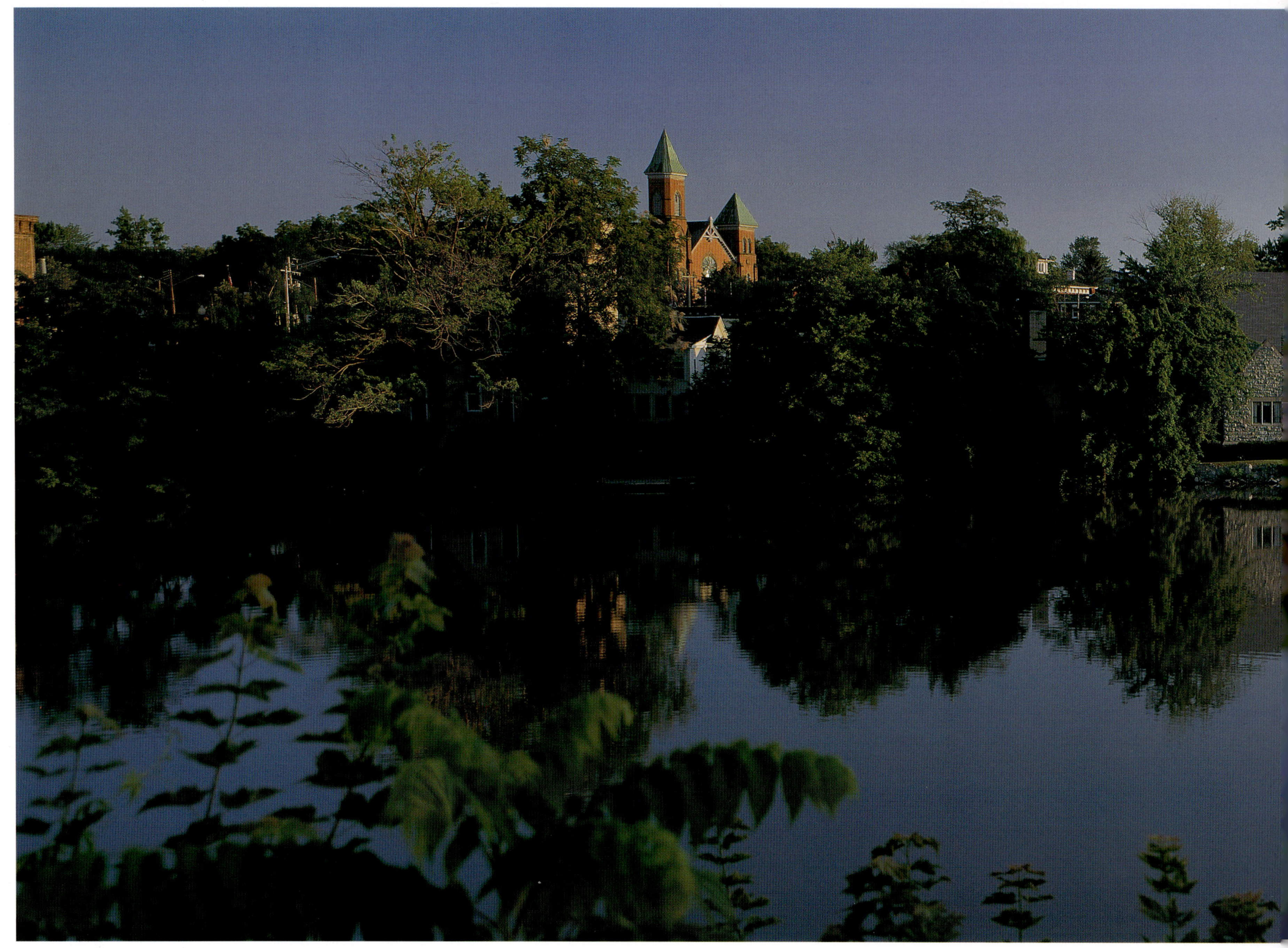

VAN CLEEF LAKE,
Seneca Falls.

Van Cleef Lake is part of the Seneca-Cayuga Canal, which links Seneca and Cayuga lakes to the Erie Canal, and ultimately to the waterways of the world.

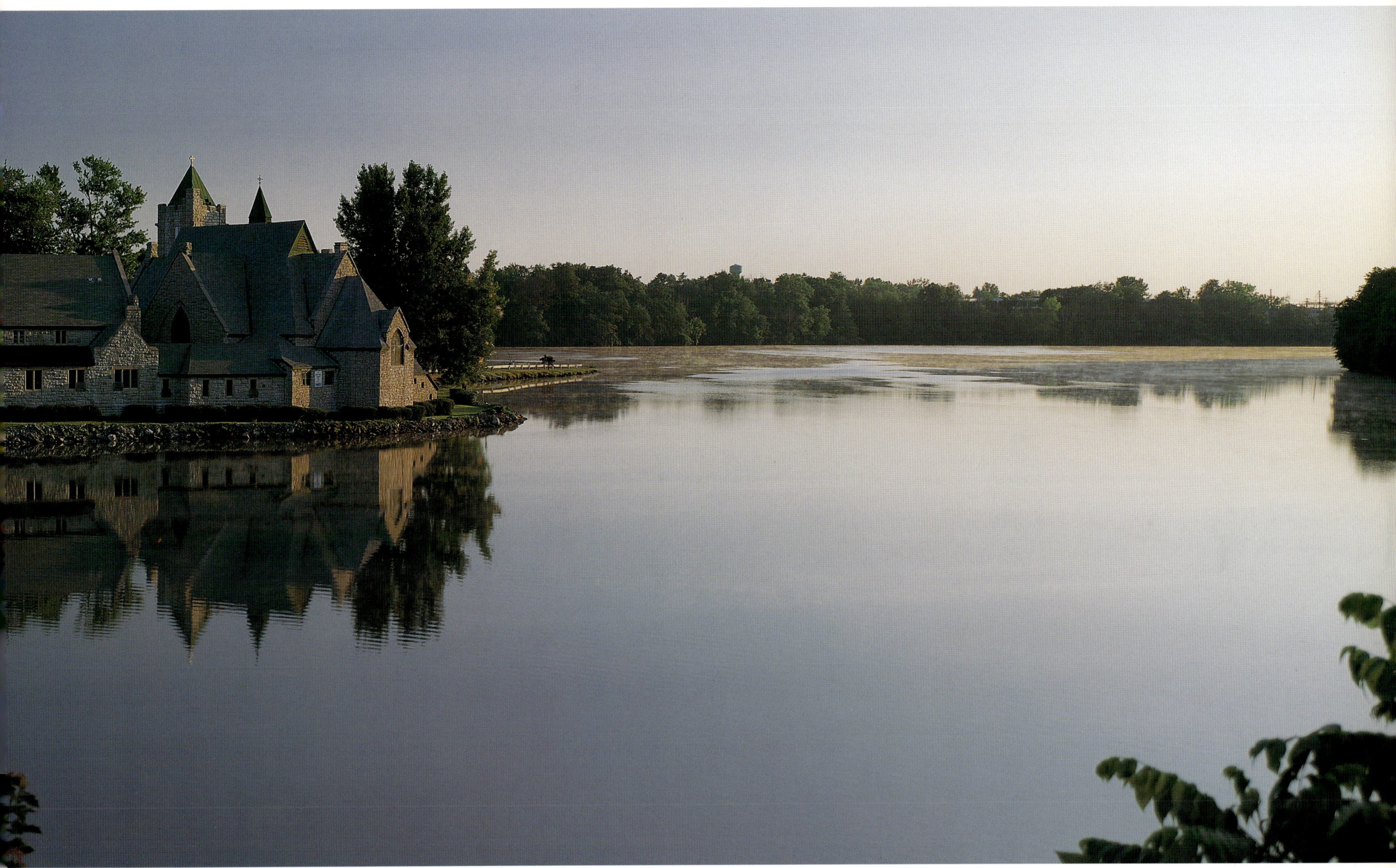

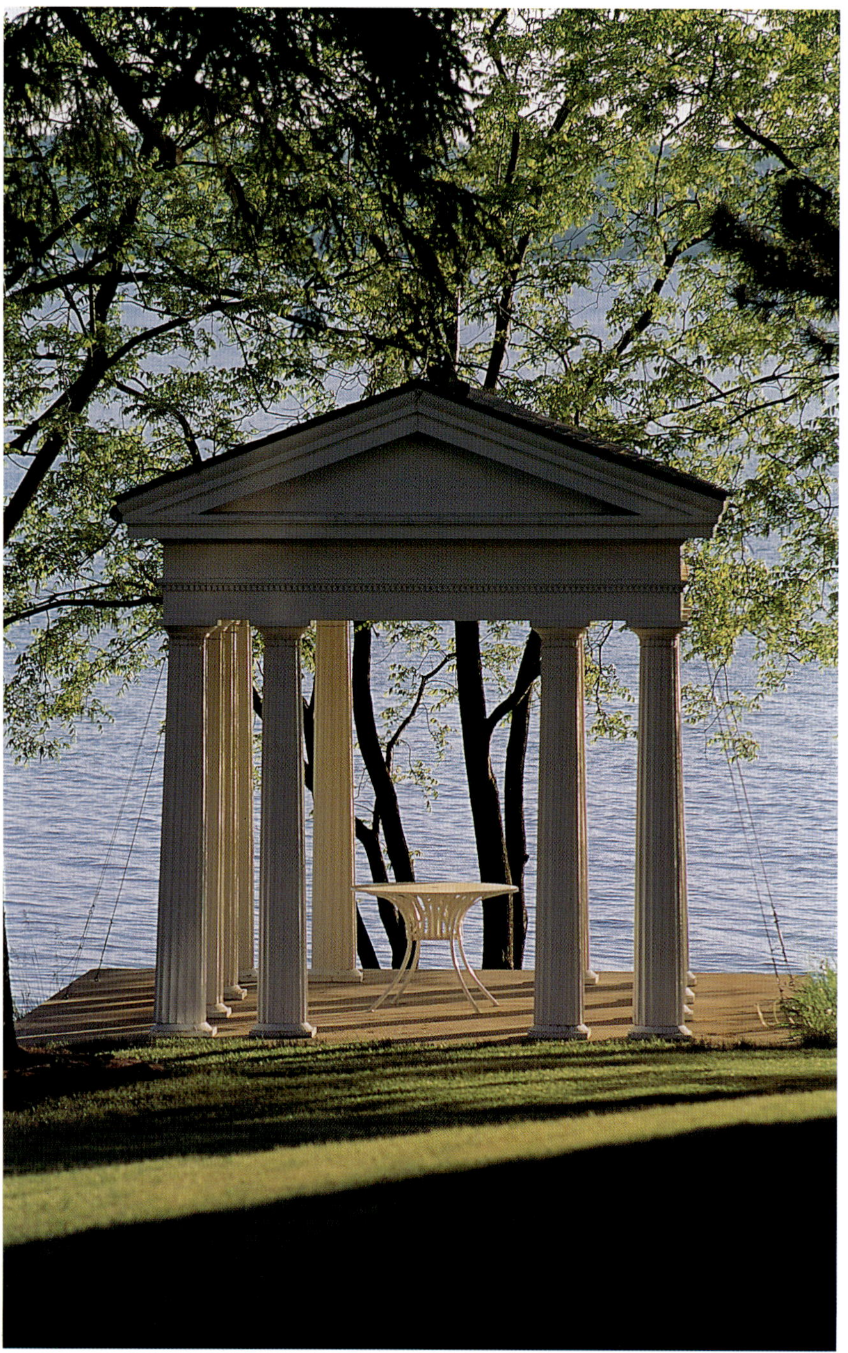

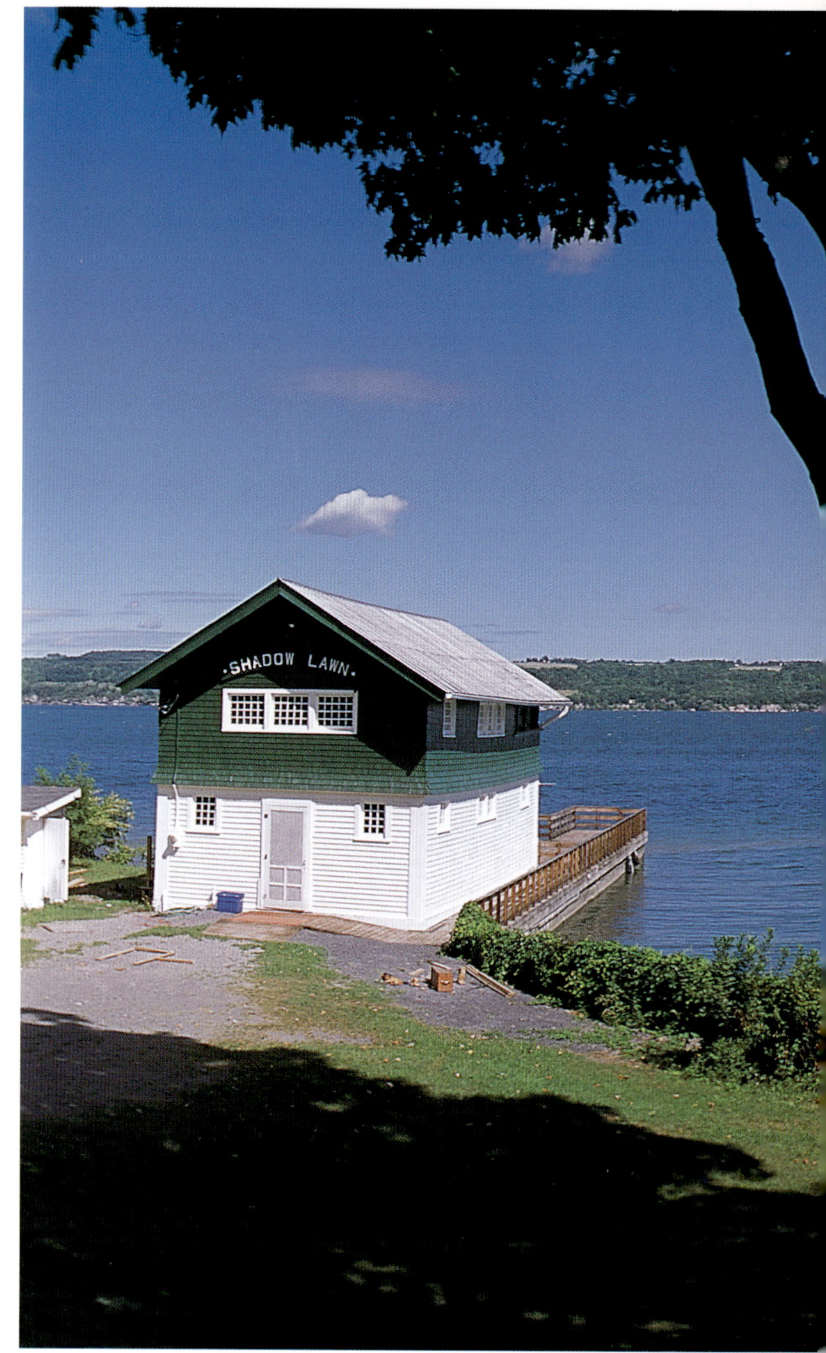

Left:
CAYUGA LAKE from Aurora, looking west.

Right:
CAYUGA LAKE from Kidders, looking southeast.

On the opposite shoreline, looking from north to south (left to right), the view stretches from Milliken Power Station, south to Lansing, and then nearly to Ithaca.

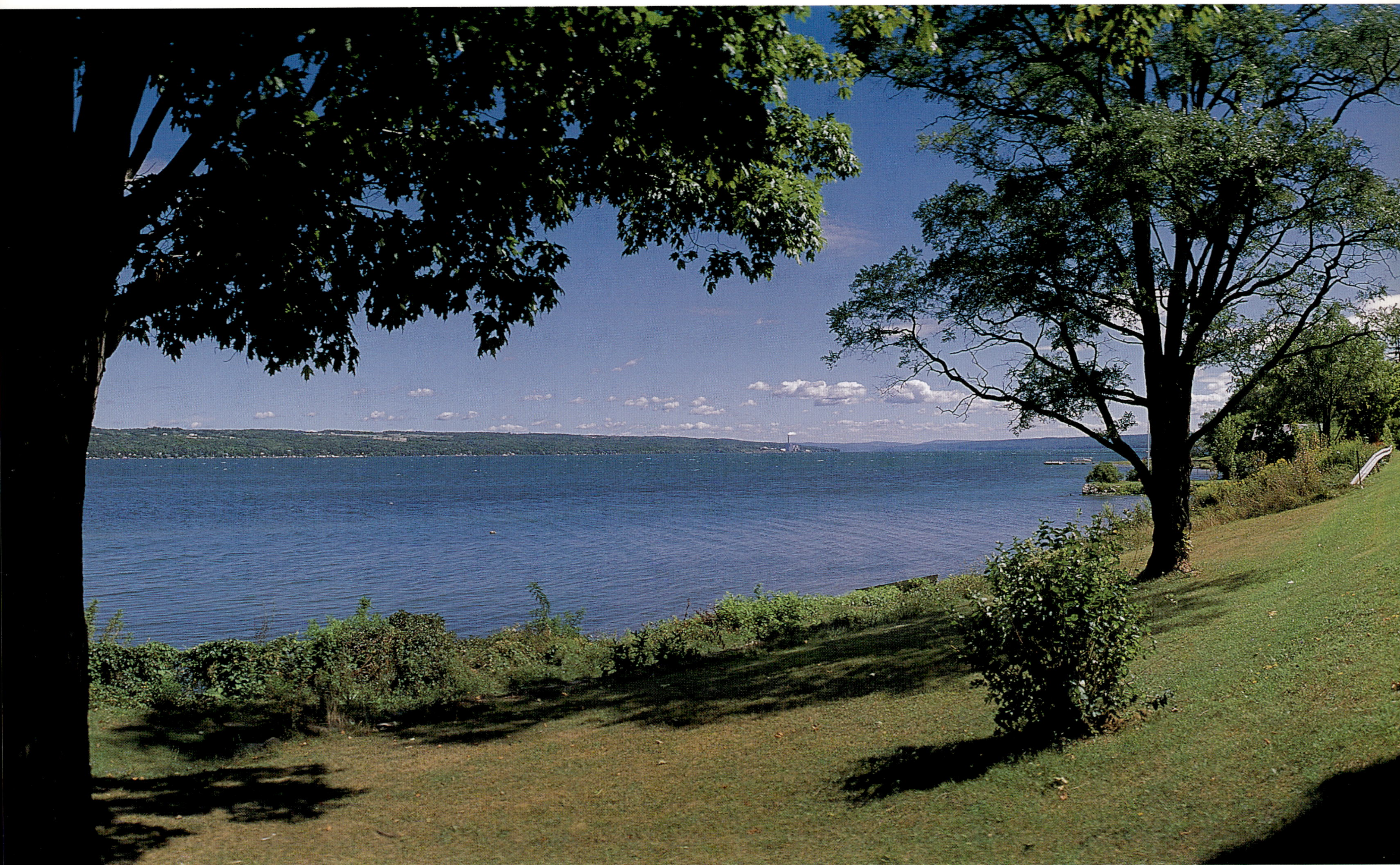

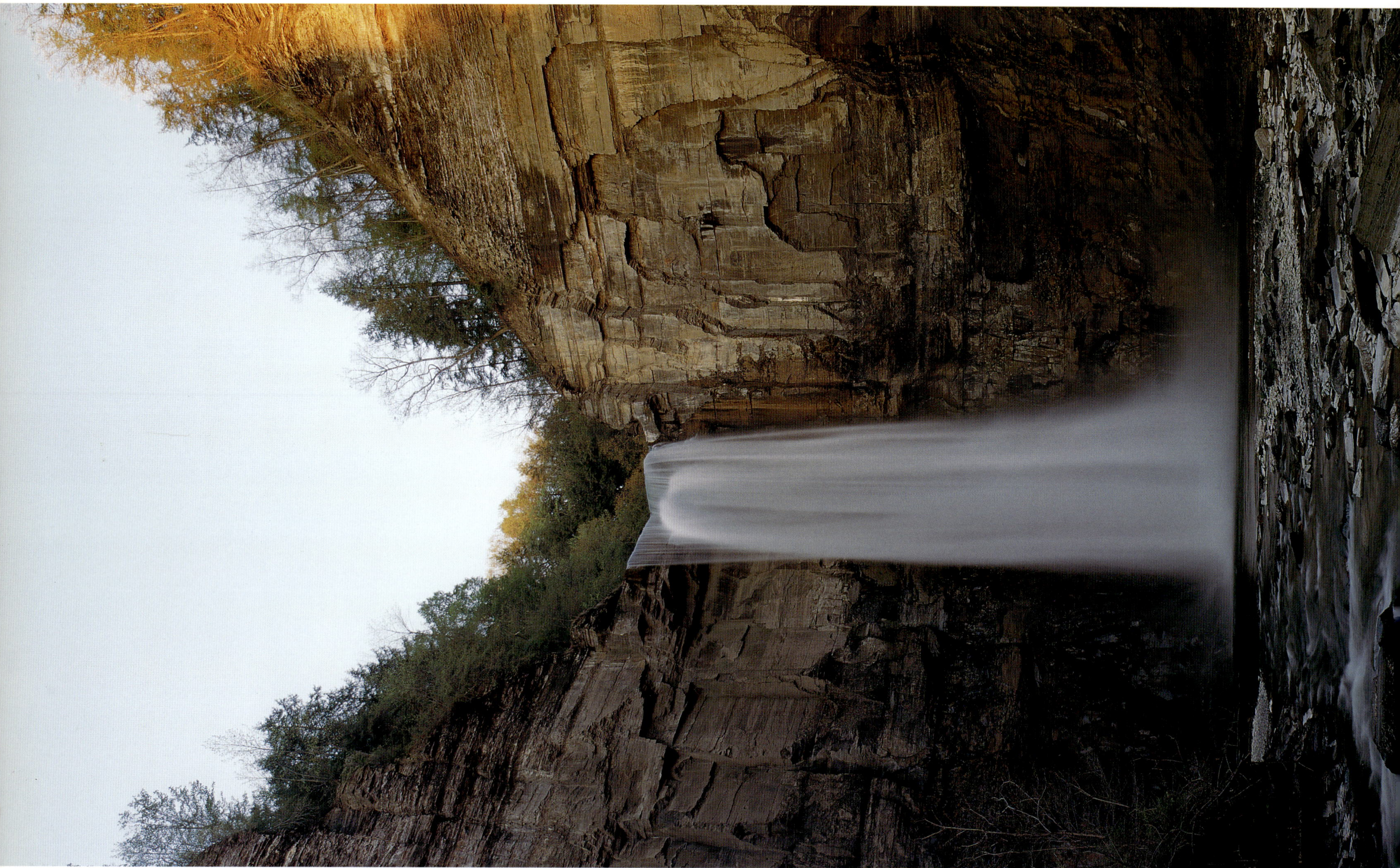

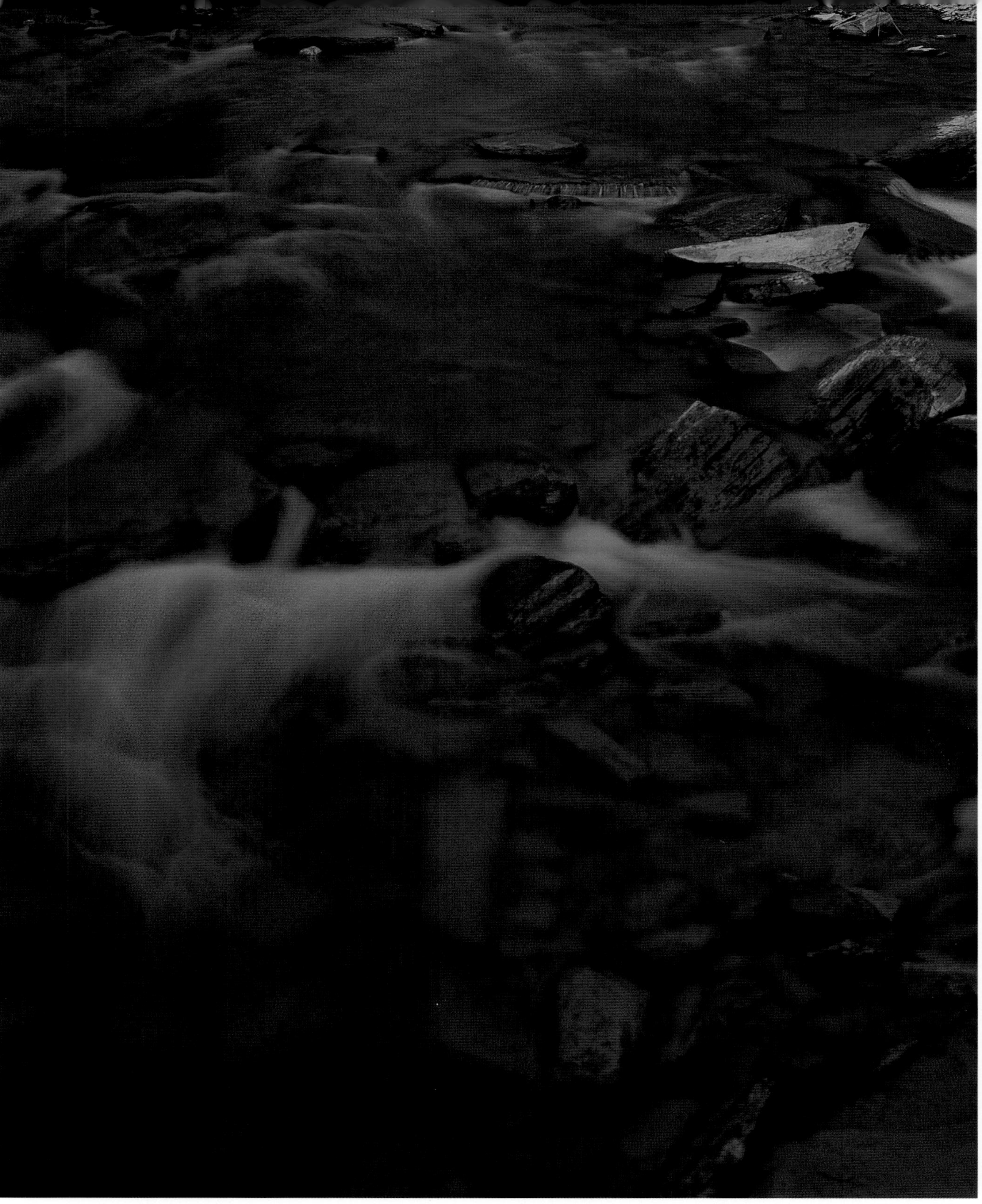

TAUGHANNOCK FALLS, Trumansburg

AT 215 feet, Taughannock's cascade is taller than Niagara Falls, making it the highest single-drop waterfall in the northeast. Sheer rock walls, four hundred feet high, create a natural amphitheater around the falls.

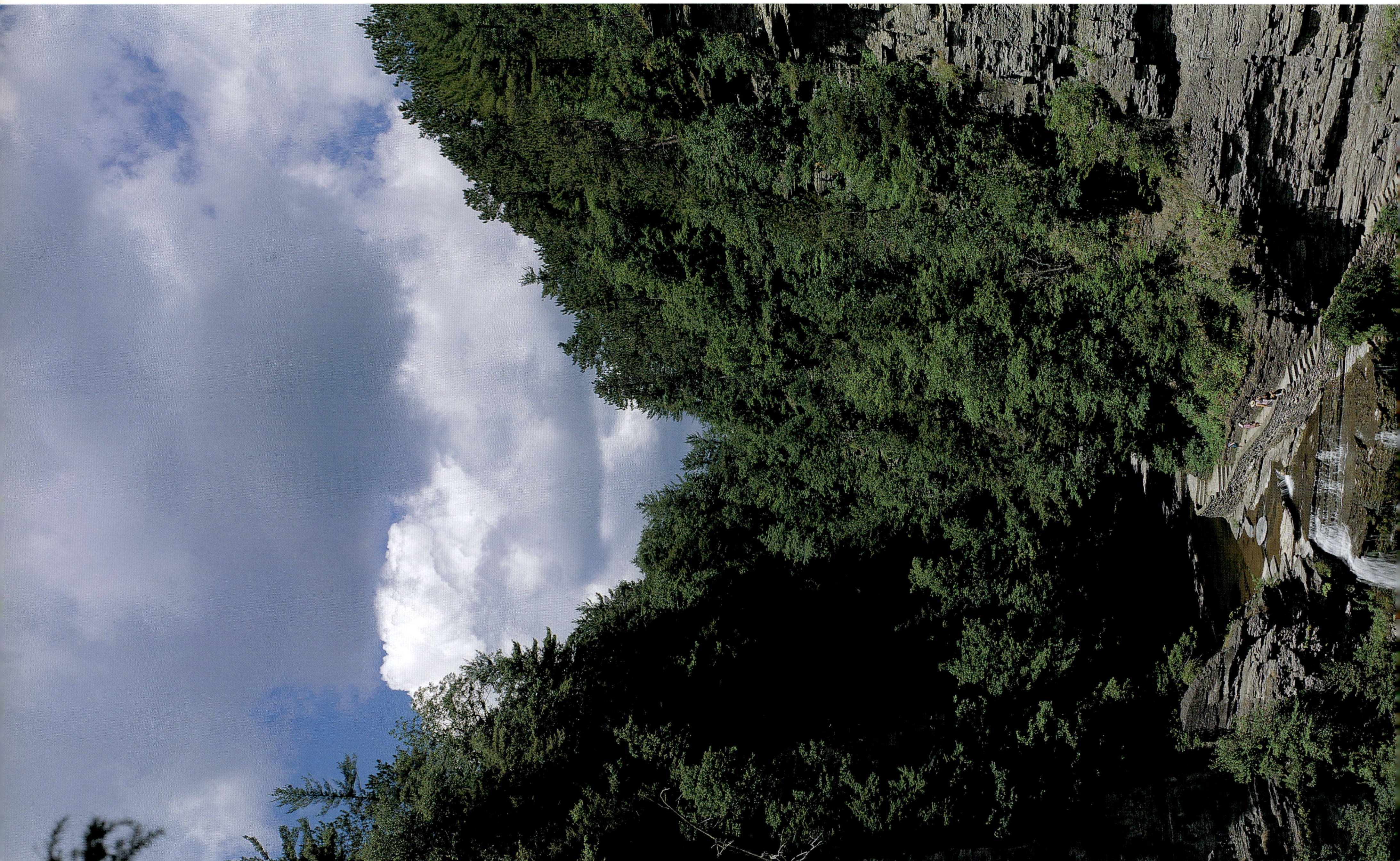

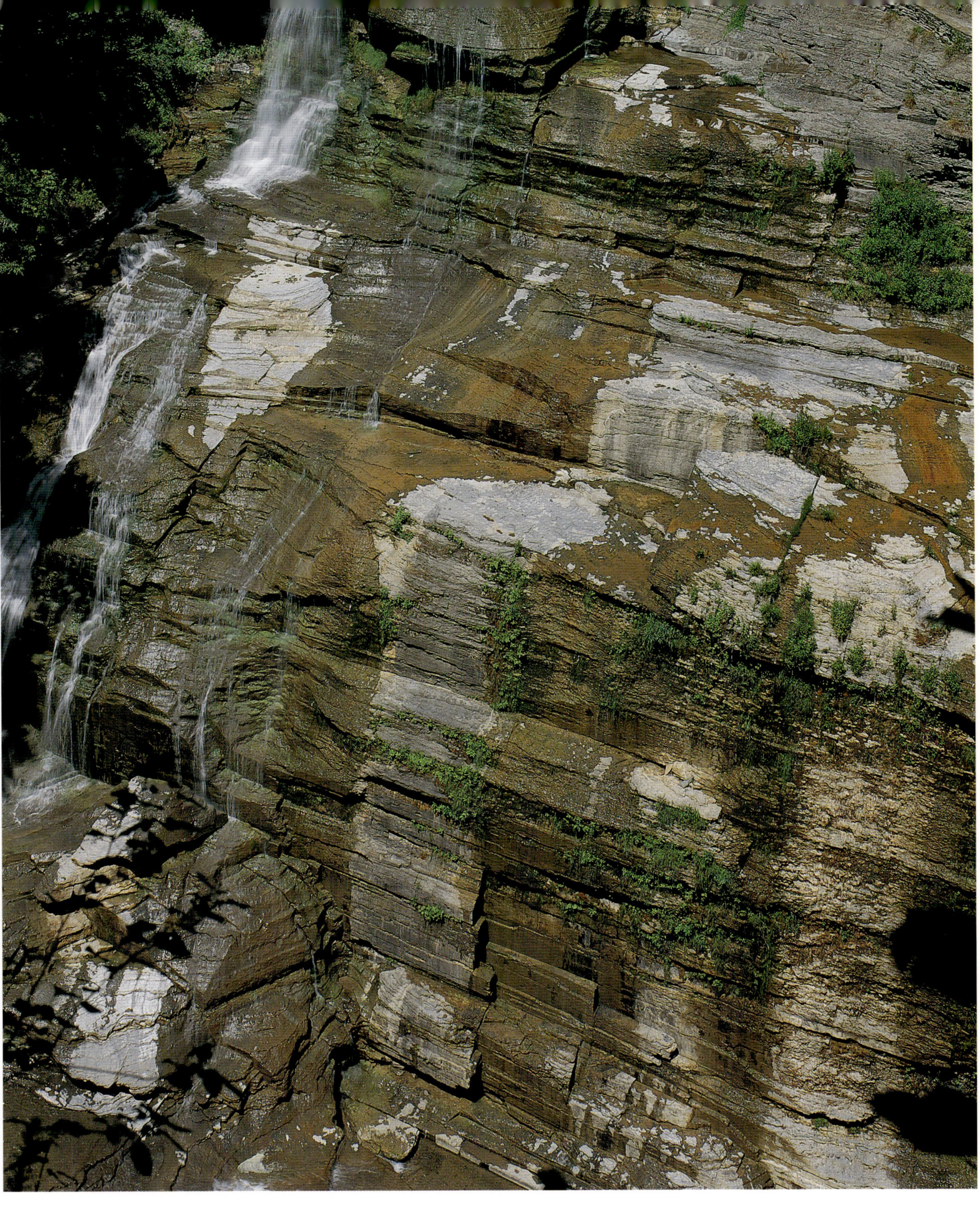

LUCIFER FALLS, Robert H. Treman State Park, Ithaca.

AT 116 feet high, Lucifer Falls is the centerpiece of Treman State Park, once called Enfield Glen. In the 1800s, the gorge provided water power for several mills to grind corn and wheat and one of these, a century old, remains as a museum in the upper park. Between 1912 and 1920, the rugged upper area of the glen was used by early motion picture companies based in Ithaca to simulate the scenery for screenplays set in Alaska and the American West.

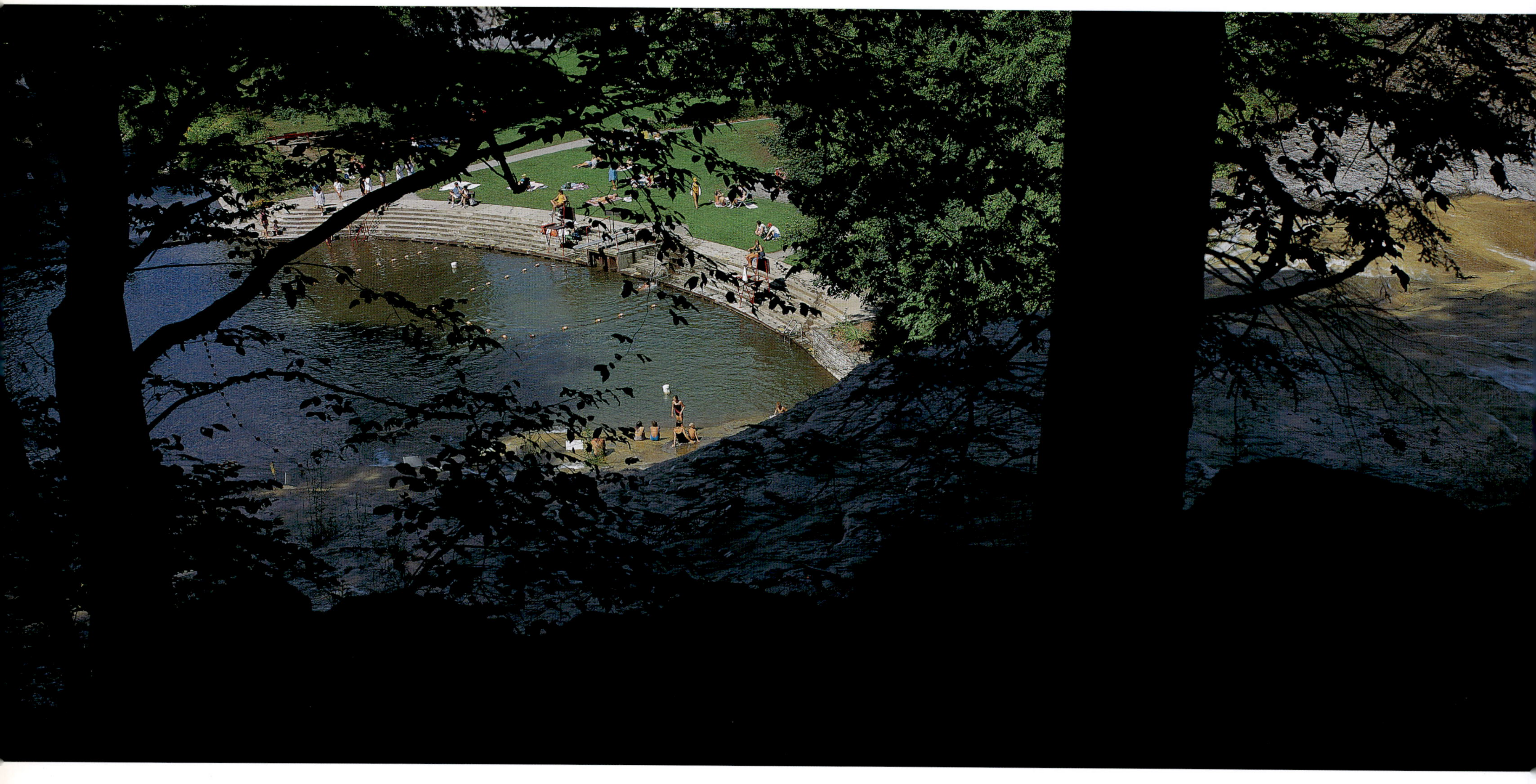

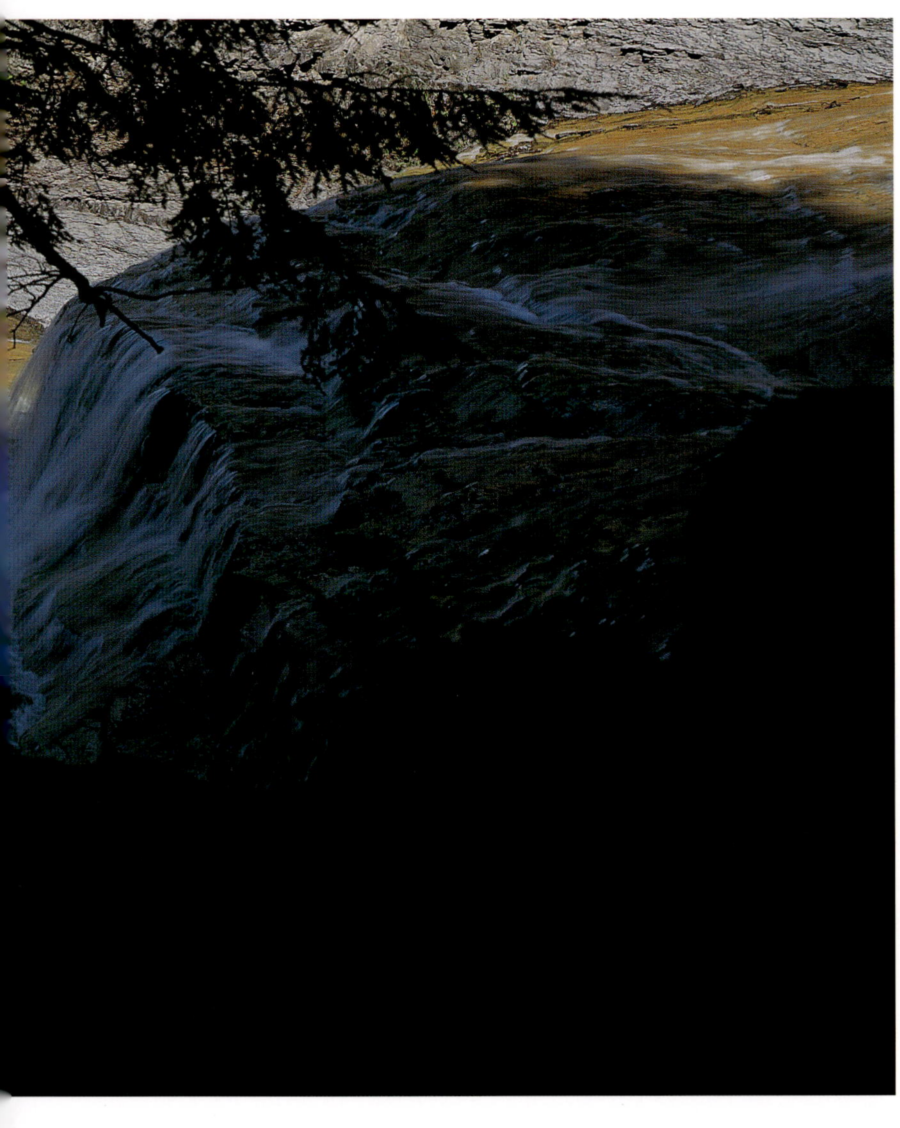

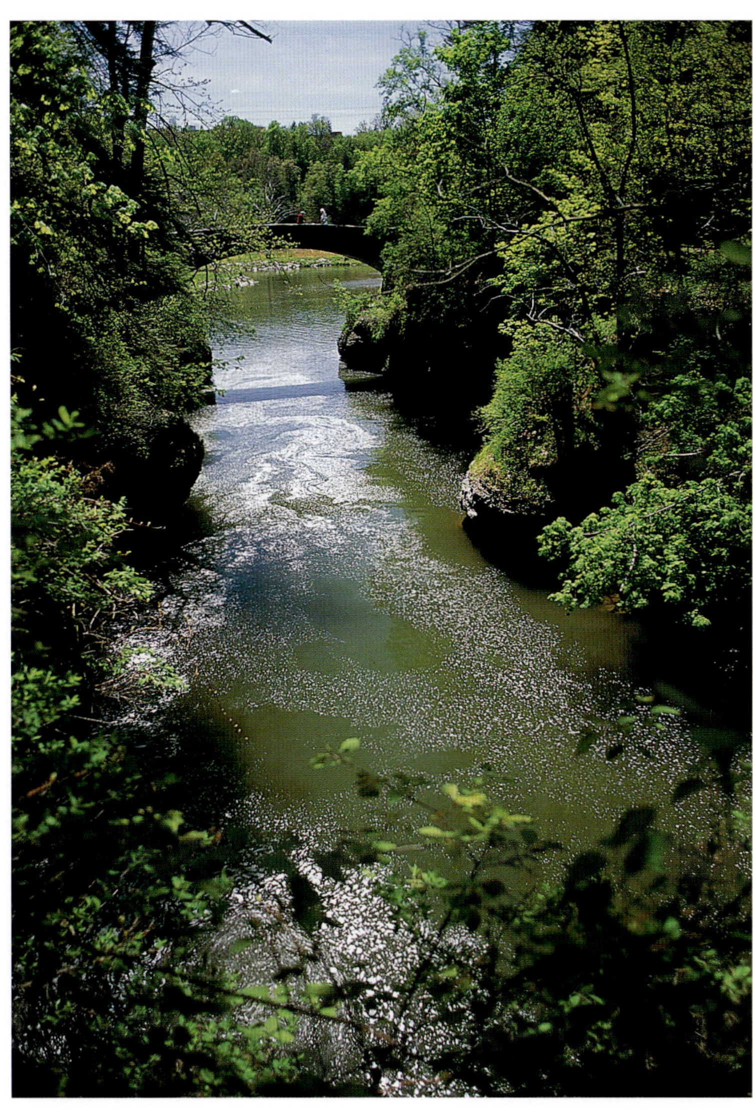

Far left:
BUTTERMILK FALLS STATE PARK, Ithaca.

Buttermilk Creek plunges more than 600 feet in a series of cascades and rapids to settle in a natural swimming pool.

Left:
FALL CREEK at Beebe Lake, Cornell University.

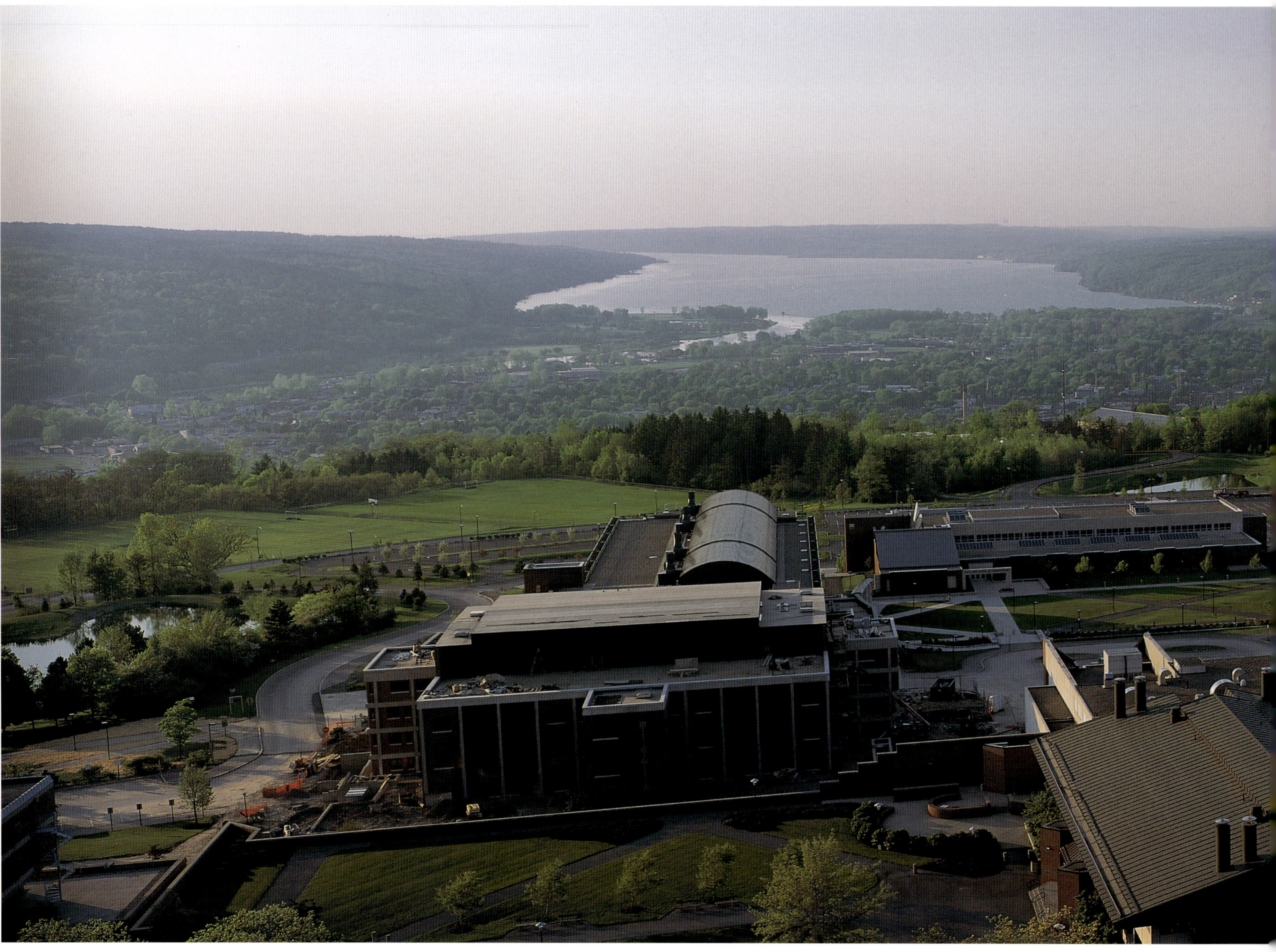

CAYUGA LAKE
from Ithaca College,
looking north.

FROM high above Ithaca on South Hill, only the first six miles of Cayuga Lake can be seen because the lake bends sharply to the north at Myers Point in Lansing. To the right, the distinctive architecture of Cornell University can be seen on East Hill.

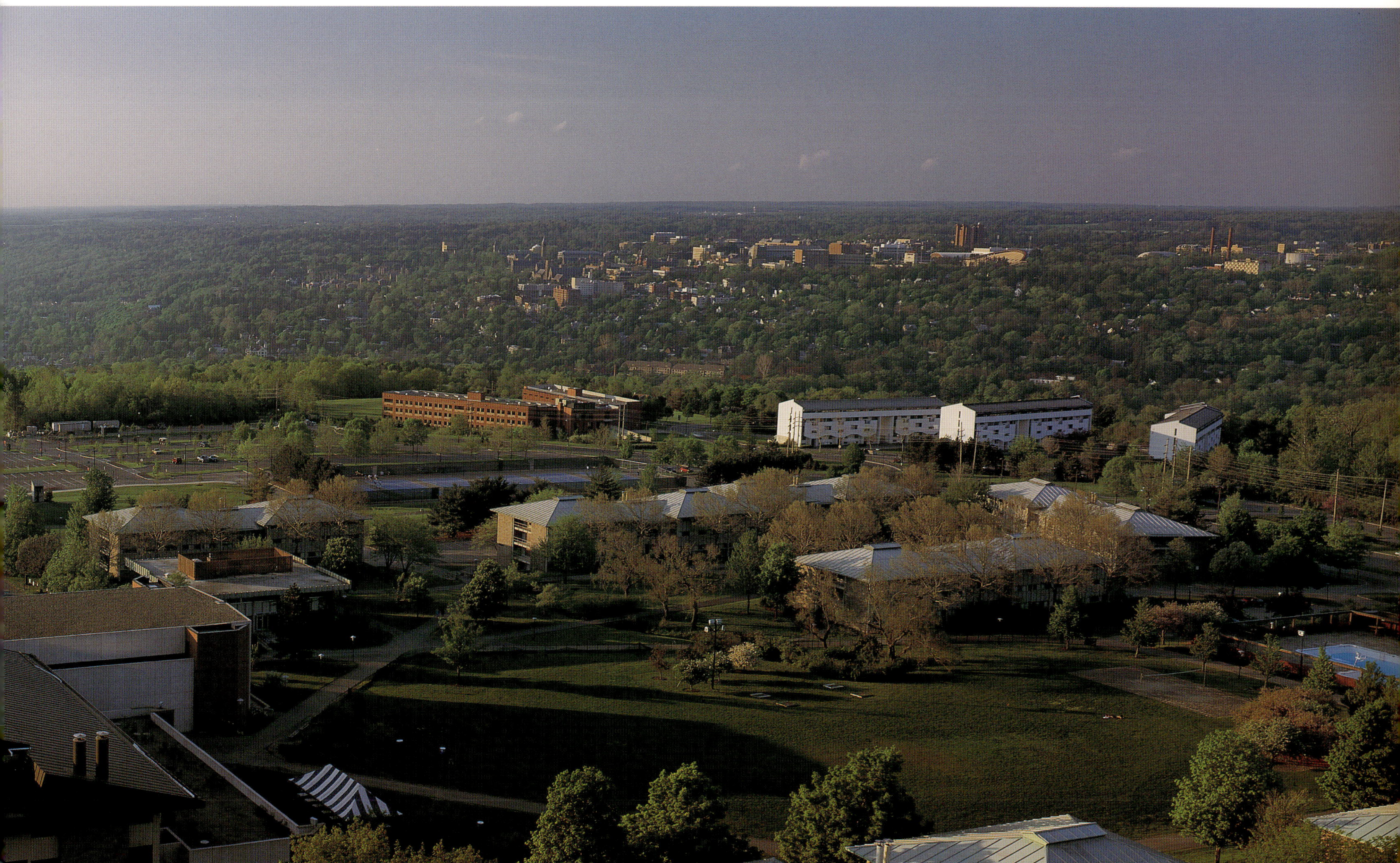

CAYUGA LAKE from Cornell University, looking north.

AT sunrise, the view from the belfry of McGraw Tower on the Cornell University campus shows clear sailing all the way to Milliken Power Station (center). For over 130 years, McGraw Tower has housed the Cornell Chimes, one of the largest sets of chimes in North America.

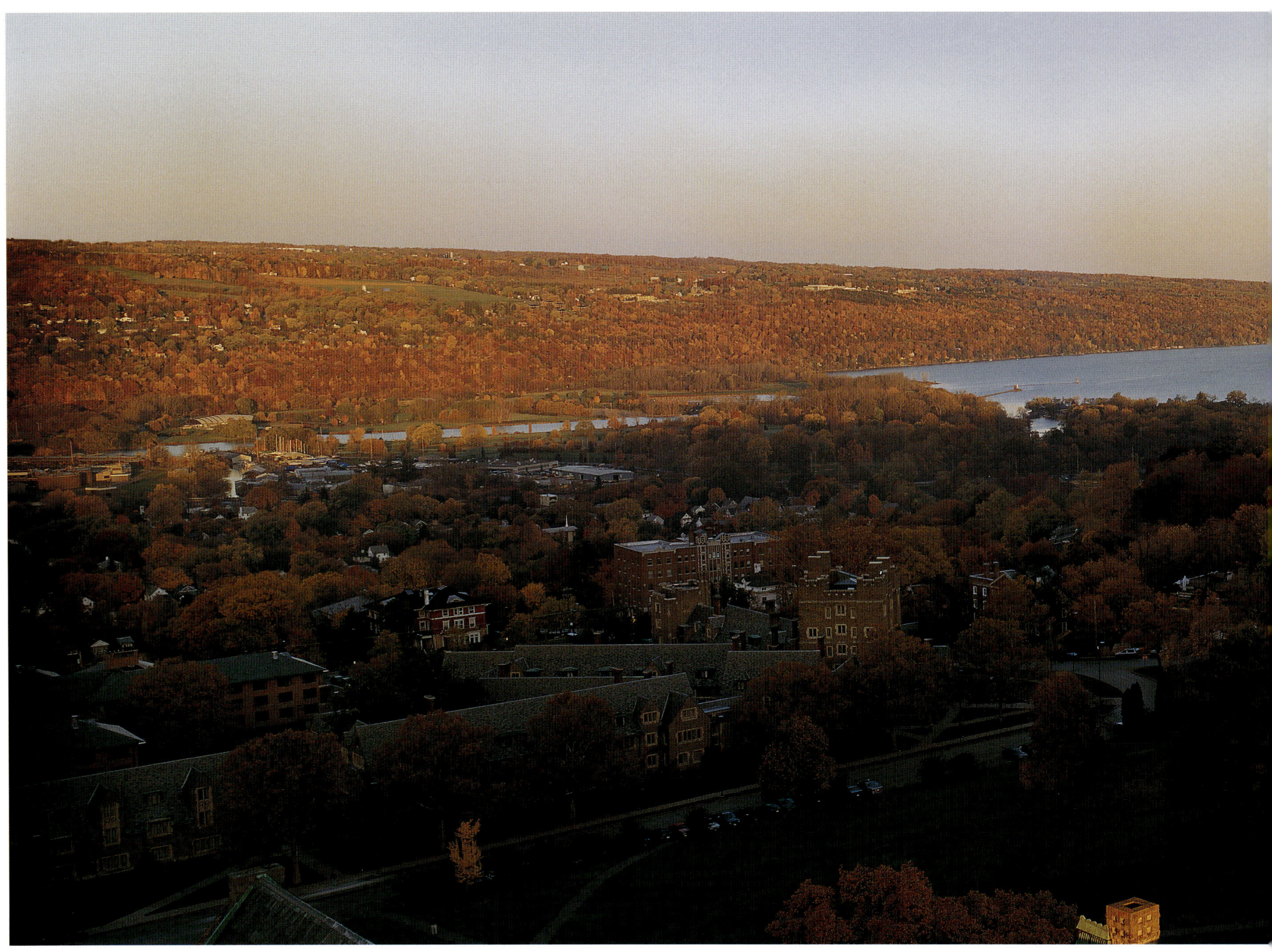

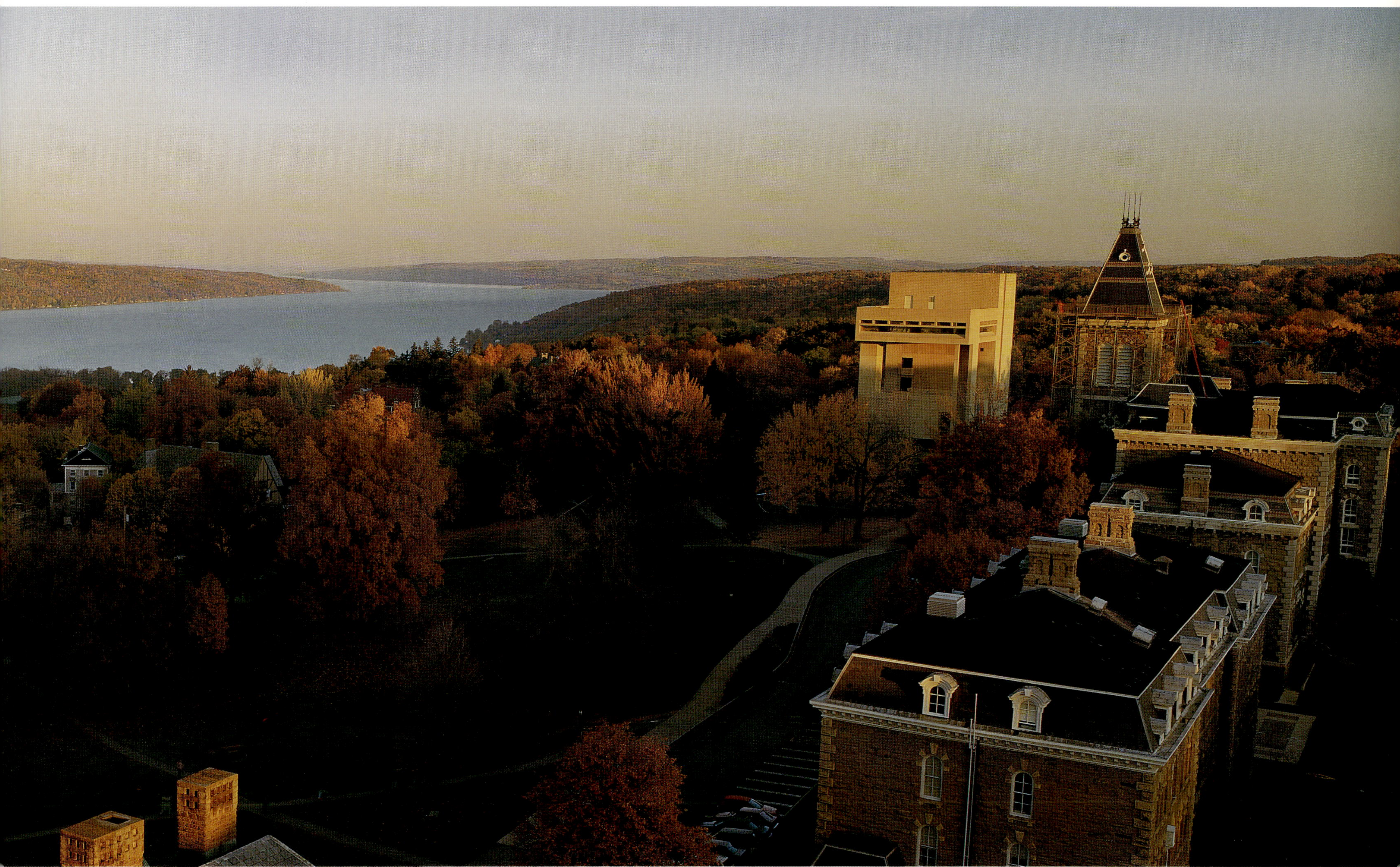

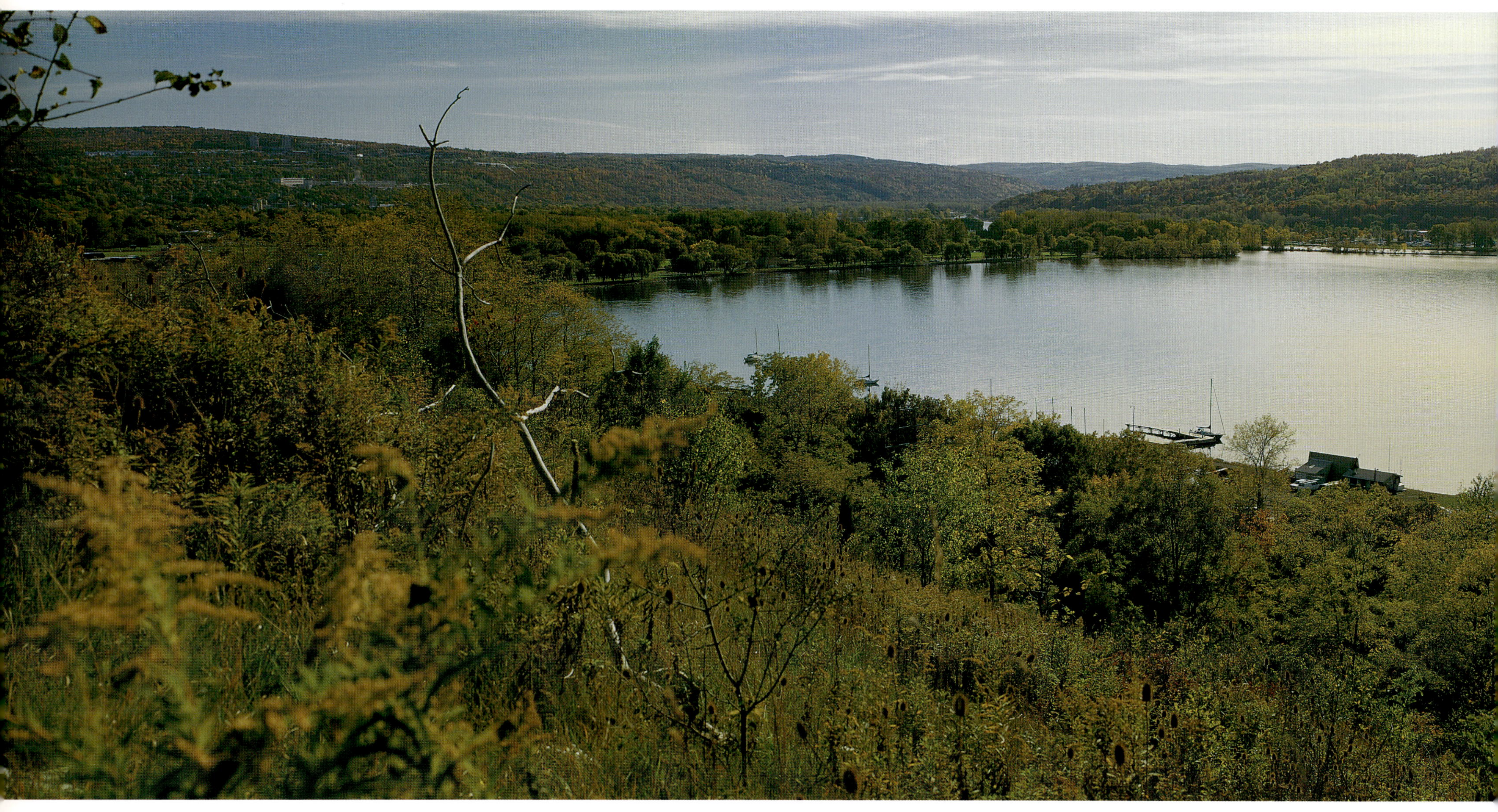

CAYUGA LAKE and Stewart Park, Ithaca, looking south.

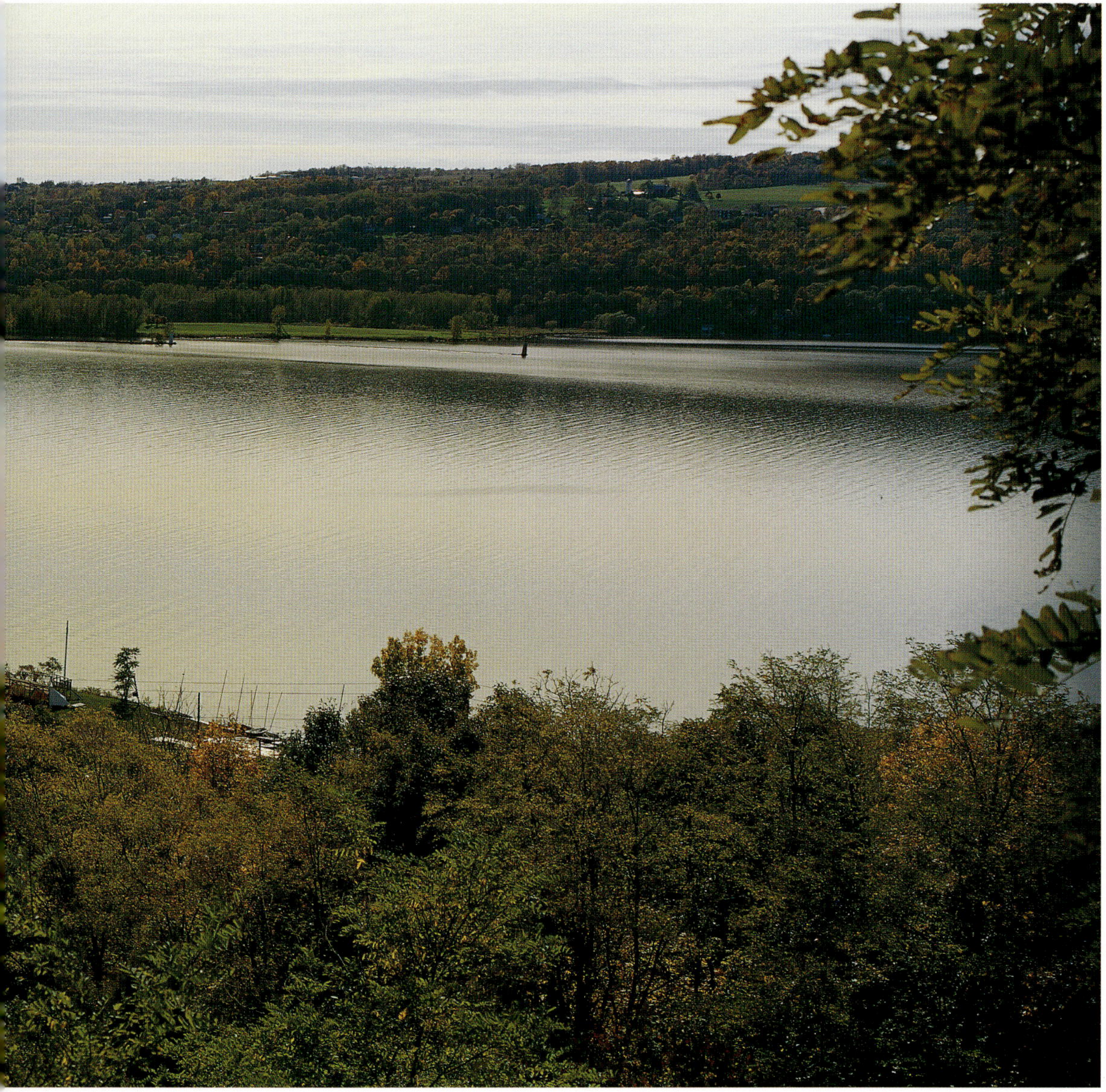

Right:
FALL CREEK GORGE, Ithaca from the Stewart Avenue bridge.

Far below the Johnson Museum of Art at Cornell University, Fall Creek rushes and tumbles after passing under the famous suspension bridge.

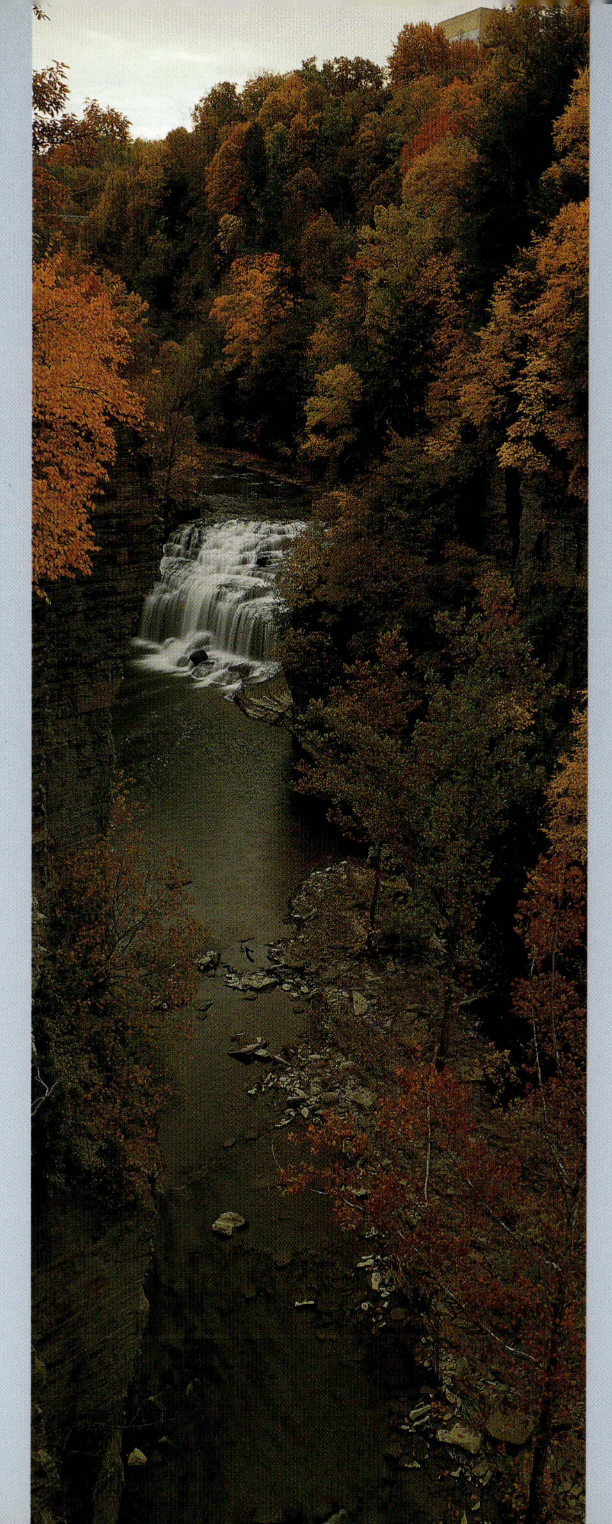

8 Owasco Lake

OWASCO LAKE, near Ensore Road, looking south.

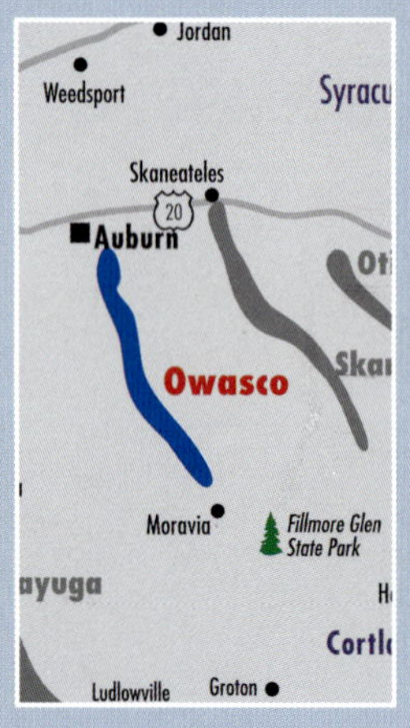

Owasco Lake is eleven miles long and 177 feet deep. Near the north end of the lake lies the city of Auburn, its streets lined with Victorian mansions, historic homes, and several important museums. Near the south end lies the village of Moravia, famous for Fillmore Glen State Park.

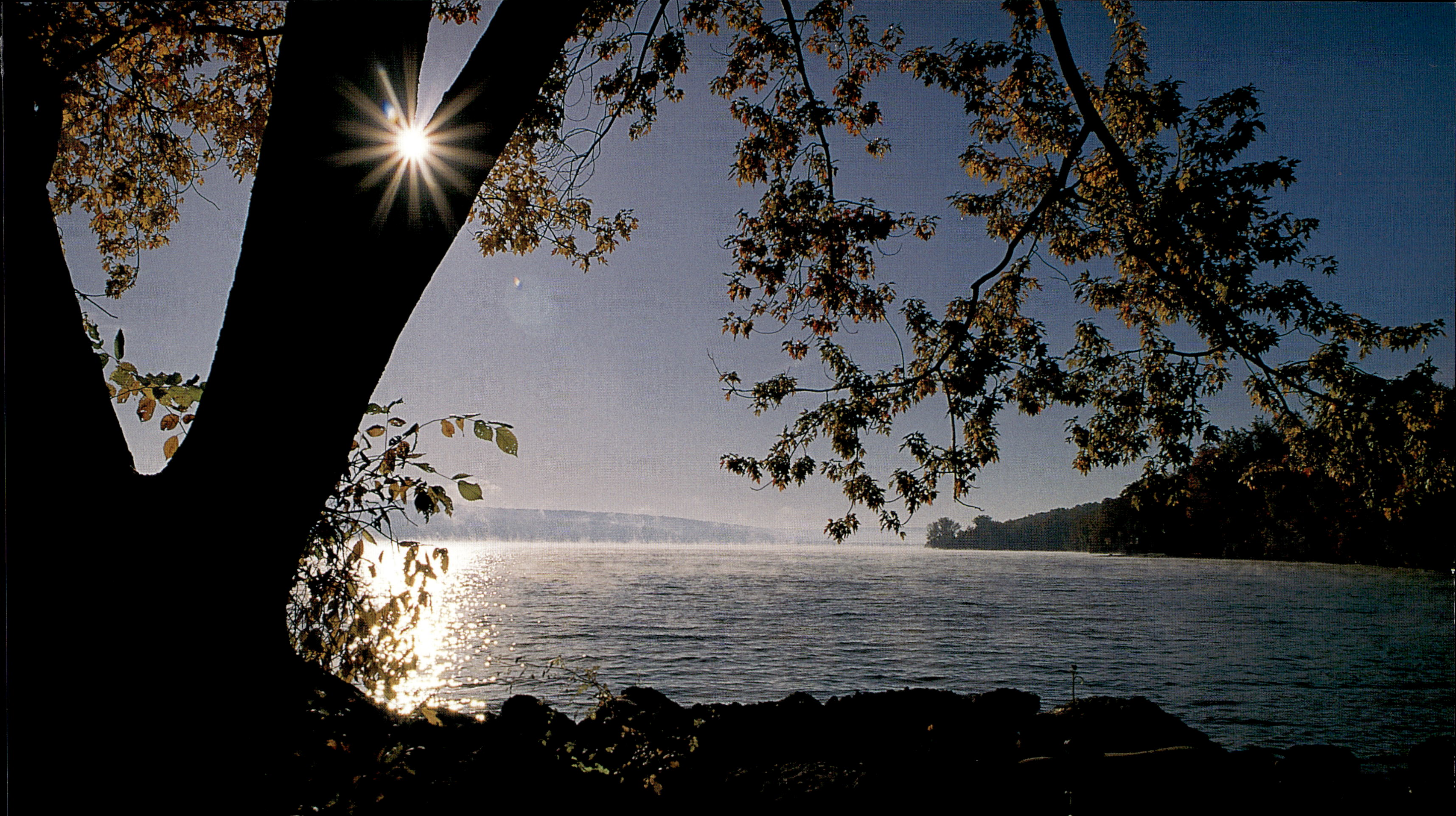

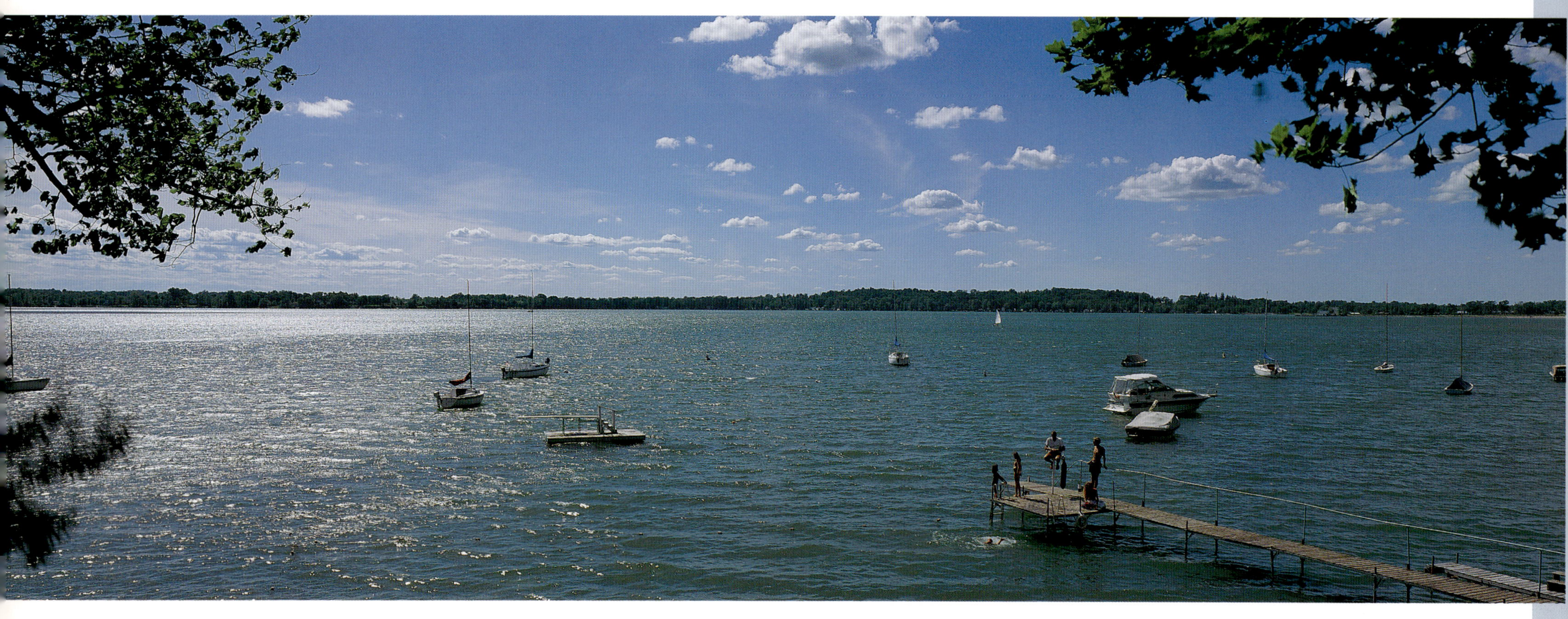

OWASCO LAKE from the Yacht Club, looking northwest.

The north end of Owasco Lake is home to the spacious Emerson Park, which offers swimming, extensive lawns, and an historic pavilion.

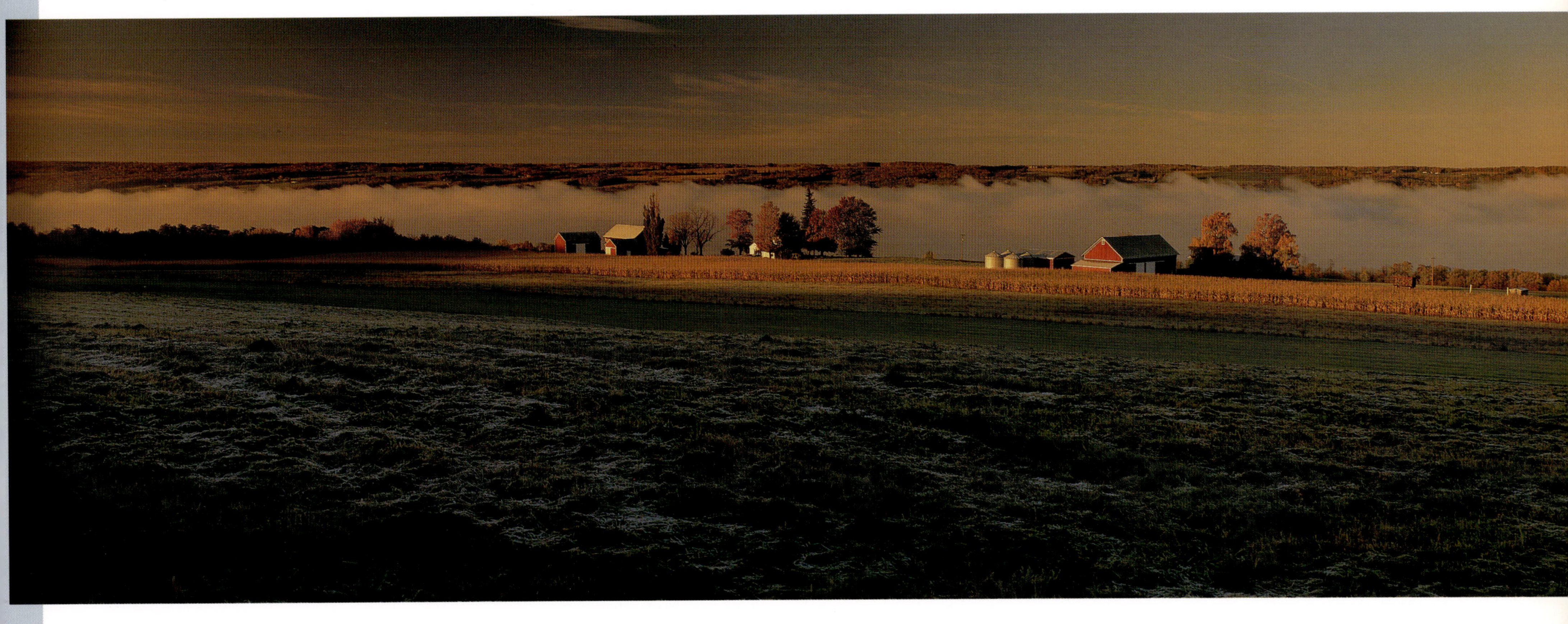

OWASCO LAKE covered in fog; from Rockefeller Road looking west.

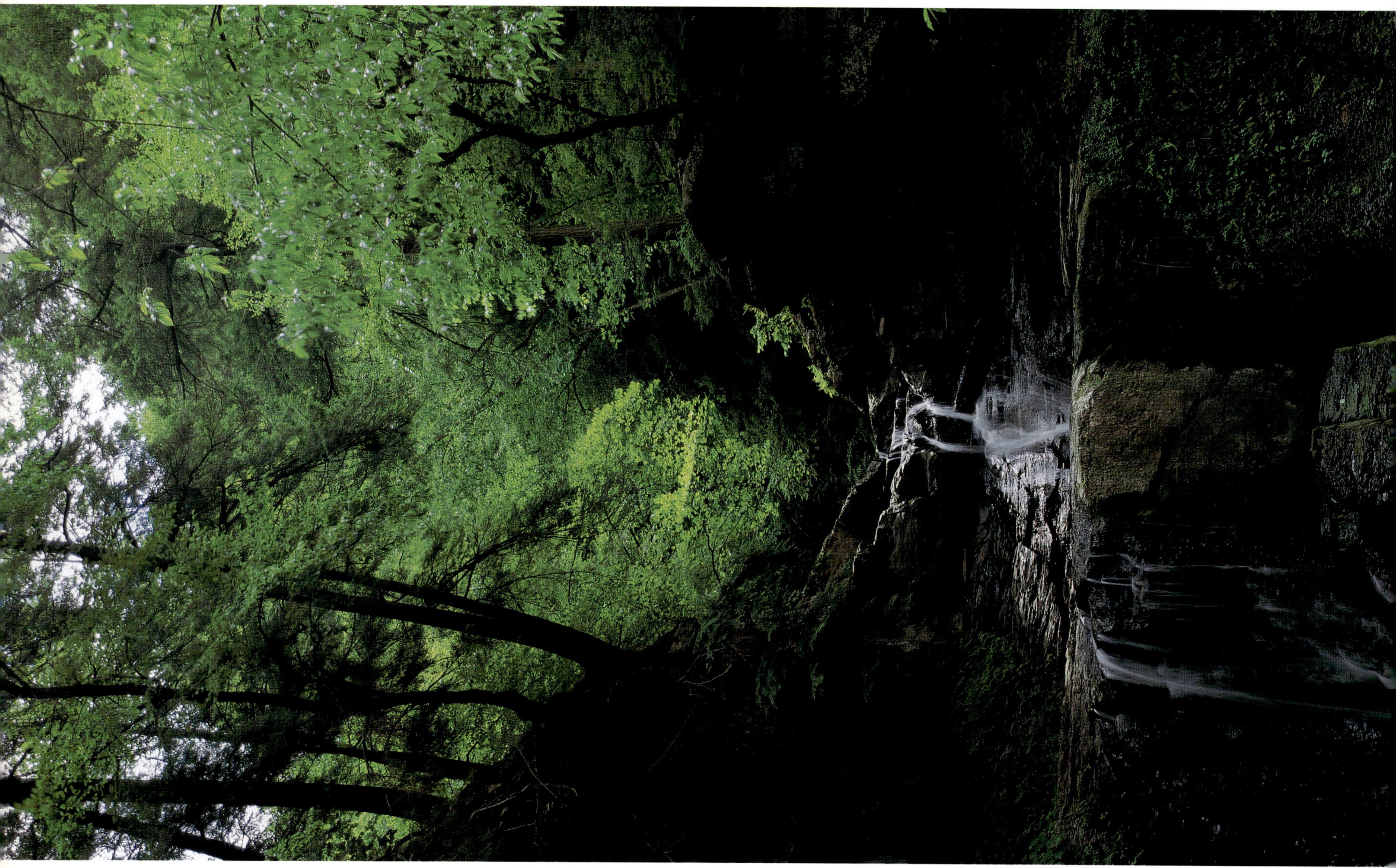

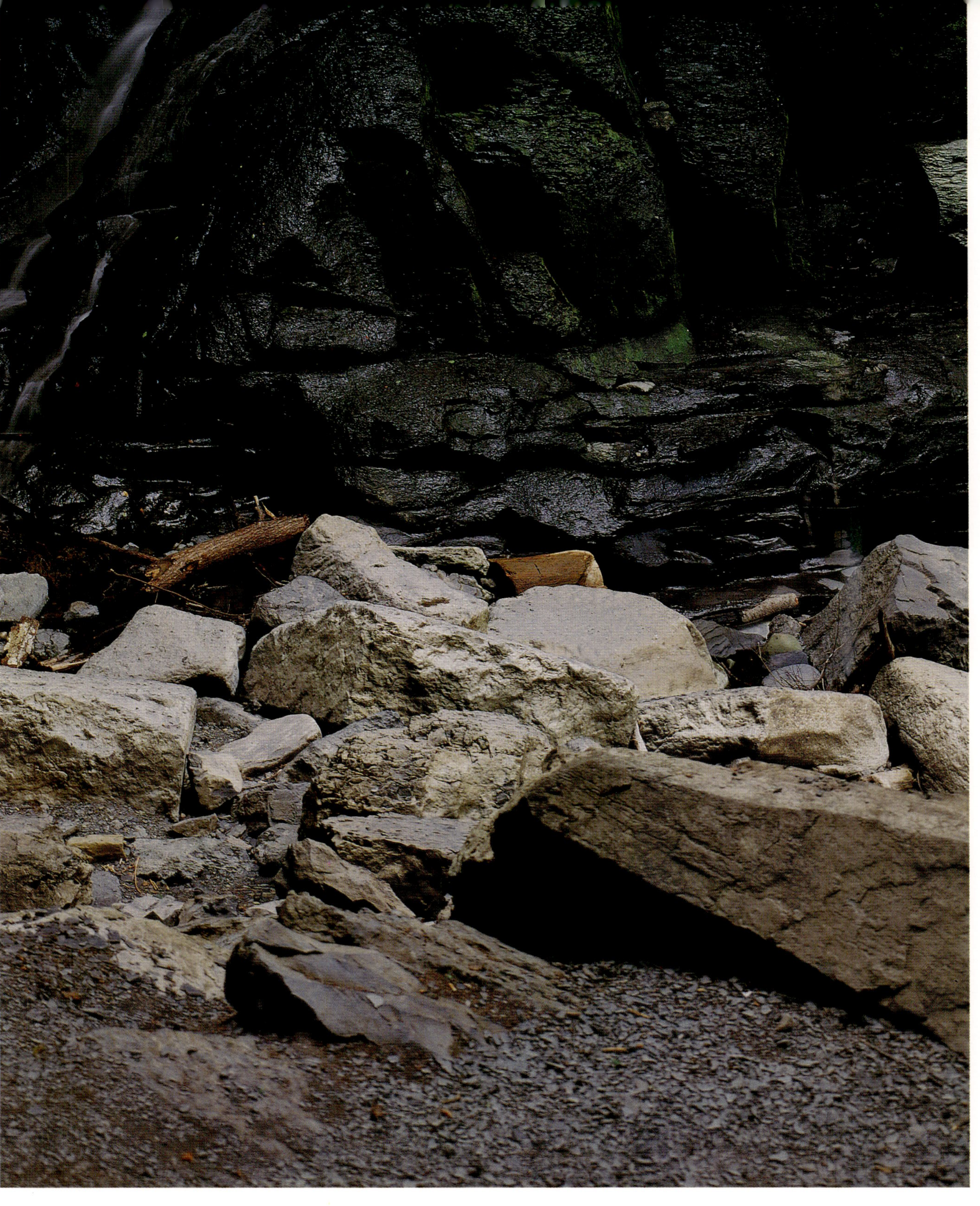

FILLMORE GLEN STATE PARK, Lower Falls.

FILLMORE GLEN was named for Millard Fillmore, 13th president of the United States who was born near the park. The narrow gorge features five waterfalls, eight bridges, and stonework completed by the Civilian Conservation Corps in the 1930s. The famous Lower Falls is seen here in a view from under the massive overhanging cliff known as the "Cowsheds."

9 Skaneateles Lake

SKANEATELES,
Main Street.

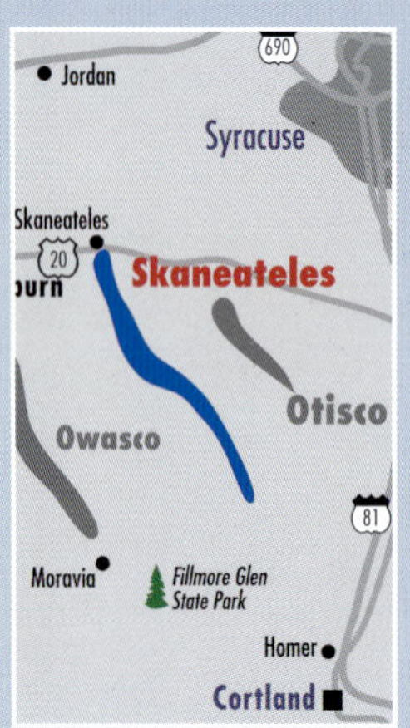

The area around this lake is best known for the charming village of Skaneateles, with its lovely old homes and quaint shops, at the north end of the lake. The lake itself is 15 miles long and over 350 feet deep, making it the third deepest Finger Lake.

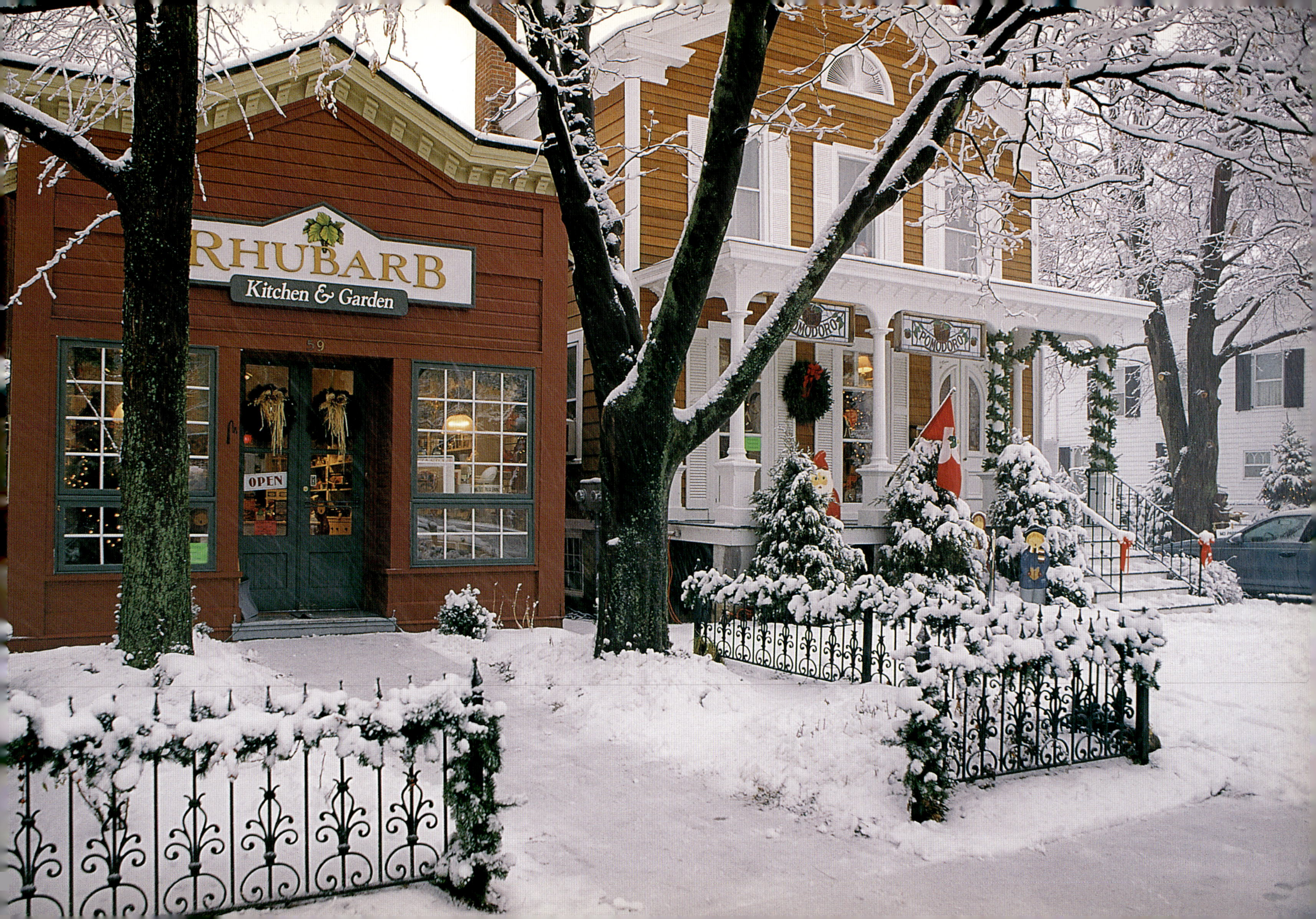
RHUBARB
Kitchen & Garden
59
OPEN
POMODORO
POMODORO

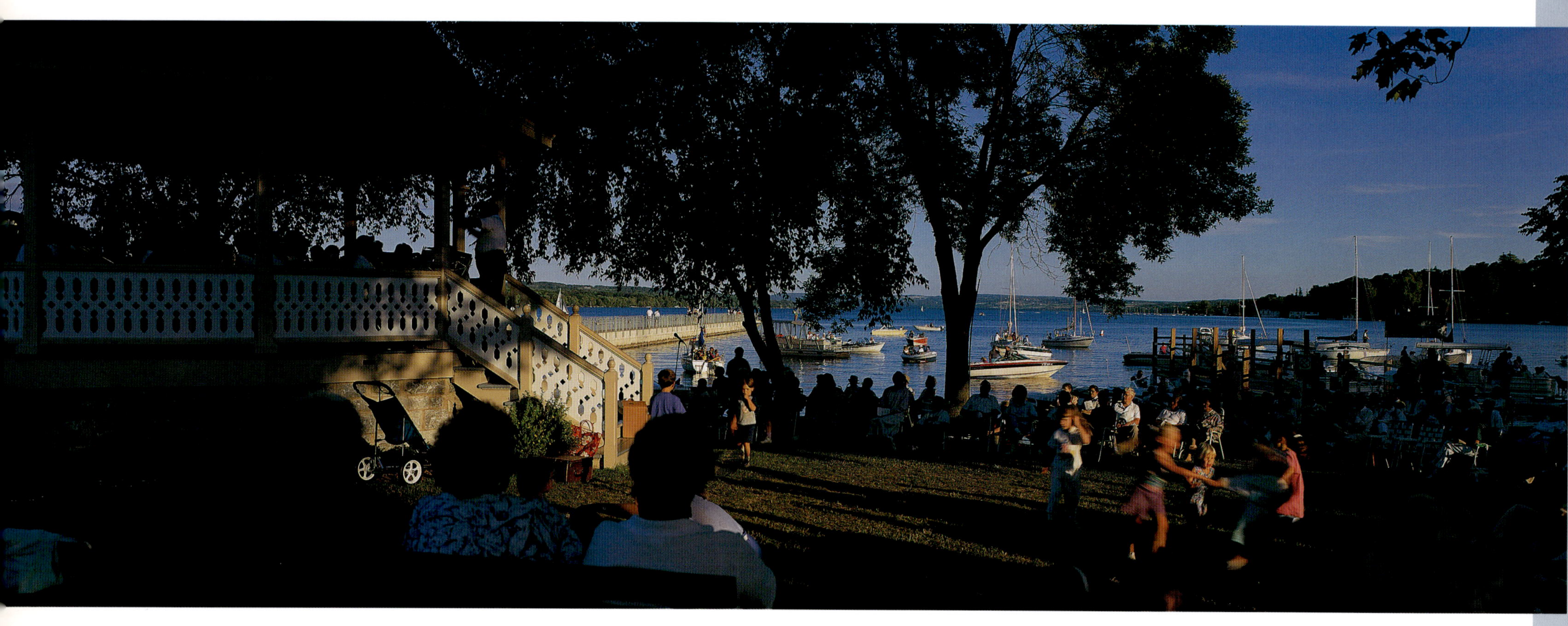

SKANEATELES LAKE from Clift Park, looking south.

At sunset in summertime, music often livens up the park and lake shore for Skaneateles residents, boaters, and vacationers.

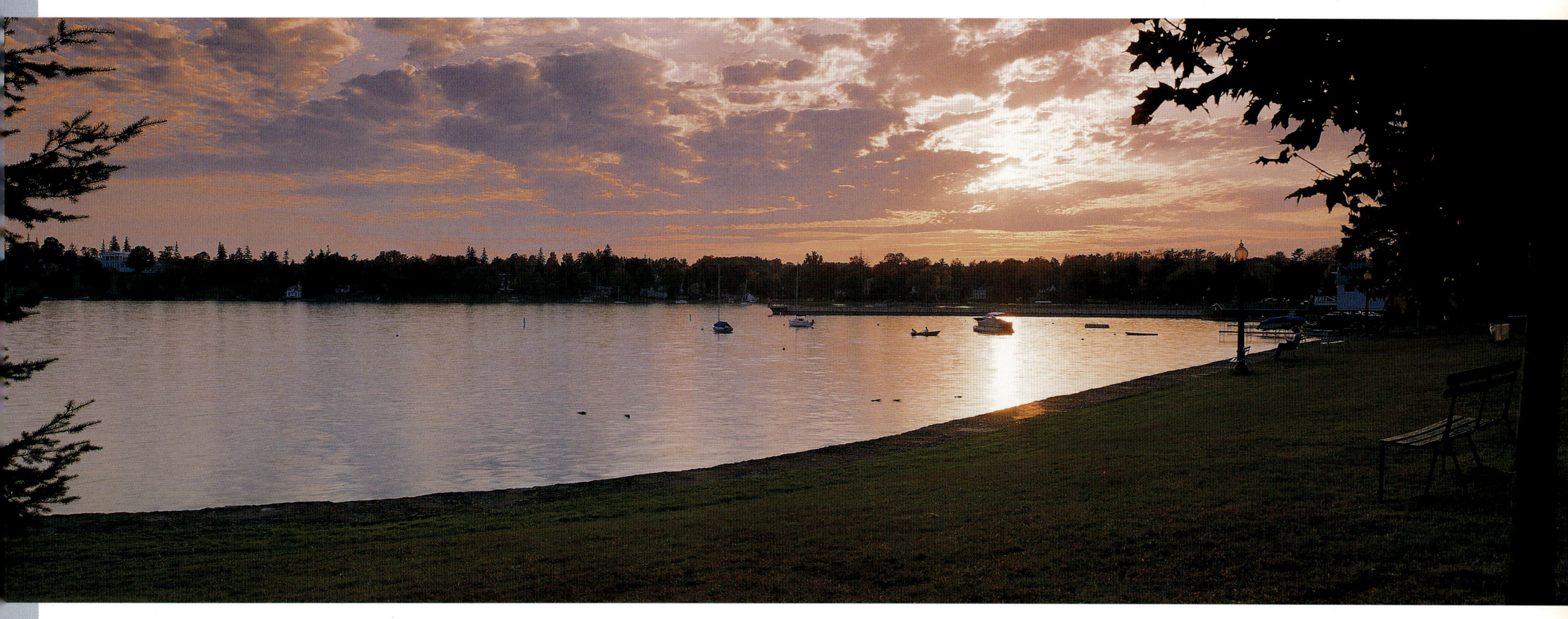

SKANEATELES LAKE from Thayer Park, looking west.

Twilight in Skaneateles shadows proud mansions and exquisite boathouses along the lake's west shore.

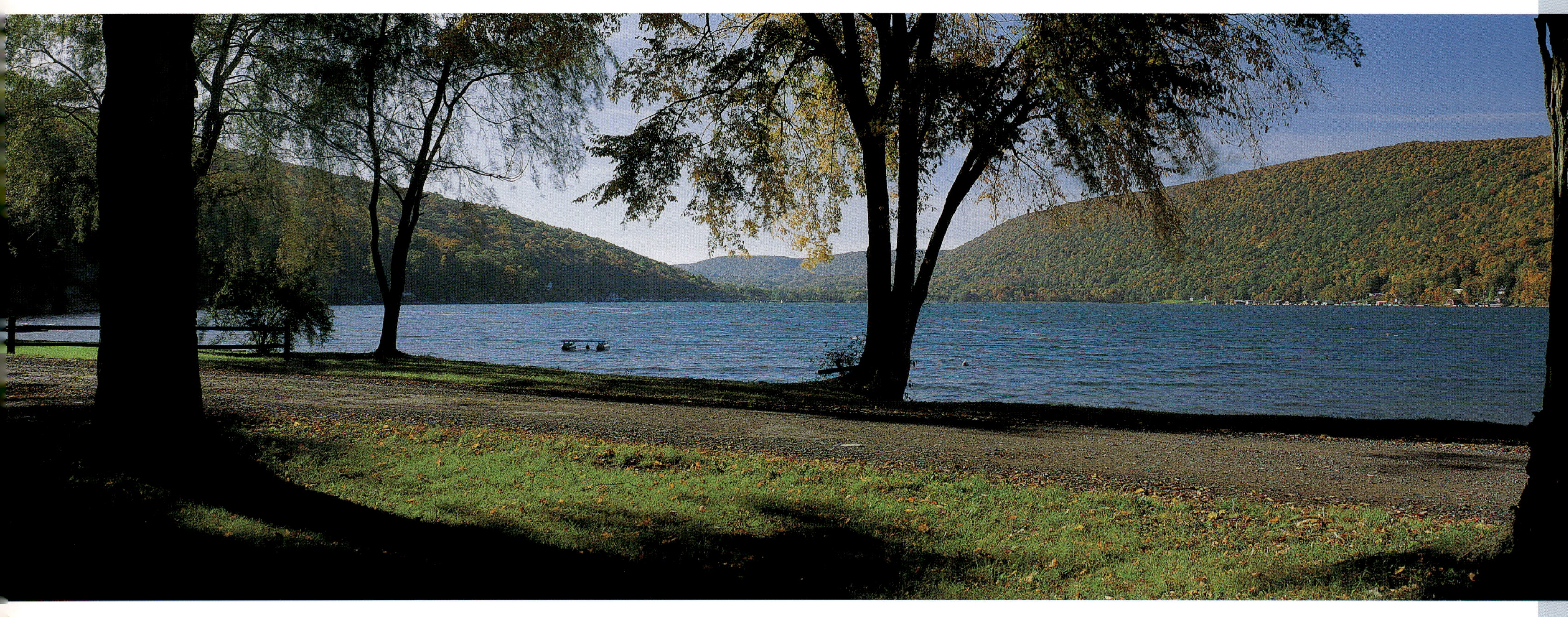

SKANEATELES LAKE, south end.

WITH its steep hills and narrow span, the south end of the lake was once the site of the elegant Glen Haven Hotel. In the late 1800s, devotees of a "water cure" traveled far to be healed by celebrated water near the hotel. In the 1930s, a small village called Ceylon briefly flourished here.

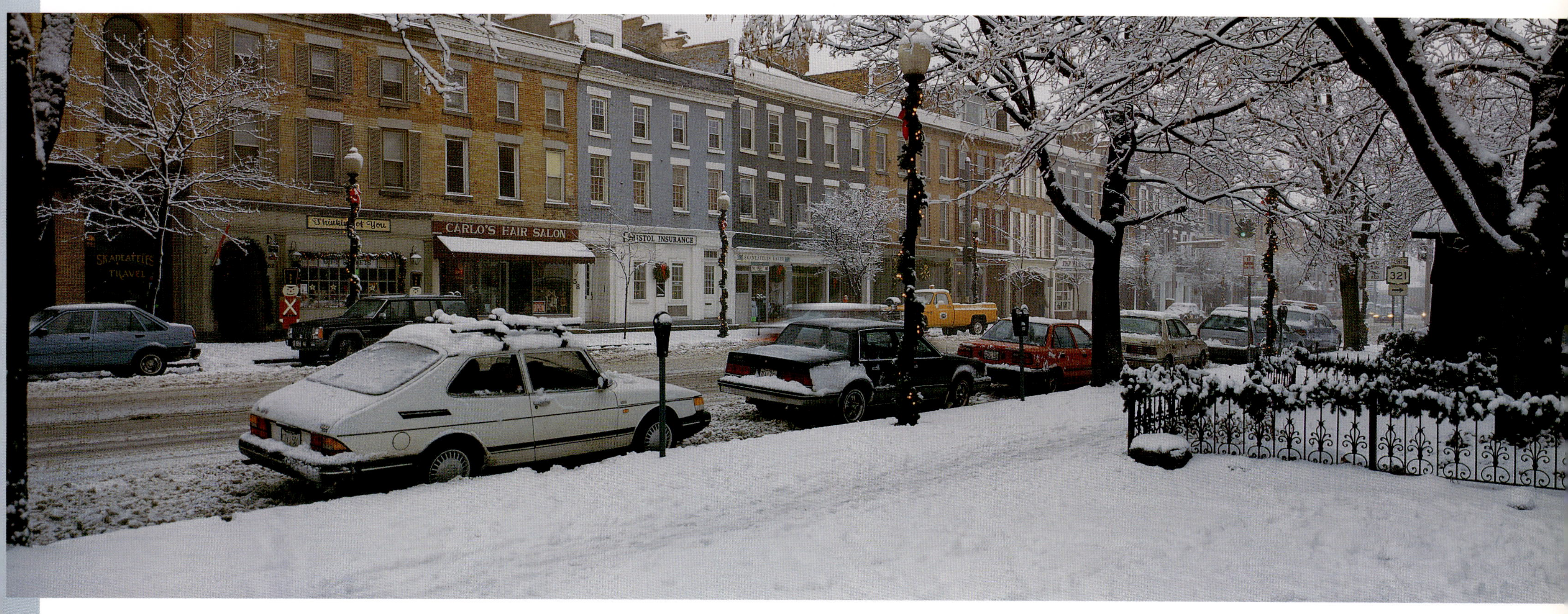

DOWNTOWN SKANEATELES.

An early winter snowstorm blankets Genesee Street.

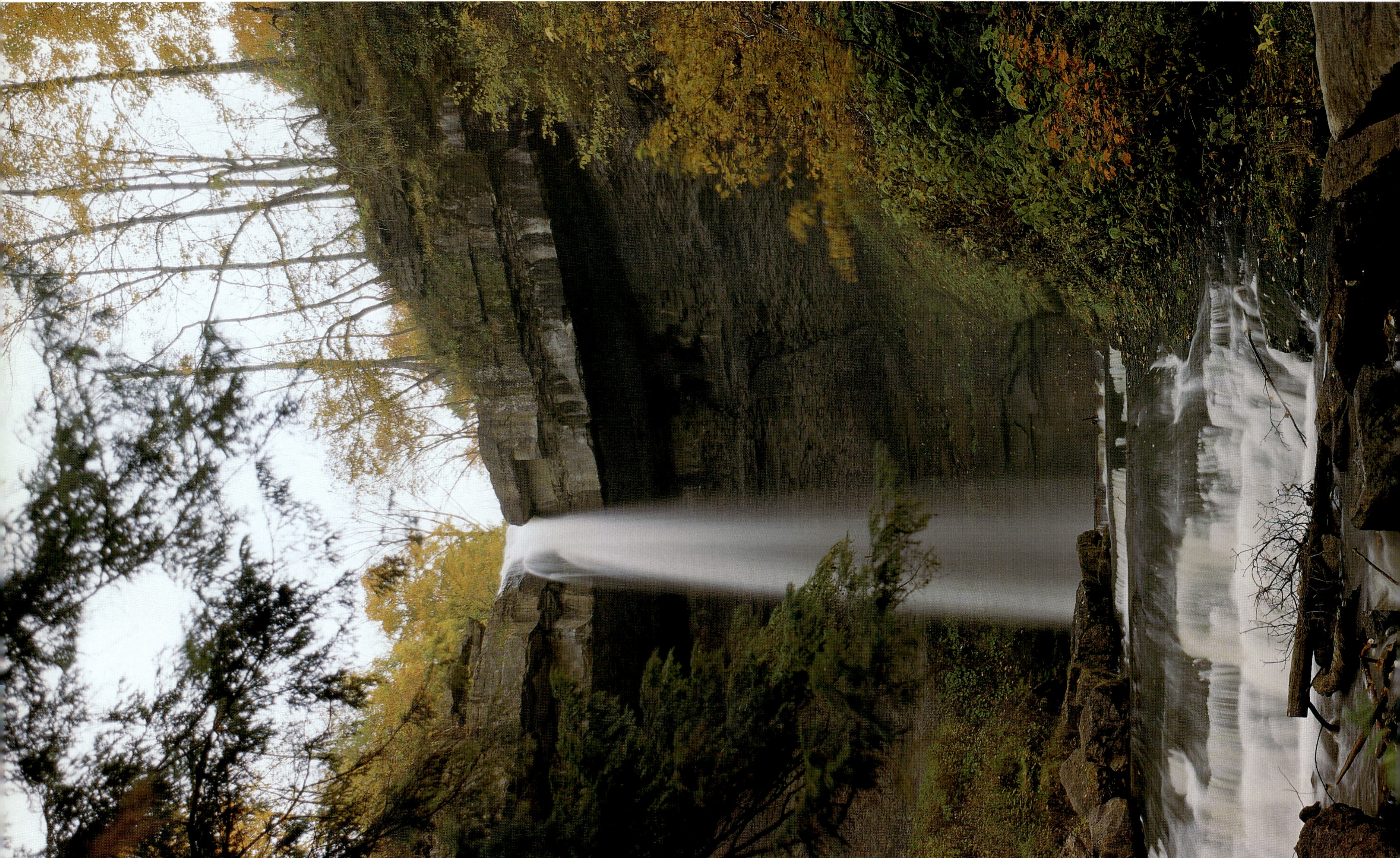

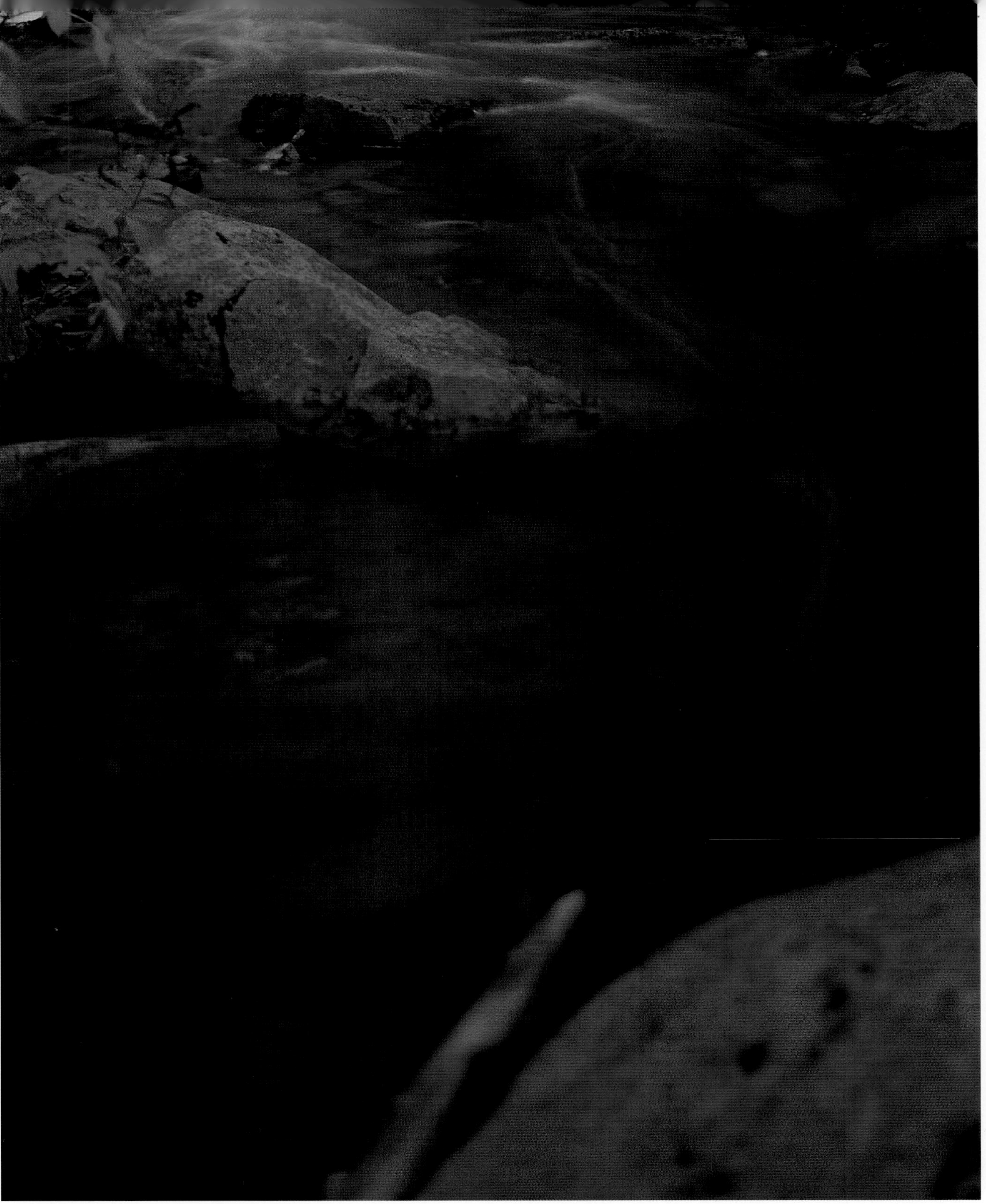

CARPENTER FALLS

THE Finger Lakes region is famous for its gorgeous waterfalls. Near Skaneateles Lake in New Hope, Carpenter Falls drops 90 feet into a basin of shale and limestone.

10 Otisco Lake
and Selected Regional Highlights

OTISCO VALLEY, looking north.

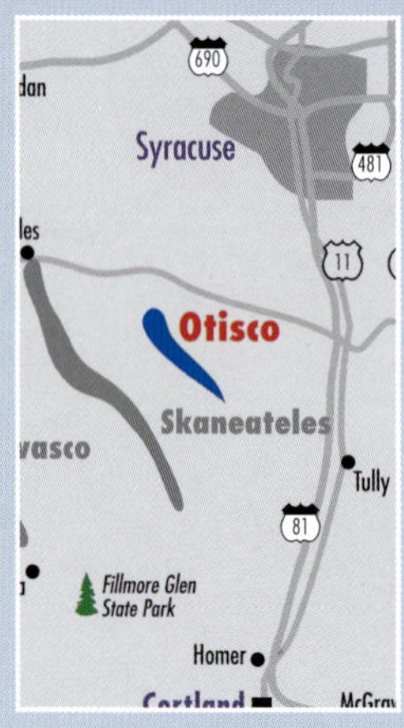

East of Skaneateles Lake lies Otisco Lake, just six miles long and 66 feet deep, the smallest Finger Lake with human habitation on its shores. Fishing enthusiasts on Otisco bring in huge walleyes, smallmouth bass, and tiger muskies.

Some of the loftiest elevations in the Finger Lakes area surround the Otisco Valley, which stretches out from the south end of the lake. At 1,986 feet, Ripley Hill (at left in the photo) is one of the region's highest points.

Beyond the lakes, no portrait of the Finger Lakes region would be complete without including several gateway cities, small towns, and state parks that enhance the character of the region.

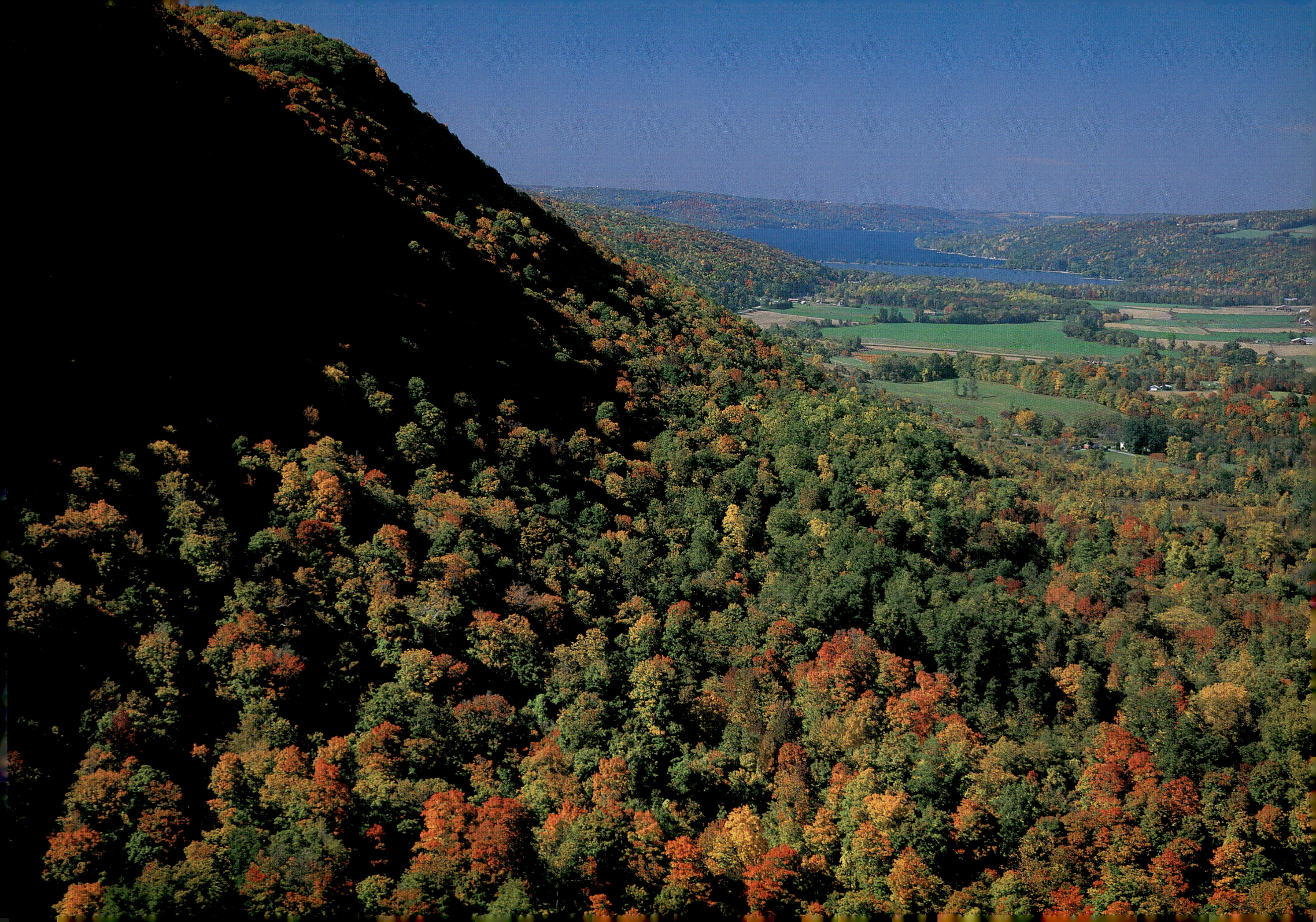

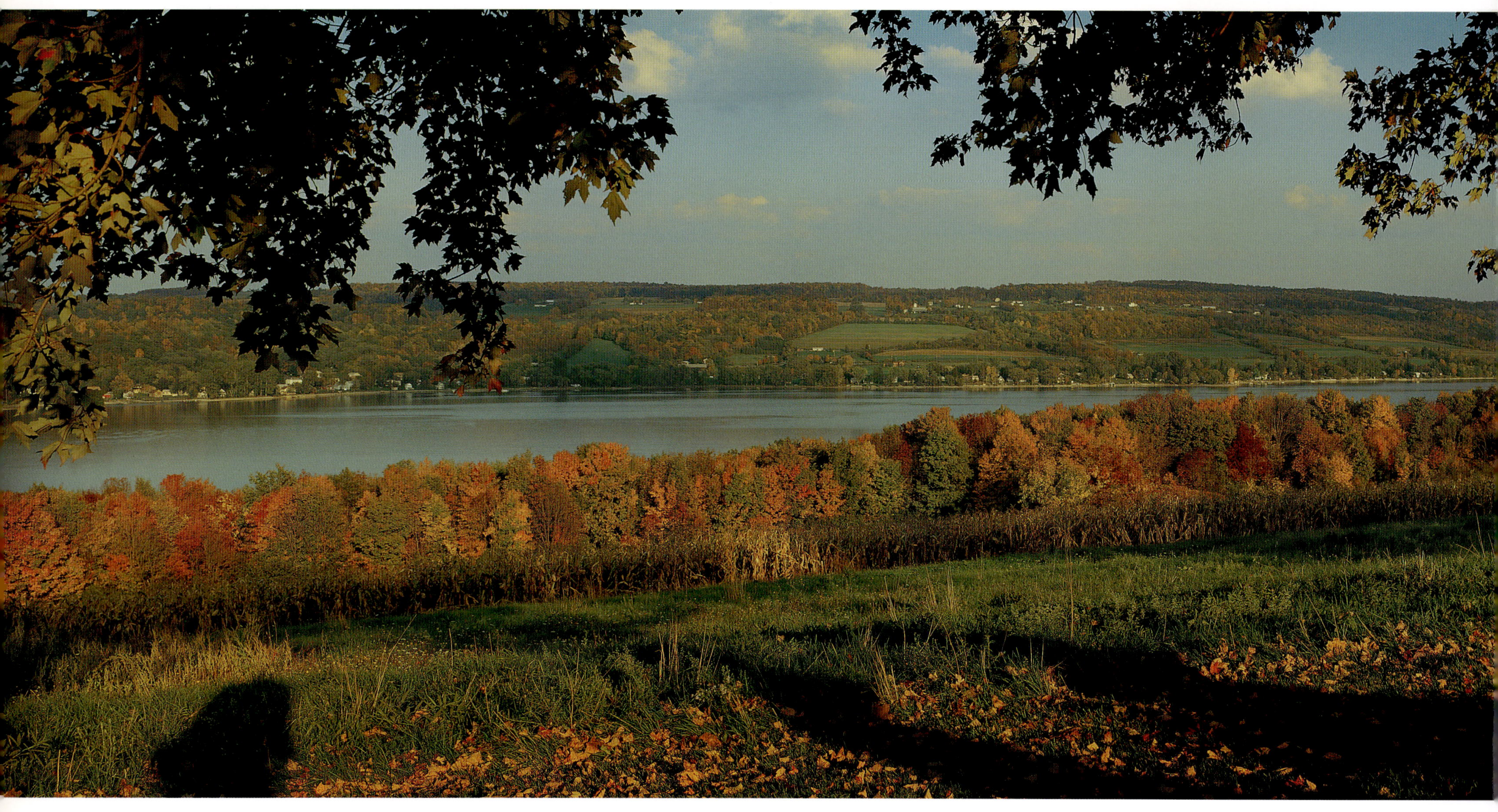

OTISCO LAKE, north end, looking southeast.

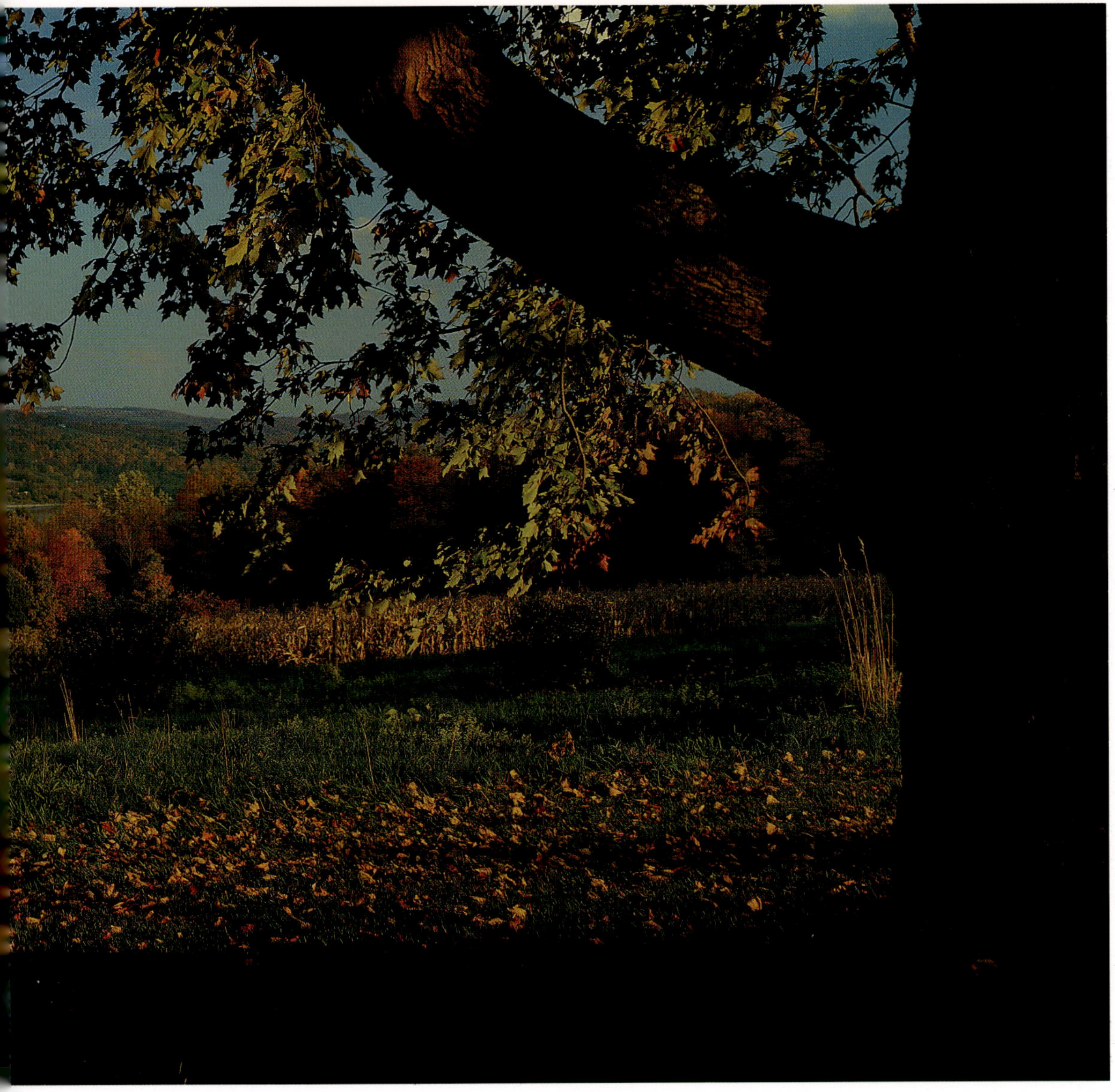

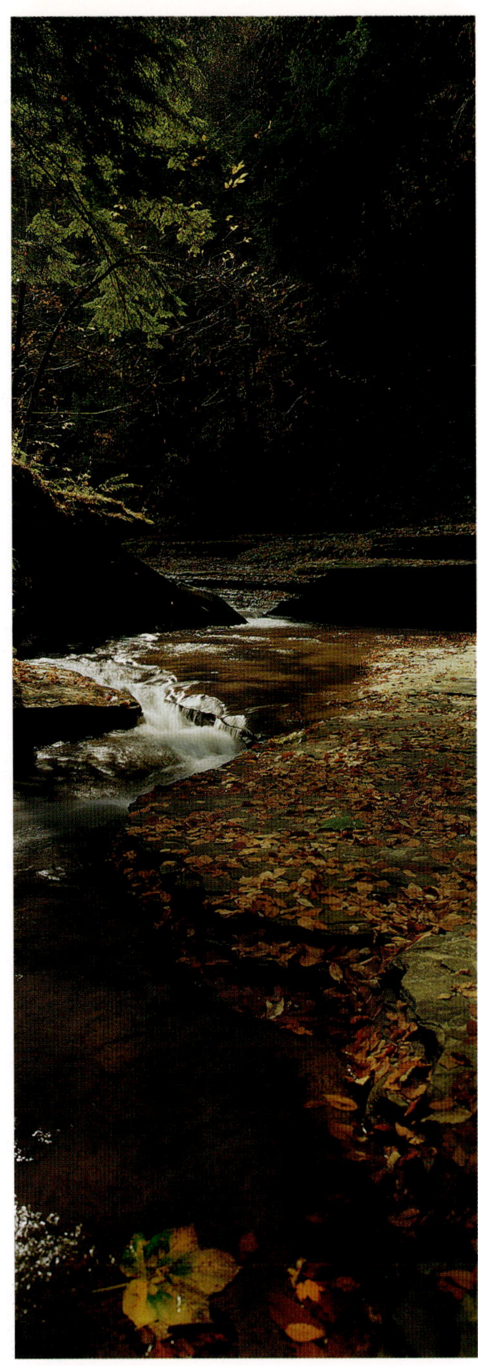

STONY BROOK
STATE PARK,
Dansville.

Once located at the bottom of an ancient sea, the rocks and sediment in this park predate the dinosaurs.

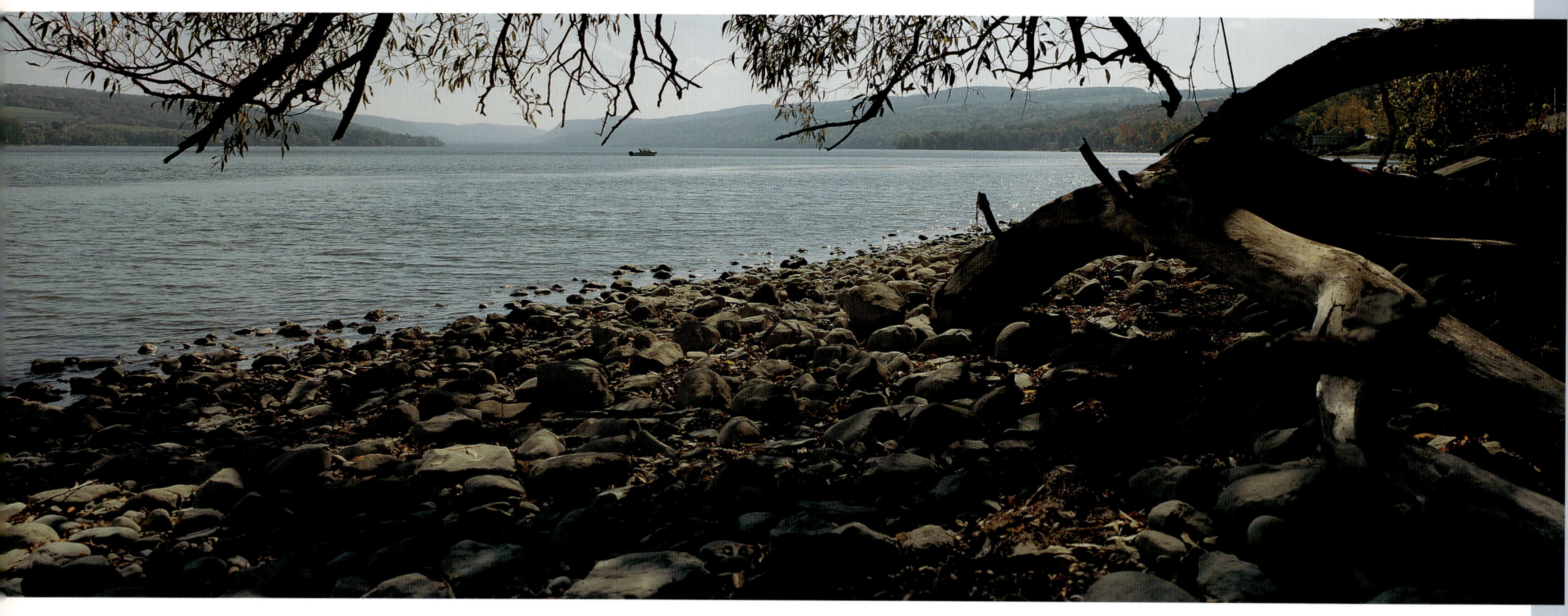

OTISCO LAKE, from the west side, looking south.

Great fishing on Otisco lasts well into the fall. The Otisco Valley (left center) can be seen stretching away to the south.

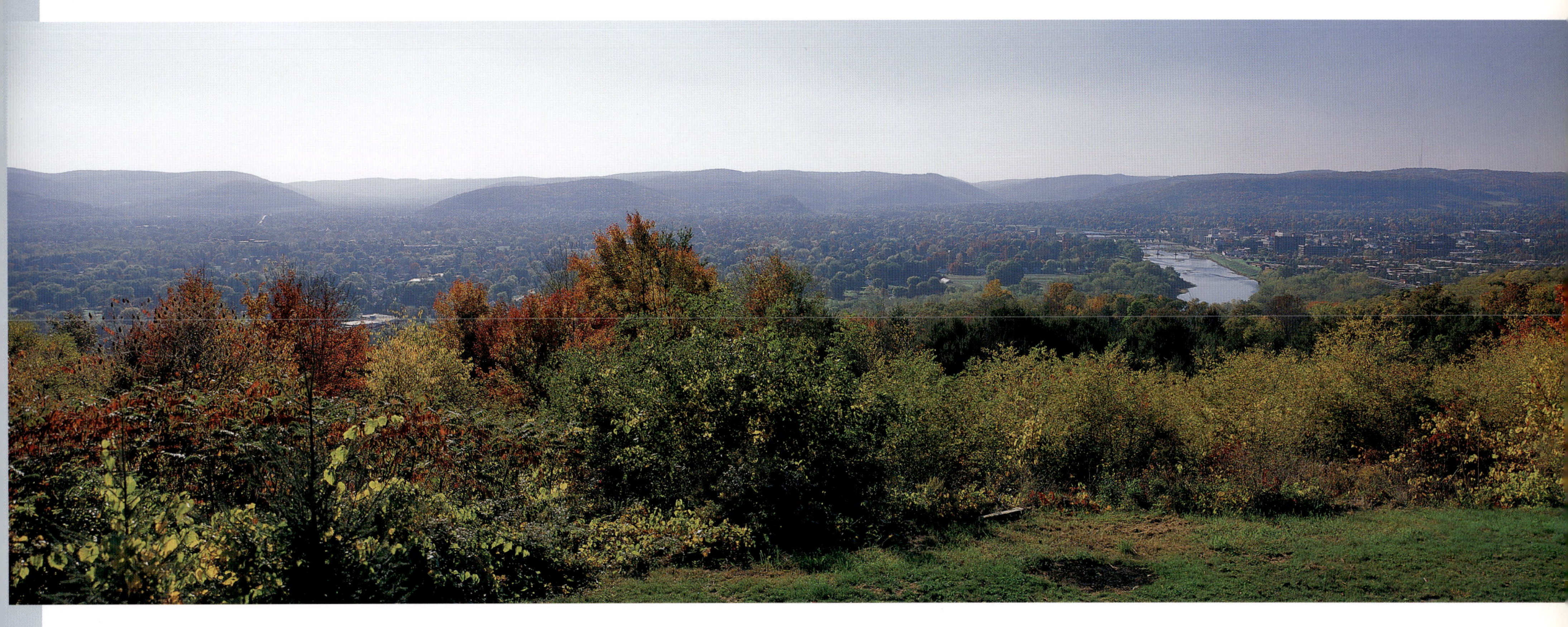

ELMIRA from Jerusalem Hill, looking west.

The Chemung River winds its way through downtown Elmira, the southern gateway to the Finger Lakes.

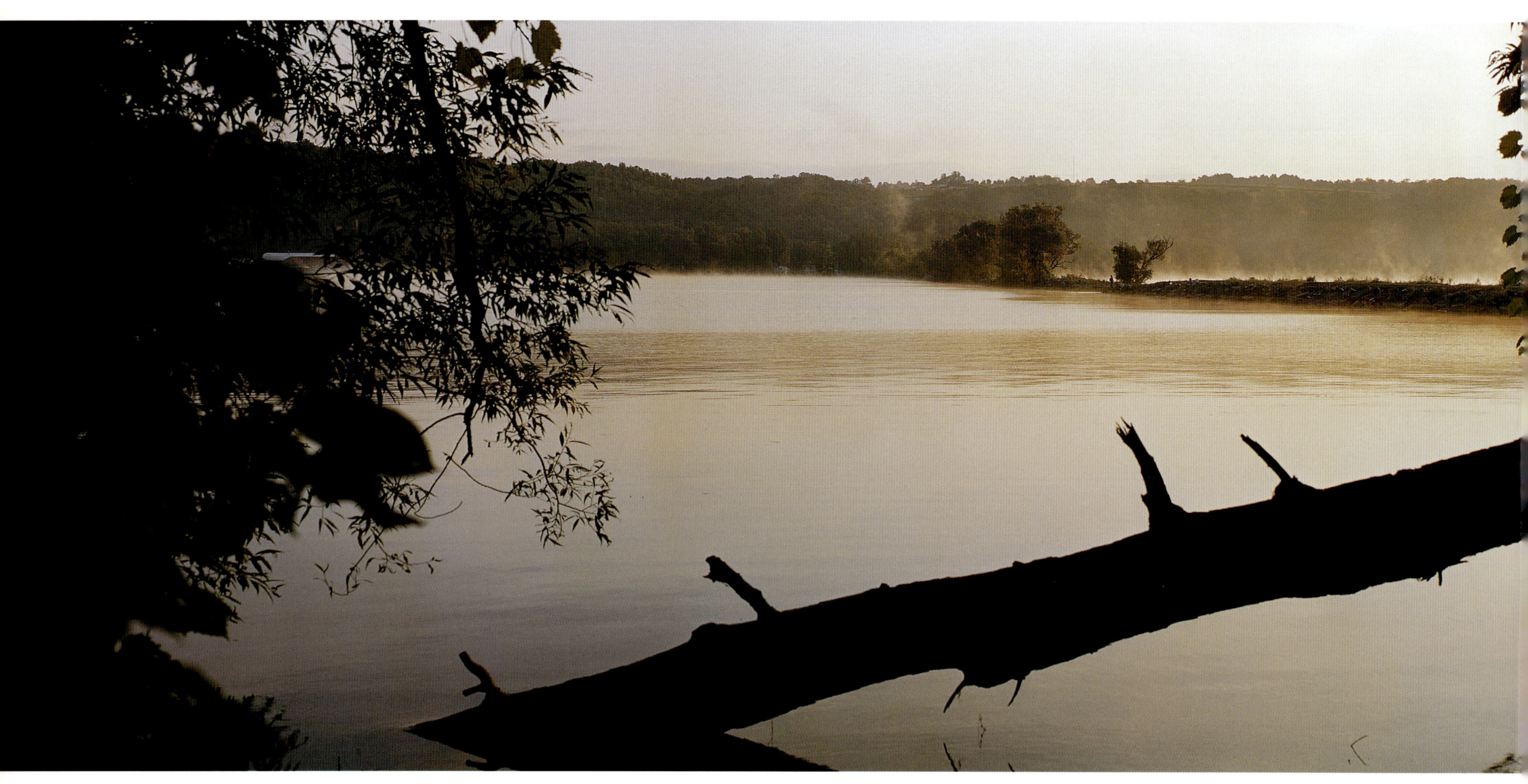

OTISCO LAKE, Causeway, looking east.

THE original foundation for the Causeway was built for a bridge in the late 1800s and used until the early 1920s by farmers and vacationers as part of the "Otisco Spafford Road." Today, it is no longer continuous, allowing boats to pass through, but it helps to retard the flow of sediment from the shallower south end of Otisco into the deeper north end.

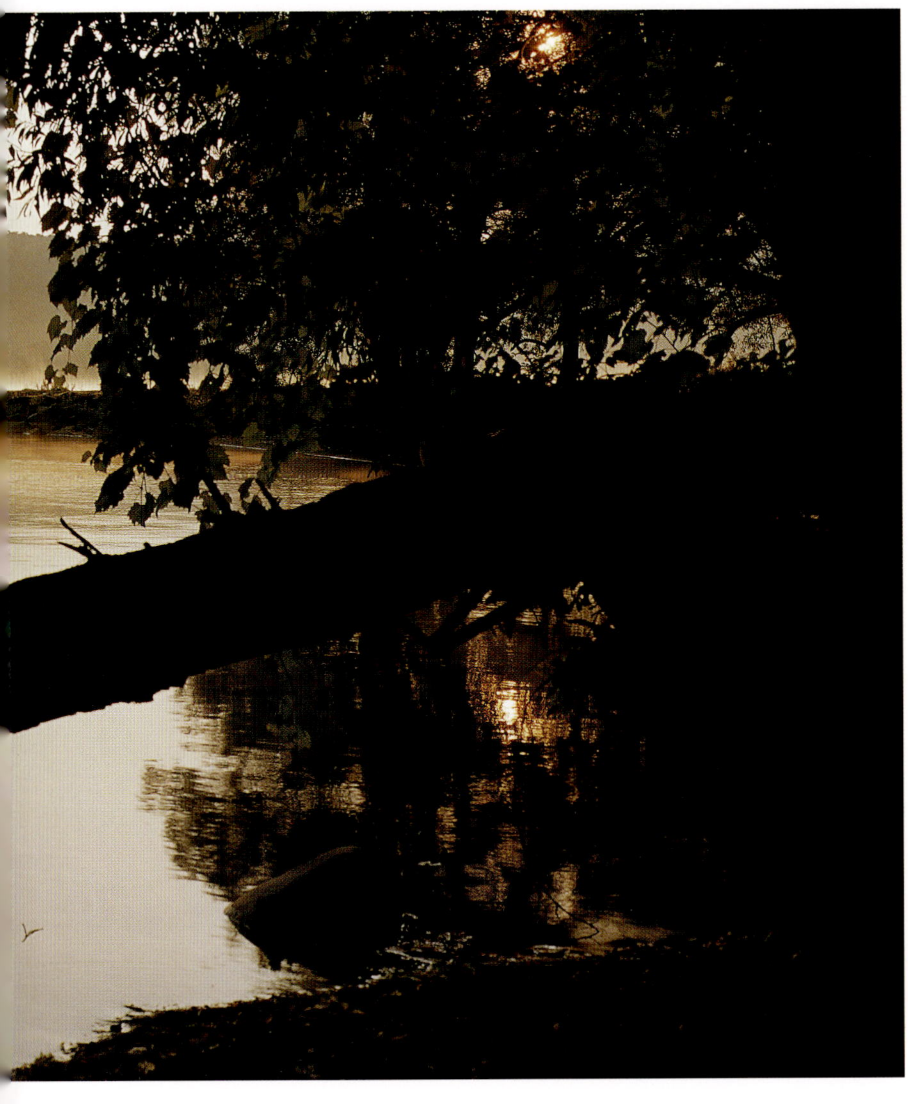

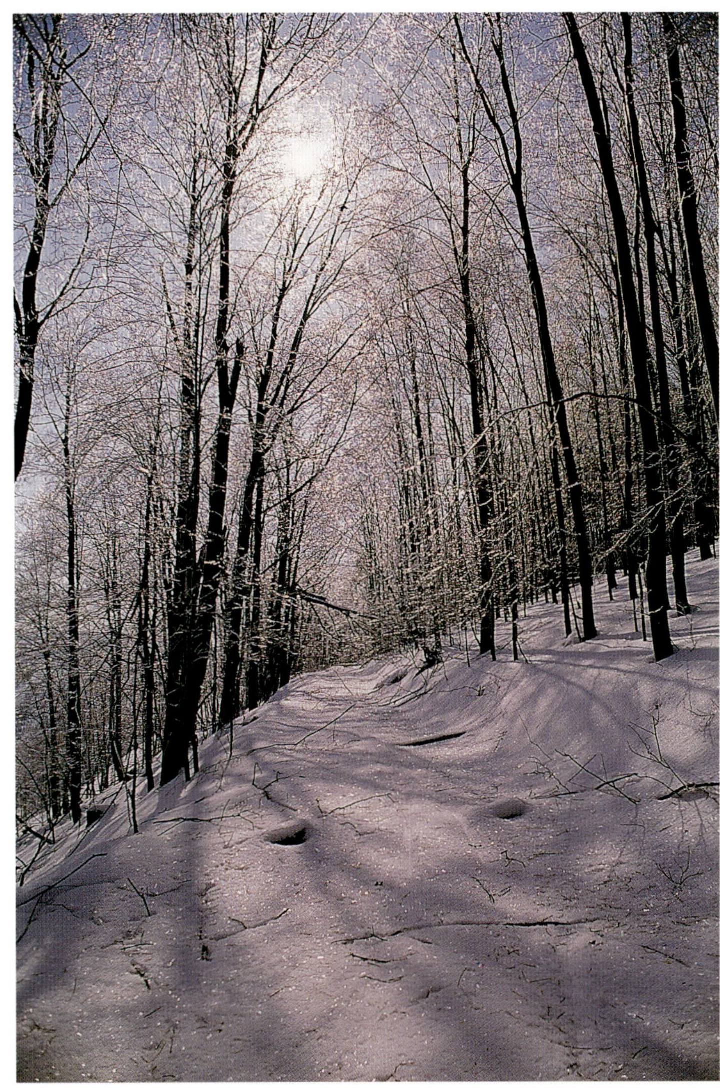

FINGER LAKES TRAIL, near Greek Peak Ski Resort.

CROSSING Virgil Mountain at 2,132 feet, the Finger Lakes Trail reaches one of its highest elevations at Greek Peak Ski Resort. Taking in branches and the main cross-state trail, the wilderness footpath system covers nearly 800 miles in Finger Lakes territory.

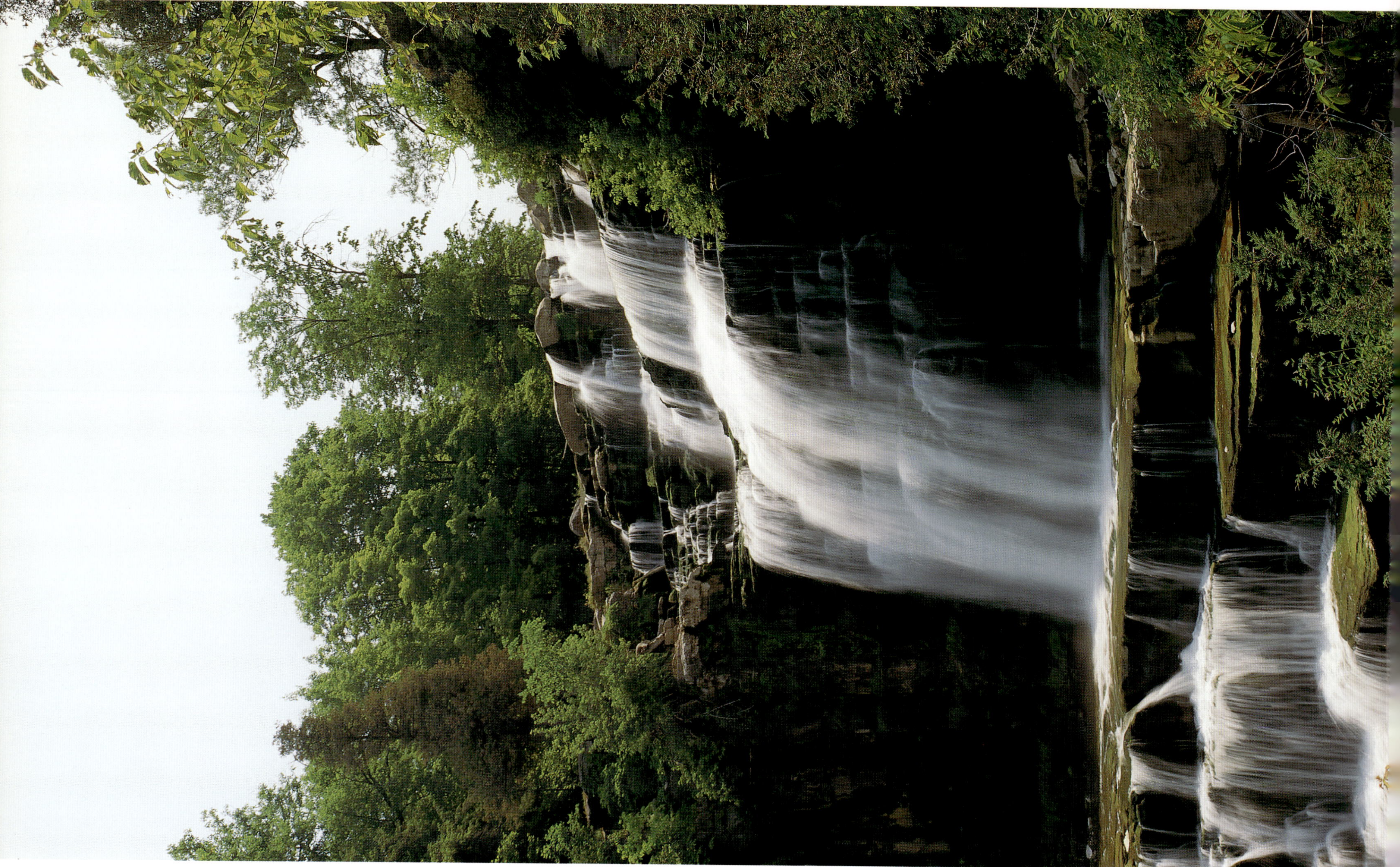

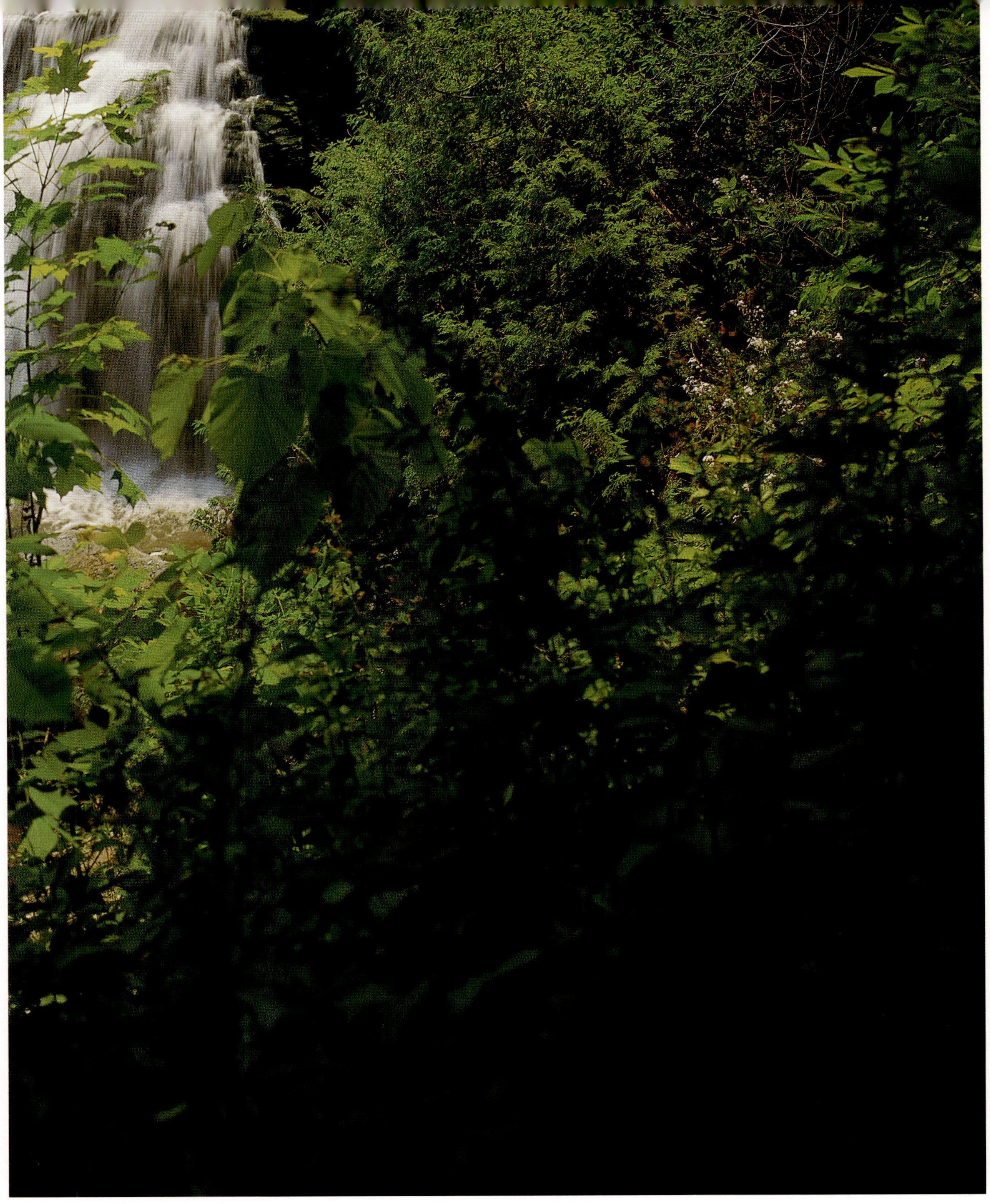

CHITTENANGO FALLS, Chittenango Falls State Park.

A short, steep circular trail wraps around the falls. Near Cazenovia, this spot is the easternmost point shown in this book.

ONONDAGA LAKE and Syracuse, looking northwest.

VIEWED from the Syracuse University campus, downtown Syracuse lies around the southern shores of Onondaga Lake and marks the northeastern gateway to the Finger Lakes region. In the foreground is the Carrier Dome, site of sports and entertainment events.

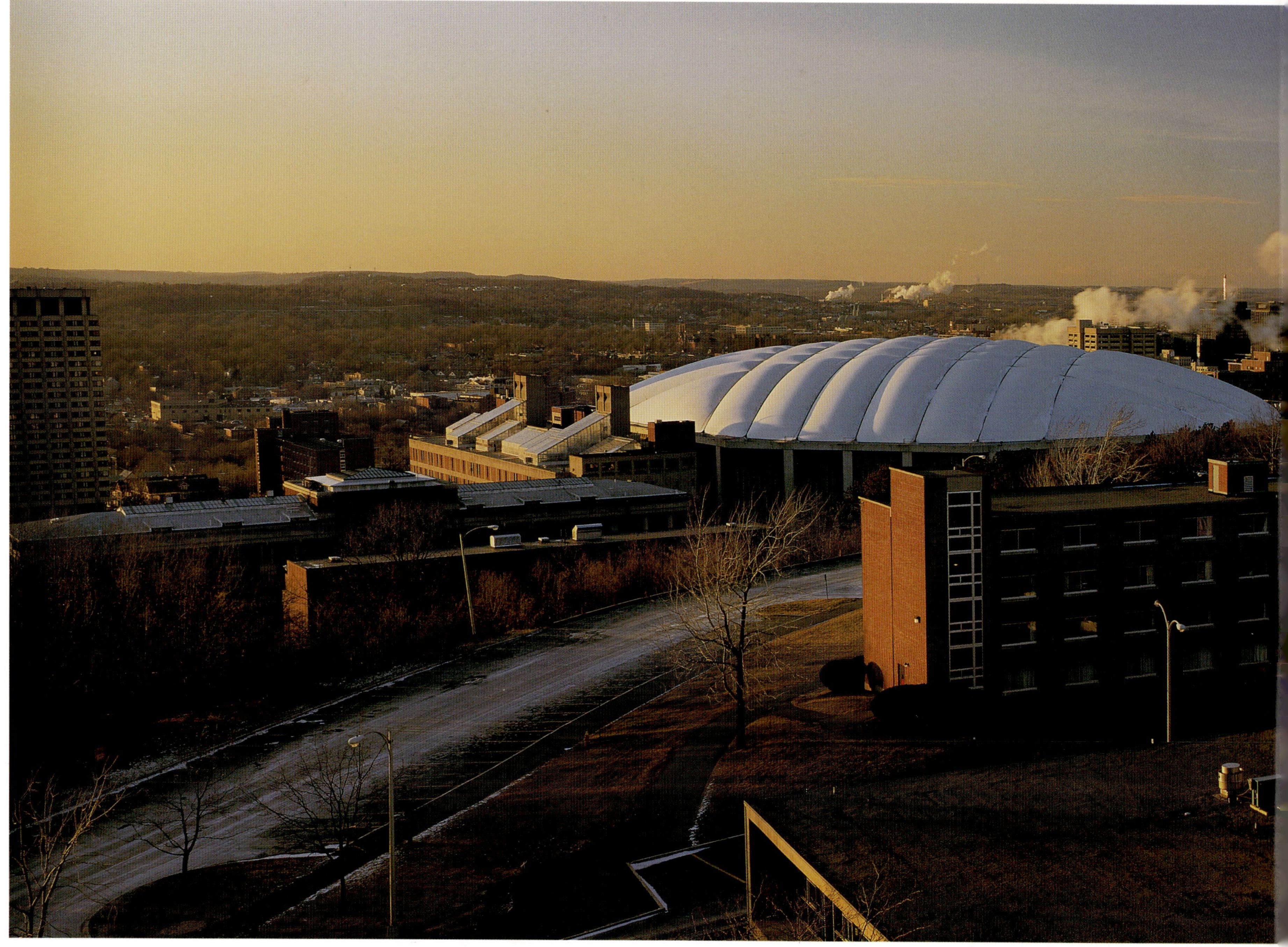

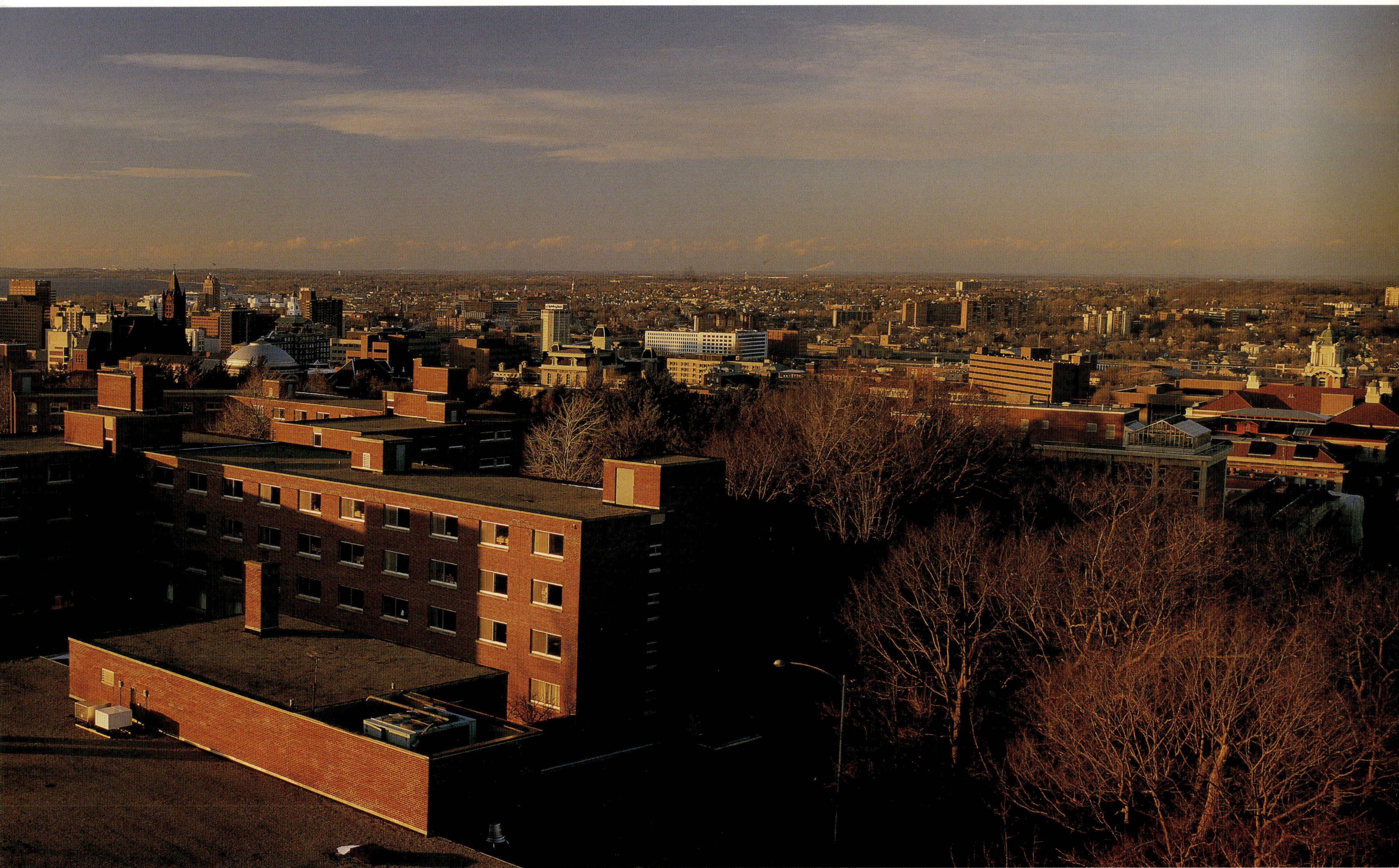

The Finger Lakes

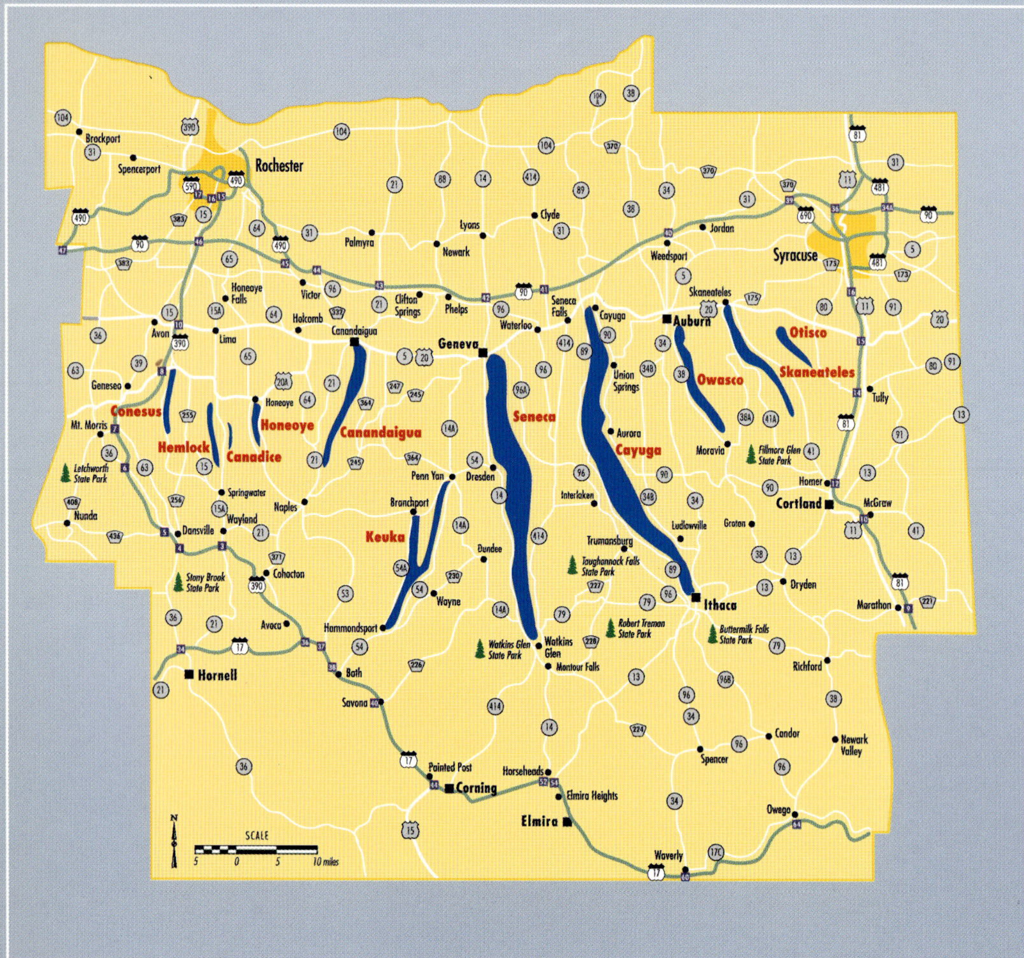

Index of Photos